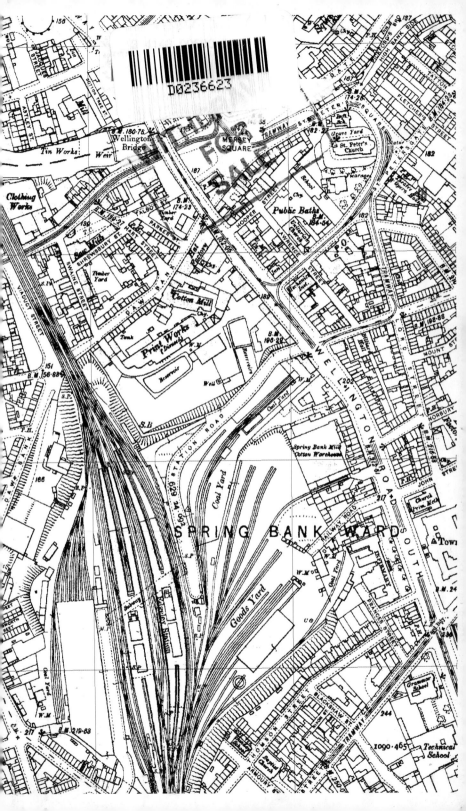

The Invisible Wall

The Invisible Wall

Harry Bernstein

HUTCHINSON
LONDON

Published by Hutchinson in 2007

1 3 5 7 9 10 8 6 4 2

Copyright © Harry Bernstein 2006

Endpaper map detail © and database right "Crown Copyright and
Landmark Information Group Ltd" (All rights reserved 2007)

Harry Bernstein has asserted his right under the Copyright, Designs and
Patents Act, 1988, to be identified as the author of this work.

This book is a work of non-fiction based on the life experiences and
recollections of the author. In some limited cases names of people, places,
dates, sequences or the detail of events have been changed solely to protect
the privacy of others. The author has warranted to the publishers that,
except in such minor respects not affecting the substantial accuracy of the
work, the contents of this book are true. Whilst the publishers have taken
care to explore and check where reasonably possible, they have not verified
all the information in this book and do not warrant its veracity in all
respects.

First published in Sweden in 2006 by Brombergs

First published in Great Britain in 2007 by Hutchinson
Random House, 20 Vauxhall Bridge Road,
London, SW1V 2SA

www.randomhouse.co.uk

Addresses for companies within The Random House Group Limited
can be found at: www.randomhouse.co.uk/offices.htm

The Random House Group Limited Reg. No. 954009

ISBN 9780091795436

A CIP catalogue record for this book is available from the British Library

The Random House Group Limited makes every effort to ensure that the
papers used in its books are made from trees that have been legally sourced
from well-managed and credibly certified forests. Our paper procurement
policy can be found at: www.randomhouse.co.uk/paper.htm

Typeset by SX Composing DTP, Rayleigh, Essex
Printed and bound in Great Britain by
Mackays of Chatham PLC, Chatham, Kent

Dedicated to Ma who gave us so much and received so little. Can this book make up for it? Can anything?

ACKNOWLEDGEMENTS

This book could not have been written without the endless love and caring of my wife, Ruby, my son, Charles, and my daughter, Adraenne. I owe deep thanks to Kate Elton of Random House for seeing in my book what others had failed to see for a long time. Thanks also to her assistant, Anna Simpson, for her patience and wisdom in the editing of my book. I am grateful as well to Allison Dickens of Ballantine for introducing the book to American readers.

Part I

Prologue

Outwardly, I suppose, our street looked pretty much the same as any other street in the working-class section of a Lancashire mill town in those days. They were all dreadfully alike, with their endless, sad rows of houses facing one another across the cobblestones, the brick darkened by age and soot, the short, stubby chimneys jutting out of slate roofs into murky skies, along with the tall, slender stacks of the mills that were sometimes half buried in the smoke and clouds.

Early in the morning, when it was still dark, you would hear people going to work in these mills, their iron-shod clogs clattering over the cobblestones with a sound and rhythm that was like a symphony. It began rather quietly as the first few pairs of clogs stepped out of the doorways, then became louder as more people joined in and louder still, until it was like a storm of hail, finally reaching a crescendo with a simultaneous blast of whistles from all the mills; then softening as they entered the mills and dying out until there was absolute silence again.

I used to lie awake often in the bed that I shared with my two brothers, listening to these noises. I would hear them again when they came home in the evening, but it had a different sound from when I was lying in bed in the morning, quicker and more staccato, and if it was summer and still daylight I might see them, the men carrying empty dinner pails wrapped in big red-spotted hand-kerchiefs, the women wearing striped coloured petticoats and shawls, with little bits of white fluff stuck in their hair, looking like snowflakes, and all of them walking separately from one another, too tired to talk, probably, and in a hurry to get home. One by one they would enter the houses on the Christian side. One by one the doors would open and close. And finally, as in the morning, there was silence again.

Our street was smaller than most of them. It had just one long row of houses on one side and two smaller rows of equal combined length on the other, intersected by another street called Brook Street. It sloped slightly on a hill that began far up in the better section of the town. It was a quiet little street, hardly noticeable among all the other larger streets, but what distinguished it from all the others was the fact that *we* lived on one side and *they* on the other. We were the Jews and they were the Christians.

Actually, what we had here was a miniature ghetto, for there was an invisible wall between the two sides, and though the distance from one side to the other, geo-graphically, was only a few yards, the streets being very narrow, the distance socially could have been miles and miles. There was very little crossing over from one side to the other; there was hardly ever any mixing. Not that there was ever any hostility shown on their part towards us. It was nothing like Back Brook Street or Bann Street or places like that where a Jew didn't dare venture if he knew what was good for him. Nor were the Christians on our street anything like the Christians on those other streets, with their constant beer drinking and fighting, and their rough ways and foul language.

For the most part, our Christians were a quiet, decent lot, and the two sides got along quite well; and for our parents, most of whom had come from Poland or Russia at the turn of the century, fleeing the pogroms there, the little street must have come as a refuge.

Just the same, there was this distance between us and it was maintained by everyone, though with an exception or two now and then. Like, for example, when Mrs Humberstone used to cross over to gossip with some of the Jewish women she seemed especially to like, or when we had to go to Gordon's grocery to buy a cob of white bread or a bottle of pop or ginger beer, or to Mrs Turnbull's sweet shop on the corner at the top of the street. Otherwise, we stuck to our side and they to theirs.

But there are few rules or unwritten laws that are not broken when circumstances demand, and few distances that are too great to be travelled; such was the case on our street and I was to play an important part, unwittingly, in what happened. It started on a summer evening, when I was about four, perhaps a bit younger, but old enough certainly to be able to get involved in the drama that began that night.

Chapter One

It was one of those rare summer evenings when it did not rain, and the smoke cleared from the atmosphere, leaving the sky a deep blue colour, and the air soft and fresh and balmy. It was the kind of evening when people brought their stiff-backed wooden kitchen chairs out to the front to sit and smoke, and perhaps listen to the Forshaws' gramophone. They were the only people on our street who had a gramophone and they left their door open so that everybody could hear. In the meantime the sun would sink, a huge red ball, behind the square brick tower of the India Mill. After it disappeared there would be fiery streaks in the sky, and these would fade gradually and the sky would become very pale, and twilight would fall gently over the street, and you would see the glow of pipes or cigarettes along both sides.

We had finished our tea, and my two sisters had quickly disappeared before my mother could get them to clear the table and wash up, and my two brothers were about to do the same. Having gulped down the last of their tea, and still chewing their bread and butter, they were halfway out to join their friends in the street, when my mother stopped them. 'Take 'arry with you,' she said.

They stared at her in astonishment, not believing what they had heard.

Well, I too was surprised. But my surprise was a pleasant one. Until now I had been the baby of the family, too young to be able to go out and play with them, though I'd always wanted to and had watched them go with silent yearning. But now, suddenly, all this was changed. I looked up at them, my finger in my mouth, waiting hopefully for my fate to be decided.

'Him?' said Joe. He was the oldest of the three boys, big for his nine years, a handsome boy, too. He spoke as if he couldn't believe what he had heard. 'Him?' he repeated.

'He's only a baby,' screeched Saul in his high-pitched voice. Saul was a bare year and a half older than I, but considered himself my senior by far.

'He's not a baby any more,' my mother said firmly. 'He's old enough now to go out and play with you and the other boys.'

'But he'll get in the way,' they both wailed. 'He doesn't know how to play.'

'He'll soon learn,' my mother insisted. 'I don't want him to stay inside on a nice night like this and I've got a lot of work to do in the house, otherwise I'd take him out myself. Go on, now, take him with you, and mind you keep an eye on him and don't let him wander off by himself.'

They had no choice, and each of them took a hand savagely, bitterly, and pulled me out with them. But once outside, and once they caught sight of the other Jewish lads from our side a little distance off, they dropped my hands and rushed towards them, forgetting all about me and ignoring my mother's warning completely. I trotted after them and that was about all I was able to do throughout the evening. I was not able to participate in any of the games

they played; I simply hung on at the fringe of the group, but
I was ecstatic at having that much, at simply being allowed
to be with them, and I shouted when they shouted, jumped
up when they jumped, imitated all their sounds and
movements.

I forget the games that were played that night, but the
locale was constantly being shifted from one part of the
street to another. We drifted down to the bottom, then
back up, and eventually we landed at the very top, at the
corner in front of the Harrises' house, where they began a
noisy game of hopscotch.

This one I do recall, and also that it had grown darker.
Twilight would linger for a long time yet, until almost
midnight, but it had reached the stage where the two sides
of the street were becoming hidden in shadow, and the
glow of pipes and cigarettes stood out strongly. The sky
looked almost white in contrast to the earth, and the
outlines of roofs and chimneys were etched sharply against
it. We could barely see the chalk marks that had been
scribbled on the pavement, but that made no difference and
the players hopped madly from square to square, screaming
and shouting to one another.

In that moment of our midsummer night's madness we
had failed to see the two people who were seated outside, a
little way off to the right on the other side of the doorway.
These were the two Harrises – old Mr Harris, who could
not have been much more than forty, a squat, heavy,
bearded man wearing a bowler hat beneath which was a
yarmulke, squinting down at a Jewish newspaper in the
fading light, and old Mrs Harris, barely forty perhaps, a
little woman wearing the orthodox Jewish woman's wig,
beneath which tiny hen's eyes peered disapprovingly
across at the Christian side.

The Harrises were possibly the most religious couple on our street. Mr Harris was an important official of the little synagogue over on Chestergate Avenue that we all attended; and the yarmulke that he wore beneath the bowler hat was concealed only because such things could draw laughter or jeering remarks from the Christians. Especially from the direction in which Mrs Harris's eyes were cast. This was the Turnbull sweet shop. Nothing had to be feared from the immobile figure of the man seated there next to the window: Mr Turnbull, who had suffered a stroke some time ago, who was brought out here by his wife to sit for hours and wait until she was good and ready to bring him in. And at the moment she was in the back room drinking beer with her boarders.

The sounds of their raucous laughter and the clinking of glasses drifted out into the street now. The boys Mrs Turnbull took in were a rough lot, a blot on the street's reputation: they were young navvies, the ones who cleaned out the middens, or chimneys, who drank and swore, and who, when they were out on the street and in a ripe, sodden mood would not hesitate to hurl a few slurring remarks across at the Jews, and at the Harrises in particular if they happened to be sitting out, as they were now.

Tonight, fortunately, they were indoors, but the lovely summer evening must have been marred anyway for the Harrises by our noisy presence. However, they said nothing and tried to ignore us while the game proceeded right next to the window. As usual, I was kept out of the game, and simply added to the din by joining in the shouting and screaming now and then. But after a while I must have grown tired of this – and perhaps it was getting a bit late for me – and my attention began to wander away from them, and suddenly it was caught by a movement from the window. The blind was being drawn up, and the white lace curtains were being parted, and a face showed dimly. It was smiling right at me and a finger was beckoning.

I didn't need to be told who this was. It was Sarah, the youngest of the six Harris girls, and a favourite among us and among everybody on the street. She was a sweet, gentle, perpetually smiling girl with lovely features, dark hair and an oval face that had a smooth, delicate complexion. She had been ill lately, and was recovering now and spent much of her time on the red plush couch in the parlour right next to the window, reading one of her little yellow-backed novels and dipping her fingers daintily into the box of chocolates that was always at her side.

. Sometimes, during the day, if we happened to be going by, she would open the window to smile and speak to us, to send some boy or girl off on an errand for her perhaps, or simply to talk and to pop one of her chocolates into a lucky mouth. I had often been one of those lucky ones. I think I was one of her favourites. I know, when she was younger, perhaps even as little as a year ago, she used to come into our house to play with my sisters, and she would always hug me and kiss me and call me her baby. Then she had stopped playing with my sisters and she had put her hair up, which on our street meant you were grown up and could go to work. Well, she had gone to work for a while in one of the tailoring shops where all the Jews worked, and then she was taken ill, and here she was convalescing, and I was staring at her stupidly through the semi-darkness, wondering what all those signals meant, for she was also putting a finger to her lips and shaking her head.

Then, at last, I understood. She wanted me to come in to her, but to do it quietly and secretly without anyone seeing me. That's what it was and I hesitated. It was much easier said than done. In the first place there were her parents seated right near the door, and in the second place you did not walk into the Harrises' parlour that easily. It was the only real parlour on our street, thanks to the fact that all the Harris girls and the one boy, Sam, were working and bringing in money. It was furnished in red plush, including even a red plush carpet, a truly elegant place, but reserved only for members of the family and for special occasions. None of us had ever been invited into it and all we knew of it was what we'd glimpsed through the window and what we'd heard of it being spoken in awe.

But there was something else. There was Sam's bike in the lobby. It stood there, shiny and gleaming, when Sam was not using it and we'd often peeped in at it when the door was open. It was Sam's great treasure and he guarded it as fiercely as a lioness her cub; and let one of us so much as dare creep an inch beyond the doorstep towards it and he'd come roaring out from the back of the house, his bushy red hair standing up like a wild golliwog's.

I'd seen it happen two or three times already and I was terrified of going anywhere near it. Yet I'd have to pass it if I went into the parlour. I stood, hesitating for a long time, my finger in my mouth, my eyes glued on her face at the window and the beckoning beseeching fingers, while the lads hopped and screeched madly over their game of hopscotch and the light on the street grew dimmer. Then finally I must have decided to chance it and I slipped in.

Old Mr Harris was still peering down at his newspaper, closer to the print than ever, and Mrs Harris was still burrowing with her hen's eyes through the dusk at the shadowy figure seated across from her, so they did not see me. I saw the bike the moment I entered the lobby, silvery highlights gleaming on the handlebars, the rest scarcely visible in the darkness. I flattened myself against the wall and crept slowly towards the parlour door to avoid touching it, and I held my breath as I went. Once I halted, hearing a sound in the back of the house, a cough, the movement of feet. But then it grew silent again and I crept on.

I groped for the doorknob, found it, turned it slowly and went in. The room was quite dark, save for the patch of light that came from the window at the front. There was a rustling and I saw the shadowy figure sitting upright on the couch. 'Over here, luv,' she whispered.

I stumbled past bulky furniture and found my way over to her. She grasped both my arms and stared at me for a moment through the darkness. 'You've grown so,' she said, keeping her voice down to a whisper. 'You're so big. You're almost too big to kiss. But I will! I will!' And she did, passionately, drawing me close to her so that I caught the familiar scent of lavender that came from the sachet she always wore tucked away in her tiny bosom.

Finally releasing me she whispered, 'Does your mother know you're out so late, 'arry?'

'Yis.'

'Would you like to go on an errand for me?'

I nodded.

She gave a glance over my shoulder first, as if to make sure nobody was there, then said, 'I want you to go to Gordon's to fetch some ginger beer for me. Can you do that for me?'

I nodded again and I might have felt some surprise. It was not an unusual request, and there seemed to be no need for all this whispering and secrecy. I may not have gone to Gordon's myself before this, but I had gone often with one of my brothers or sisters. Especially when somebody in the family was sick, because it was believed that ginger beer had medicinal qualities.

However, she did not lessen her whispering tone and in fact glanced over my shoulder once more before she resumed. 'Take this empty back with you,' she said, thrusting a bottle into my hand. 'But first, 'arry' – she brought her mouth so close to my ear as she went on that I could feel the warm breath coming from it – 'before you go in the shop look to make sure Freddy's there. I don't want you to give the bottle to anybody except Freddy. Not Florrie, not the old man. Just Freddy. Do you understand?'

'Yis,' I said, speaking this time because the urgency of her tone seemed to demand it.

'And here's a thripenny bit.' She put the tiny coin into my other hand. 'There'll be a penny change and you can keep it.'

My heart leaped. A whole penny! I couldn't wait to be off. But she held on to me a moment longer and whispered in my ear, 'Be very careful, 'arry. Don't tell anybody where you're going and remember what I said, don't let anybody wait on you except Freddy. You look through the window first to make sure he's there and if he isn't you just wait until he comes along before you go in. Do you hear me now?'

'Yis.'

Then finally I was off and I made my way out of the room much faster than I'd come in. My excitement over the penny was so great that I bumped into Sam's bike and immediately there came a great roar from the back of the house: 'Who's there?'

I must have flown out of the house. I know I put all caution aside as I dashed out and the two Harrises, catching a glimpse of me as I went past them, must have been utterly bewildered and were probably never able to make out what had happened, or where I'd come from, or even who I was. All they saw was the small figure of a boy dashing across the street and disappearing into the Christian darkness.

I trotted. I half ran. Perhaps this was due less to the hurry I was in than my fear of being on the Christian side. I had never been here alone and certainly not at night. The doorways were open as I trotted along and strange odours came out of them, the smells of bacon and lard and ham and other forbidden foods. I caught glimpses of crosses on walls and pictures of Jesus. Fires glowed inside, with kettles boiling on them. I could hear the Forshaws' gramophone further down the street.

The people sitting outside glanced at me curiously as I went by. A Jewish kid running down their side at night. It must have seemed odd to them. But they said nothing. Christian children were playing just as noisily as the ones across the way. I wove my way among them and hurried, clutching the empty bottle in one hand, the thripenny bit in the other. The sound of the gramophone grew louder, and then I came to the Forshaws' house and simply had to stop.

The gramophone was placed right near the open doorway on a small table, with the Forshaws sitting on either side of it. I had often stared fascinated from across the street, listening to the squawking sounds that came out of the big green horn. Close up, I found it even more fascinating. I could see the disc twirling round and round, and the voice coming out of the horn, singing, was so real I thought perhaps there was a man inside. The two Forshaws were watching me, though they were pretending not to, and they were smiling a little. Mr Forshaw was holding a mug of beer in his hand and took a sip every now and then, and wiped his moustache with the back of his hand. Mrs Forshaw simply sat erect with her hands clasped in her lap, a tall, slender woman with dark hair tied in a bun at the back of her head.

It was rumoured on our street that they'd once been well off and it was Mr Forshaw's drinking that had brought them down to our street. Anyway, they were decidedly a cut above the rest of us and they seemed to have very little to do with their neighbours, though they were friendly enough with everybody, and nodded and smiled, even though they never said more than a word or two. They had just one offspring, a boy, Arthur, who'd won a scholarship to the Grammar School. He was a nice-looking boy, about fourteen at the time and big for his age, and friendly like his parents, but one who minded his own business and was studying all the time.

He was sitting in the room behind his parents, reading at the table under the gaslight and scribbling notes, and my attention wandered over to him and away from the gramophone for a moment.

Watching him with his head bent under the gaslight coming from the mantle above, I couldn't help thinking of the argument that had taken place between my mother and Lily, my older sister, earlier that day. It had been on account of Arthur. Lily, who was twelve, had never spoken to Arthur in her life, but she fairly worshipped him from a distance, and that was chiefly because of his accomplishment in winning a scholarship – something nobody on our street had done before – something she intended to do herself.

Yet she must have spoken of Arthur once too often and my mother lost her patience. She had been struggling against it all this time, saying nothing when Lily had mentioned him, but now she burst out, 'That's enough. I

want you to stop talking about Arthur Forshaw. I don't
want to hear his name in this house again.'

My sister looked at her in astonishment. Well, we all did.
We had never seen our mother so angry before. 'Why?' Lily
asked. 'What's wrong with it?'

'What's wrong? He's a Christian, that's what.'

Lily gaped in astonishment for a moment, then said, 'Of
all the stupid things to say. What difference does it make if
he's a Christian?'

Then my mother slapped her face and Lily ran upstairs
crying.

So I was thinking of all this and looking at Arthur when
Mrs Forshaw's voice interrupted, saying, 'Would you like
to sit down on the doorstep for a little while, 'arry, and
listen to the gramophone?'

'And have a sup of beer while you're at it,' Mr Forshaw
put in, winking.

'Oh, you shut up,' Mrs Forshaw said to him, then turned
back to me. 'Go, on 'arry, sit on the doorstep.'

'I'm going on an errand,' I said.

'You are?' She seemed surprised. 'All by yourself? Does
your mother know you're going?'

'Yis,' I lied and instinctively cast a glance across the
street at our own house, which was almost directly
opposite this one. But my mother was not sitting outside.

'Well, go on then,' Mrs Forshaw said, smiling. 'You're
going to Gordon's for ginger beer I can see, and you'd better
hurry before it gets too dark.'

I hurried on. I ran, trying to make up for the time I'd lost
standing in front of the Forshaws' house. About to pass the
Greens' house I stumbled and fell. Mrs Green was sitting
outside with her daughter Annie, who was holding her
baby (the fatherless one that had caused so much whisper-

ing on the street). Mrs Green was the toothless old woman who made up our fire on Friday nights and Saturday. Every Jewish family on our side had someone on the Christian side to do it for them, since Jews were forbidden to light a fire on the Sabbath that began Friday at sunset. We called them 'fire goyahs' and Mrs Green was our fire goyah. Seeing me fall, she let out a cackle of amusement.

But Annie, always a nice, quiet girl, who sometimes substituted for her mother on the Friday nights and Saturdays, sprang up at once to help me, holding her baby under one arm.

'Did you hurt yourself, 'arry?' she asked, pulling me up with the free hand.

'No.' I'd landed on my knees, but my only thought was for the bottle that had fallen out of my hand. Fortunately, it was one of those durable stone bottles and had not broken. I picked it up and, without bothering to thank Annie, ran on.

The gaslight had been turned on in the Gordons' shop, and it spilled out on to the pavement. I stood there in the light and looked through the window. Old Mr Gordon was seated close to the window, dozing over his newspaper, his head on his chest, his glasses slipped down to the end of his nose. He was a very fat man with a huge, sagging belly that heaved up and down every time he wheezed and coughed asthmatically in his sleep.

Otherwise, the shop was empty. There were no customers inside, no Florrie and certainly no Freddy. I had been warned by Sarah not to go in unless Freddy was there, so I waited. I glanced uncertainly round the corner. There were two entrances to the Gordons' place. The one round the corner led to the taproom and this one appeared to be busy. People were coming and going, some with jugs in their hands that they'd had filled up, and every time the door opened the noise from within came out along with the smell of beer.

Freddy was almost certainly in there, waiting on customers, but it was one place I would never have dared to enter. It was a place where only Christians went. I turned back anxiously to the grocery window and suddenly, to my relief, I saw the door at the rear that led to the taproom open and Freddy came backing out of it, lugging a heavy case filled with bottles.

I went in at once, the bell on the door ringing as I opened it. Mr Gordon awoke with a start and began struggling out of his seat, but Freddy, who had swung round at the sound of the bell, said quickly, 'Don't you trouble yourself, Da. I'll take care of him. You just sit there with your paper.'

The old man didn't seem to mind staying where he was and settled back in his chair, wheezing and coughing. Freddy's hand reached out across the counter. In a low voice he asked, 'Did Sarah send you?'

'Yis,' I said.

'Gi' it to me,' he said.

I handed him the empty bottle and watched him as he half turned away from me with it. Freddy at that time must have been about eighteen, a rather short, stocky fellow with thick blond hair. Ever since their mother had died, he and his sister Florrie had been running the shop and the taproom, and it had kept them busy. The old man was too sick to be able to do much. Freddy's face was flushed, and perspired right now from the exertion of rushing about and lugging the heavy case in, and though his back was partly turned towards me I could see it clearly, and I could also see what he was doing.

I know it struck me as a bit odd and my mouth must

have opened a little, as I saw him take the cork out of the empty bottle I had given him and slip a finger into the opening. He seemed to bring something out. It was a small slip of paper that he unfolded and read. Then he did another peculiar thing. First he gave a swift look at his father, who had already dozed off again, then he bent over the counter and wrote something on another piece of paper, which he folded up into a strip. Now, he took a bottle from the case he had brought in, opened it, spilled a little of the ginger beer out of it on to the floor and began pushing the slip of paper into it.

In the midst of all this, unseen by him but seen by me, the door leading to the taproom opened and Florrie came bustling out. She stopped short at sight of him and stood watching. Florrie was about two or three years older than her brother, a buxom girl with the same colour hair as he. She had been engaged to a man from Birmingham for several years, the wholesale grocery salesman who serviced their shop, and it was believed that it was the responsibility she felt towards her sick father and the shop that kept her from getting married.

She had entered in time to see all the strange things I had seen, the writing of the note, the spilling of the ginger beer, and it was just as he was thrusting the note inside that she burst out, 'What the bloody 'ell are you doing, Freddy?'

He swung round sharply at the sound of her voice and the red in his face deepened. 'What's the matter with you, Florrie?' he muttered.

'Oh, you bloody fool!' She had started to shout, but suddenly remembered her father, glanced towards him and, seeing that he was asleep, went on, but with a lowered voice that was filled, nevertheless, with passion, 'I know what you're up to, and maybe you think you're smart, but

I warn you you're not messing around with any mill girl or with another Annie Green. Those people across the street wouldn't let you get off easy like Mrs Green did . . .'

'You shut up, Florrie,' hissed Freddy, also glancing at his father and at me too. 'You just shut your big mouth and mind your own bloody business.'

'Mind my own business?' she said, her voice almost choking. 'And whose business is it if you go to prison, which is what those people across the street are going to do to you if they catch you messing with one of their girls? Who's going to have to run this place and take care of Da? It's me, that's who. Me, who could be married by now and living in Birmingham with an 'ouse of me own if it wasn't for this place.'

Freddy didn't answer her this time. He was afraid that I was hearing too much and he hurried to finish what he was doing. He put the cork back into the bottle of ginger beer and gave it to me. He took my thripenny bit, handed me the penny change and said, 'Be sure you give that bottle now to the one who sent you here and be off with you.'

I hurried out and as I closed the door behind me I heard their voices again clashing sharply in anger. But I was no longer interested. I was in a hurry now to get back and spend my penny. I was clutching it tightly in my hand. I ran back up the street. Now it had grown darker still and a few pale stars were visible in the sky. The lamplighter was going round with his tall tapered pole. He had lit the lamp on the upper corner of the street and was now marching down to light the one at the other end. The lamp, right next to the Turnbull sweet shop, cast a thin glow of light around its base and hardly touched the buildings.

The street was quieter too. The children had dis-appeared. Fewer people were sitting outdoors. Yellow light showed at windows behind drawn shades. When I reached the Harris house it was empty there too. My brothers and his friends had gone, and the chalk marks on the pavement were vaguely seen through the darkness. Old Mr and Mrs Harris were no longer there either. I was half afraid that I'd have to go inside again, but suddenly the window opened and I heard Sarah whisper, 'Right here, luv.'

Eagerly, glad to see her, I turned towards the window with the bottle. She reached out for it, took it from me and asked in another whisper, 'Did you give the empty to Freddy?'

'Yis,' I said.

'Oh, that's wonderful. Thank you so much, 'arry. Here, let me give you a kiss.' She drew my face to hers with both hands, pressed her lips against mine and held me tightly, smothering me in her lavender smell. Then she let go of me and said, 'You'd better hurry on home now, luv. I think your mother is looking for you.'

Indeed she was. My whole family had been scouring the street for me and Sarah knew that only too well, but hadn't dared say anything to them for fear of getting involved. However, I hadn't the slightest intention of going home yet. Not with that penny burning a hole in my hand. I ran back across to the Turnbull shop. Mr Turnbull was still seated outside and he threw me a beseeching look as I went past him into the shop. I don't think I even noticed him.

Inside, I stood uncertainly. The shop was empty. From the back room came the sound of men's voices, hoarse guffaws, the clinking of glasses, with Mrs Turnbull's own hoarse, almost masculine voice dominating the others.

I tapped on the glass counter with my penny to get her attention, timidly at first, then louder and bolder, until one

of the men must have heard me and peered round the doorway, for I heard him say, 'There's a little Jew boy in th' shop.'

'The bloody little buggers.' Mrs Turnbull's voice came to
me, bitter and complaining. 'They're always bothering me.
I don't get a minute's peace.'

She appeared in a moment, shuffling in slippers, a large,
heavy woman with thick arms folded over a massive
bosom, fleshy face creased with displeasure, her breath
smelling of beer. 'Now what do you want?' she snapped at
me. 'Y'ought to be in bed this time o' night, instead of
bothering me. You're always bothering me, the whole lot
of you. Go on and pick what you want and don't take all
night at it. I've got lots of other things to do.'

I gazed down through the glass case at the assortment of
sweets, with the usual dilemma over what choice to make,
but more frightened and flustered than ever at her
impatience. My eyes went from one to the other, the clear
mixed gums, the aniseed balls, the licorice allsorts, the
Kali suckers (with a balloon included), the Devonshire
caramels, the Turkish Delights and the bon-bons and the
humbugs, the big humbugs and the small humbugs and the
chocolate dragées. And all the time she chafed and
muttered, and finally burst out savagely, 'I'll gi' ye five
seconds more . . .'

I jumped at the sound of her voice and in sheer panic
made a random choice, the humbugs, the large ones. She
filled a bag with them, took my penny and almost pushed
me out; and as I left her gaze must have fallen on her
husband and reminded her of him, for I heard her mutter,
'There's him, too.'

Outside, I crossed back to my own side, but paused to
open the bag and pop one of the humbugs in my mouth. It
was so big it caused both my cheeks to bulge and I slowed

my pace as I went on, because I wanted to finish it before I entered the house. I had no intention of letting my brothers and sisters know I'd come into possession of a bag of humbugs and be forced to share it with them. In fact, I immediately thrust the bag deep down inside my trouser pocket.

But by the time I reached my house I was in trouble. I'd only managed to whittle the humbug down a fraction of its original size and my cheeks still bulged. Yet I knew I could not delay entering much longer. Sounds came out of the house that were ominous, my mother's angry voice berating my brothers and the latter wailing protests, and I knew it was over me.

There was only one thing to do. I took a deep breath and swallowed it. I nearly choked as it entered my throat, but I managed to gulp it down and it sank into my stomach like a rock. Then, wiping off the tell-tale marks from my mouth with the back of a dirty hand, I went in.

My mother was still shouting at them, blaming them for letting me out of their sight, and they were both sniffling and protesting, and she was preparing to go out herself and search for me, when I walked in and stood for a moment blinking in the light, unseen as yet and listening to the argument raging.

It was Saul who saw me first. 'There's the bloody little sod,' he shrieked.

All eyes instantly turned on me and Joe glared hatefully, then strode towards me and gave me a clout on the side of the head. 'You bloody little bugger,' he said. 'Why'd you run off?'

Saul would have followed suit with another clout if my mother hadn't stopped him, pushed him and Joe aside, grasped me by both shoulders and said, 'Where have you been? We were looking all over for you.'

I hung my head and muttered, 'I went on an errand.'

'Who sent you on an errand?'

'Sarah.'

'That's where we saw him last,' interjected Joe. 'That's where the bloody little bugger was standing when we were playing hopscotch outside the Harrises' house.'

'Where did she send you?' my mother asked.

'To Gordon's.'

'What for?'

'A bottle of ginger beer.'

'She's got some nerve sending you there alone,' my mother said angrily. 'I'm going to have a talk with her when I see her. And I'm going to tell her mother, too. She shouldn't be sending you off to Gordon's for ginger beer all by yourself at night. Now, all of you go up to bed.'

She was very angry, otherwise she might not have said that. On summer nights she always let the older children sit up a bit longer to read after they came in from play, and there were loud protests from my sisters and Joe, from Saul too, who considered himself an older one already, but especially Lily. She was the oldest in the family, but besides that she had a lot of studying to do. She was always reading books and preparing herself for the scholarship exam.

'It's not fair,' she protested. 'It's just not fair.' And then, notwithstanding the argument she'd had with her mother earlier that day and the warning that had been given her, she said bitterly, 'I'll bet Arthur Forshaw's mother didn't tell him to go to bed early when he was studying for his exam.'

Perhaps if she hadn't said that she would have stood a

screamed with delight as they fell on her. Some she managed to catch with her open arms, others rained down on her head, hit her in the face, or scattered on the floor round her feet, to be gathered up by her, the rest of the game to be played by her alone under the gaslight, sewing and mending and washing until late into the night.

As for us, we scampered off to our beds, the two girls to theirs in one room, the three of us to the one we all shared in another room. It was not comfortable sleeping, especially for me, since my place was at the foot of the bed where their feet stretched out to me and often caught me in the face. There was a lot of wriggling and twisting and shouts of protest before finally we settled down to sleep.

That night my two brothers soon fell asleep, but I remained awake, still excited by the events of this strange night in my life. They passed through my mind as I lay there in the darkness, all those kids playing out on the street, running from one spot to another, jumping and shouting and running, the hopscotch game in front of the Harrises' house, old Mr Harris and Mrs Harris sitting out there in the dusk, then that face at the window and the finger beckoning to me, and slipping into the house, and the lavender scent that came from Sarah's bosom. Then crossing over to the Christian side and seeing crosses on the walls, and the Gordons' shop and the argument between Freddy and his sister, and finally Mrs Turnbull, and her boarders and the sweets. And suddenly I remembered my humbugs. They were in the clothes hurled down the stairs at my mother. Instantly, I shot up in bed. Luckily, I was on the outside of the bed and did not have to step over one of my brothers. I got out swiftly and padded out of the room. I went past the bucket placed on the landing for nocturnal use and down the stairs, and turned into the kitchen. I halted for a moment in the doorway.

There she sat, her back towards me, at the table under the gaslight, the mantle turned down low to save on gas, the light so dim I don't know how she could have seen. She was surrounded by the clothes we had thrown down at her, her head bent over them, her right arm going back and forth with the needle. She had not heard me coming down and did not know I was standing there. Nor did I give her a chance to find out. I dashed forward suddenly and began tearing at the pile of clothes, scaring her so that she jumped violently and put a hand to her heart.

''arry!' she gasped. 'What are you doing here? What is it? What are you looking for?'

I was tearing madly at the clothes, throwing them aside, scattering them in all directions, in an effort to find what I wanted. 'I'm looking for me trousers,' I said.

'Well, don't throw everything about like that,' she said. 'I'll find them for you. What do you want them for?'

'I've got something in them,' I muttered.

'All right, here they are.'

She had found them without any difficulty, and she handed them to me and watched curiously as I dug into pockets, first one that was empty except for a rusted nail that I had been carrying around for several days, then the other in which I found the bag of humbugs. I pulled it out quickly, and I would have turned right round and gone back up to bed with it if my mother hadn't stopped me. 'What is that?' she asked.

I showed it to her, opening the bag for her to peer in. 'Why, they're humbugs,' she said in surprise. 'Where did you get them from?'

'I bought them in Mrs Turnbull's shop.'

Her eyes widened. 'Where did you get the money?'

'Sarah gave it to me. She gave me a penny for running the errand.'

'Oh!' She was not altogether displeased and it was a relief to me. I had somehow felt that she might have objected to this as much as she had to the errand itself. But she even seemed interested in the contents and kept peering down at them. 'Can I have one?' she asked.

'Yis.' I let her take one, then asked, 'Can I have one too?'

She hesitated a moment. 'You should be in bed sleeping not sucking humbugs this time of the night, but I don't suppose you'll be able to sleep until you do have one, so go on and take it, and I'll let you sit with me for a while until you've finished it.'

The first one I'd swallowed down in such a hurry had long since been digested and forgotten, and I was good and ready for a second one. I dipped into the bag eagerly. The next half-hour or so was a memorable one for me, not only sucking a humbug late at night, but being alone with her and having her all to myself for once. How often did that happen in our busy household with her love shared among five of us? She let me sit on her lap too, and went on sewing as we talked and sucked our sweets, and we talked of various things.

I told her of my trip to the Gordons, and how I'd stumbled in front of the Greens' house and nearly broken the bottle. I didn't tell her anything, though, about the strange things Freddy had done with the piece of paper, and the quarrel between him and Florrie. I don't know why. I hadn't forgotten it, but somehow I felt I should not mention it.

My mother smiled, paused in her sewing for a moment to stroke my hair and said, 'You're getting to be a regular big boy now. And soon you'll be going to school.'

'When?' I asked, not too sure that I wanted to go.

'In the autumn,' she said. 'In September.'

'Will I go to St Peter's?' I asked.

'No, I don't want you to go there. They have too many little batesemas in St Peter's.' We called the rough and more openly anti-Semitic Christians 'batesemas', a name that has no origin in any other language and that Lancashire Jews must have coined. 'I want you to go to a better school,' she said, 'and I'm going to try and get you into the one up the park, the big one called the Hollywood Park School.'

I listened to her open-mouthed. It was the first time I'd heard of her plan and my feelings were mixed. I would much rather have gone with my brothers and sisters, yet I'd heard so many stories of the beatings they and the other Jewish children got from the ragamuffins – the batesemas – who went to St Peter's that I had been dreading it also.

'Who'll take me there?' I asked.

'I'll take you,' she said. 'I'll take you every day until you learn to go by yourself. I've already spoken to the head-master there. He's half promised to take you in, although he says they don't take in many Jews. But he warned me you're going to have to wear nice clothes and that means you're also going to need a pair of shoes.'

'Can I have clogs?' I asked eagerly. I'd always wanted a pair of clogs, the kind the Christian boys wore, the same as their parents wore, wooden with iron soles that could make sparks fly up into the air if you struck them across the cobblestones. How I'd always envied them!

But my mother shook her head firmly. 'No, clogs are for batesemas. Jewish people don't wear clogs. Although they're much cheaper. No, I'll have to get real leather shoes for you and I don't know where I'm going to get the money from. I suppose I'll have to ask your father for some.'

An unhappy look spread over her face as she said this and she seemed preoccupied with her sewing once more; and watching her I knew of the thoughts crossing her mind and the worry she felt over having to ask my father for money. I'd heard her trying often before and I'd shivered at the repercussions.

Yes, clogs were for Christians only. Jews considered it beneath them to wear clogs and I was the one exception that my mother reluctantly made, chiefly because she had no choice and clogs were better than nothing. The shoes my brothers wore were those handed down from my father, save for the rare times when my mother could scrape together the money to buy new ones. The more children that came, the less money there was to scrape together, and I was last in line.

And just as I was thinking of this, I heard the sound outside, the heavy footsteps in the street, the halt at the door and the temporary silence before the faint clicking came of a key being fitted into the lock.

She heard it too, and instantly put down her needle and thread, and pushed me off her lap. 'Go upstairs, 'arry,' she whispered. 'Go to bed.'

I didn't have to be told twice. The fear had rushed through me at those very sounds, and I dashed up the stairs once more and got into bed.

It didn't take long before I knew he was in the house. I heard the rumbling of his voice, then the faint pleading sounds of my mother's. She would be asking him about the shoes, I thought. The rumbling grew louder and louder, and erupted into violent roars and curses.

The trembling went through my body. I did what I always did during these moments. I pulled the covers over my head to shut out the sounds.

Chapter Two

O ur house was on the corner at the bottom of the first
short row of Jewish houses, where Brook Street came
to a cul-de-sac at our street. Like all corner houses it
boasted a lobby, with a door leading to the front room that
was empty and unused most of the time. Now and then it
became a playroom for us, for Rose especially, who was
next to Lily in age and who often created fantasies about
the room, turning it into a fancy drawing room and herself
into a duchess, and acting out scenes in which we became
her servants and she would order us about in a haughty,
aristocratic voice: 'Do tell the coachman to prepare the
horses and carriage. I am going to a ball.'

When brought out of her dream world to wash some
windows or sweep a floor she would fly into a violent rage,
and I think my mother understood how she felt and would
feel sorry for her, and try to comfort her by saying, 'Some
day, we'll have a real parlour, with proper furniture in it,
and you won't have to just pretend.'

'Yes, when?' Rose would say bitterly, only half believing
her.

'Yes, when?' we'd all demand, because it was something we all wanted and yearned for, a parlour like the

Harrises', red plush furniture and red plush carpet. And perhaps even a piano, like the Blanks had. 'Yes, when, Ma?' we'd nag.

And she would say confidently, 'Some day.'

I think she meant it. She had her dreams too. Her one big dream was to go to America, where we had relatives. She wrote to them often. She herself could not write, but she had one of us do it and her letters always asked the same thing – steamship tickets for all of us – and when their letters came, far less frequently than hers went to them, they were filled with optimism about the future, but there were no steamship tickets and nothing was said about them.

Still, my mother continued to hope, to write and to wait anxiously for the postman to knock on the door. Perhaps, after a while, she came to have another dream about which we knew nothing for a while. She kept it secret from us all.

In the meantime she struggled to make ends meet. My father earned little money at the tailoring shop. Well, none of them did. Nor did the others at the mills. It was the one thing the two sides of our street had in common: our poverty. When the landlord came to collect his shilling rent on Sunday afternoon there was panic on both sides. He owned all the houses on our street. He was a little shrunken man with a yellowish moustache and he tapped on each door with the end of his pencil, making a formidable sound. In the other hand he carried a notebook in which he recorded each transaction.

I can remember how, as soon as she heard the rapping come closer, my mother used to start searching in her apron pockets, and then under the oilcloth on the mantel-piece where she kept an odd copper or two sometimes.

Finding none anywhere one day, she gave me a little push and said, 'Go to Fanny Cohen's and ask her if she can lend us a shilling for the rent.'

I ran at once. Halfway up the street I met Philly Cohen coming towards me. He was a little red-haired boy about my age and my friend. We both stopped and eyed each other silently for a moment, like two puppy dogs meeting nose to nose.

Then I asked, 'Where you off to?'

'T'yours,' he said. 'Me mam sent me to borrow a shilling for th' rent. Where you off to?'

'T'yours,' I said. 'Me mam sent me for a shilling for th' rent too.'

'Then I'll see you later,' he said. 'Ta-ta.'

'Ta-ta,' I said.

And off we went in opposite directions, too stupid to realise the futility of our respective errands. My mother and his mother were also close friends, and later when they met to discuss this episode they burst into gales of laughter. The two of them doubled over and shrieked until tears came to their eyes.

It was strange how they could laugh over their misfortunes and yet they did, often, but just as often they wept too. I know my mother did. Never in front of us if she could help it. But I sometimes saw her surreptitiously wiping her eyes. Perhaps she was a bit worse off than some of the other women, because my father only gave her a small portion of the little that he made. The rest went for drink and gambling. He gave her little of love, too.

He was a strange man, not at all like other Jewish men, who rarely drank or gambled or swore as he did. He was like a boarder in our house. He came and went. He was big and dark and surly. He always wore a cap pulled low over his brow so that you could hardly see his face. He left early in the morning to go to his tailoring shop. He came back late in the evening and he ate his supper alone at the table, with his head bent low over his plate, never saying anything to us. When he spoke it was only to my mother and always with savage curses.

Barely had he finished his supper than he pushed his chair back with a scraping sound and was off, and in such a hurry that one sleeve of his coat was left dangling behind him and he was fumbling for it as he rushed out. When the door closed behind him with a bang we all felt relief. He was off to a pub or some card game and would not be back until late at night.

We always fought with one another when it came to taking his tea in the afternoon. This was a daily routine among all the Jewish children on our street. The Christian children did not have to do this. The mill workers were not allowed to take time off to have tea. They had no union as the Jewish tailoring workers did.

About four or five o'clock you would see a long line of Jewish children struggling along Brook Street in the direction of Daw Bank where the workshops were located, all of them carrying steaming cans of tea and little packages containing bread and butter, enough to tide the men over until they came home for supper. The other boys went eagerly, glad of a chance to see their fathers, but in our family there was a constant battle over who should go. We hated the job because we feared being with the man who was our father even for the few moments it took to deliver the tea. We sometimes cried and pretended to be sick, and indeed often my mother herself would have to go, tearing herself away from her numerous other chores to rush to the shop.

Now that I was grown up I had to take my turn. I always went shivering with apprehension, tagging along after the other boys, and as we approached Daw Bank my fears grew. It was a disreputable neighbourhood to begin with; the rows of houses, built probably long before ours, were in a tumbledown state, doorways leaning, window panes missing. The middens were in the front here, giving off a foul stench that sickened us the moment we turned into the street.

Worse than anything else was Old Biddy, a huge, slattern of a woman with stringy unmade hair dangling down the sides of her face. She came out of the dark hole where she lived, looking like a huge bear emerging from hibernation, and glared at us as we came along with our tea cans and muttered, 'Bloody Jews.'

I would never have dared go by there alone. I was terrified of this woman and clung closely to the others, who were just as afraid as I was and hurried by quickly.

The Jewish tailoring shops were at the back of these houses. They were flimsy wooden structures built on stilts. A tall, narrow flight of rickety steps led up and into them. We tramped up these steps in single file, holding on to the handrail with one hand. We entered into a roar of machines, the thin wooden floor vibrating beneath our feet. The men, bent over their machines, feet treadling, looked up and gave little cries of relief at sight of us. The treadling stopped and the room grew quieter, save for the noise of the men greeting their children.

How they ran towards their fathers, sometimes throwing arms round their necks and hugging them, and how I envied them! I myself had simply halted and waited a moment, trying to pluck up courage to go up to my father. He was the only one among them who had not stopped treadling, and

his machine alone still hummed and clattered, and he was
bent over it with his dark, glowering face.

I went up at last, and timidly placed the can of tea and
the package of bread and butter on the machine beside him.
He said nothing. He did not look at me. I turned away and
went back to the door to wait for the others. It would not
be for too long. The men were not given much of a respite
for tea. Yet the boys could not tear themselves away from
their fathers and clung to them as long as they could, and
my envy grew still deeper as I watched them sitting close
together, laughing and talking, and occasionally helping
themselves to little bites of the bread and butter and sips of
tea.

When it was at last time to go and I began to turn away
with them, I noticed that my father had finally stopped
working and was now unwrapping the bread and butter and
picking up the tea can. I caught this last glimpse of him as
I followed the others through the door and down the
rickety stairs. They were all in high spirits, racing and
yelling at the tops of their voices, but I went quietly and
there was a heavy feeling inside me.

Growing up that summer, but still very young, I could
not have been conscious of the darkening clouds hanging
over England, over the entire world in fact, as war broke
out. I was much too absorbed in myself, in other things
that were happening to me, and in how sorry I used to feel
for my mother – that more than anything else, especially
when I saw her crying quietly to herself and trying not to
let us see – and how it used to upset me. The war, the
Germans, the men being sent off to fight, were still more
remote to me than the discovery of how poor we were.

I was still young enough to be going shopping with my
mother and to be holding her hand as we went along King

Street. It was a busy street. Horses and carts went rattling by. Occasionally a motor lorry lumbered along. A delicious aroma came from Owen's bakery shop and my mouth watered at the sight of the currant buns in the window. We passed Kemp's fish and chip shop and the aroma there too, and the sizzling sound of the frying, taunted me. My mother didn't stop at any of the shops until she came to Hamer's shoe shop, and there she paused a moment before entering.

Mr Hamer was a lean, lantern-jawed man, stooped, with green braces over a collarless shirt, and he wore spectacles that were shiny in the dimness of the shop. It smelled of leather and there were white boxes on shelves, and two chairs to sit on with footrests in front of them.

'I just came to ask how much you'd want for a pair of shoes for him,' my mother said, almost apologetically.

'For him?' He pointed a finger at me, and then whatever it was he said made my mother gasp a little and shake her head.

'I could never afford that,' she said.

'Well, you'd better get 'im something,' Mr Hamer said, casting a look down at my feet. I was wearing a pair that Saul had outgrown, and they were pretty far gone. 'Otherwise', he added, 'those things are going to fall off his feet.'

'I know,' said my mother. 'But I can't afford to pay that much.'

'Well, what about clogs, then? he said. 'They don't cost half that much.'

But she was already shaking her head and halfway out of the shop. 'I'll just have to wait a bit,' she said, 'until I have the money for shoes.'

'Well, don't wait too long,' he called after her. 'Or that fellow'll be going barefoot.'

I was disappointed. I wanted clogs more than anything else. 'Why can't I have clogs?' I nagged outside.

'Because you can't,' she said. She had told me once before why I couldn't have clogs and she refused to discuss it again.

Besides, she was in a truly desperate situation that day and couldn't have had enough to buy even clogs. We crossed over to the kosher butcher shop. It was crowded inside and my mother stood back with me against the wall, not too anxious yet to be waited on until all the others had gone. The customers were mostly from up the park, the well-to-do – the wives of the tailoring-shop masters, the jeweller's wife, the landlord's – and she must have felt self-conscious among them.

Behind the counter the butcher hacked away furiously at a haunch of beef. He was a big, heavy, muscular man with red cheeks and red snapping eyes. He wore a long white apron stained with blood. There was fury in his movements as he hacked and slashed at the beef, cutting expensive steaks that his wife beside him was wrapping. She was a tall, slender woman, who wore no apron over her fancy dress, and seemed quite out of place there behind the counter amid all the blood and raw meat. In fact, there was a certain elegance to her manner, and the way she wrapped packages and kept up a running conversation with the women; her speech feigned a haughty aristocratic British accent that sometimes blended incongruously with her Russian accent.

And yet, despite all her airs and aloofness, she was known to be a sharp businesswoman and always kept a pencil tucked in her hair behind one ear, and also a ledger book close beside her to record every transaction she made. It was she who caught sight of my mother standing at the back of the crowd and immediately whispered something to her husband, who threw a sharp, ugly look in our direction.

Craning her long, graceful neck, the butcher's wife called out over the heads of the others, 'Yes, madam, is there something I can do for you?'

Everyone turned to look and my mother, flushing a little, stammered, 'That's all right. I'll wait till you have more time.'

'We always have time for our customers,' the woman said, smiling a little.

'But it's not my turn,' my mother protested.

'Now it's your turn.' And still the same smile. 'I am making it your turn, so please tell me what it is I can do for you.'

There was cruelty in every word and in her smile. She knew full well what my mother had to say and she was forcing her to say it in front of all the other people, and my mother had no choice.

The flush growing deeper, she stammered, 'I just wanted a pound or two of neck meat, and perhaps some bones for a soup . . .'

'And you want it on tick, I suppose,' the butcher's wife finished for her.

'Yes. I thought perhaps, just for a few days . . .'

She was wasting her time. In her best haughty British fashion, the butcher's wife was saying, 'Madam, unfortunately you are behind on your account too much already, so I cannot give you any more tick. After all, we are not a charity organisation.'

But now, suddenly, my mother was pulling at my hand and we were on the way out, with all the women staring. Outside, we walked swiftly. Her cheeks were flaming and she was looking straight ahead, and I'm sure she was

struggling to keep back the flow of tears. We went back up
the street, and we did not halt until we reached Levine's
grocery shop. Nor did my mother hesitate before she went
in. She was truly desperate that day.

Levine's shop was untidy and always smelled of herring.
The smell came from the large open barrel of herring
standing near the counter. Customers could help themselves, dipping their hands in and pulling out a herring, or
the Levines would do it for you. Boxes and sacks of things
cluttered the place, leaving hardly enough room in which
to move about. The shelves had never been dusted and
cobwebs hung from the corners. Mrs Levine sat behind the
counter, nibbling poppy seeds that she clutched in a hand.
She was a short, fat, sloppy-looking woman with frowsy
hair that fell into her eyes. Her husband, pacing idly up and
down behind the counter with hands clasped behind his
back, was equally short and fat, and bald, with a sickly
complexion.

It was, fortunately for my mother, empty of all other
customers and I could sense her relief. To spare herself any
further humiliation she got through with what she had to
say quickly. 'I must tell you right away,' she said, 'I'm
going to need tick. I know I owe plenty already. But I can't
help it. I've got to have food for my children. I'll pay you
back as soon as I get some money. I promise you.'

At first they did not say anything. They looked at one
another. Then Mr Levine muttered, 'Give her.'

Mrs Levine put down her poppy seeds and stood up, and
my mother told her what she wanted. Her voice trembled
as she spoke, showing the emotional state she was in, and
towards the end, as the big brown shopping bag was filled
up, she broke down altogether and wept. 'How can I thank
you?' she said, but she could not go on, and wept hard,

while there was an uncomfortable silence from the other two and myself.

After a while, apparently feeling she had to say something, Mrs Levine sighed and said, 'There is much sorrow in the world.'

Mr Levine had begun his pacing again and came to a halt in front of my mother, who was dabbing at her eyes with a handkerchief. 'Why don't you open a little business of your own?' he said. 'You would always make a little.'

'What could I do?' my mother asked.

'You should go on the markets,' he said. 'You go to the wholesalers and buy some dry goods. A few dozen bloomers, some drawers, stockings, camisoles – ladies' things especially – they always sell good. Perhaps some towels, curtains. Then you rent a stall in our market, in the Bolton market, in Manchester, Salford – there's a different one each day. And you go from one to the other. You'll do all right I tell you.'

My mother listened with interest, but Mrs Levine broke in suddenly, scoffing, contemptuous. 'Meshugana,' she said, 'where is she going to get the money from to start the business? And how is she to go around to the markets? She has five children. Who'll take care of the children while she's running around to the markets? Stop draying her kop.'

Mr Levine shrugged. 'All I know is a business is the only way to make a living. You can't starve when you have a little business.'

When we left and were walking back home, my mother hugging the big brown paper bag to herself with one hand and holding my hand with the other, she seemed lost in thought, and hardly aware of my presence, and she was walking so fast I had to trot to keep up with her. I didn't say anything, but from time to time I looked up at her and wondered. She seemed far away. How was I to know that she was thinking of something then that would change our whole lives in the years to come?

*

The approach of the weekend brought on a bustle of activity on both sides of the street. The Jews were preparing for Saturday, their Shabbos, the Christians for Sunday. It began actually on Friday morning with the arrival of a little one-armed man leading a donkey and cart, and bawling through the cupped good hand, 'Be – boo – ragbone!'

Instantly, children came running out of houses carrying bundles of rags and bones. There were plenty of rags on the streets and more bones than meat. They clustered around the cart and the little man took their bundles deftly with the iron hook that protruded from the armless sleeve and tossed them on to the cart. Payment was made in the form of little slabs of coloured sandstone that were used for colouring doorsteps.

We were allowed to help ourselves and, amid much excited chattering, hands fought with one another as we scrambled for the gaudiest, brightest, newest colours.

Soon afterwards, the girls who were old enough, or the women, were on their hands and knees in front of each house, scrubbing the doorsteps and a small area of pavement around them. There were reds, blues, greens, yellows, a wild variety of all sorts of colours among them and by the time they were done there were two long rainbows running down each side of the street, of which we were immensely proud. Other streets, less respectable than ours, did not bother. But we did, even in the worst of times.

On that same day, towards evening, the Jewish houses

began to exude the pungent smell of hot chicken soup and later on, if you had looked through windows on our side, you would have seen women lighting candles and waving their hands in front of them and muttering something that was a prayer, a strange ritual that always mystified the Christians opposite us.

Soon, now, there began the calling of the fire goyahs. Once the sun was down and the candles had been lit we were not allowed to touch the fires in our grates and lift a pot on or off them, so a Christian had to be called in to do it for us and we paid them a penny or two for it. Each family had its own fire goyah. Ours for many years was Mrs Green and I was the one now who went out to summon her.

A number of other boys and girls were doing the same thing. We stood at the kerb and called across, our voices forming a chorus.

'Oh, Mrs Green,' I called, 'will you please come over and do the fire?'

A moment later her door opened and she ran across, huddled in her black shawl. She was always in a bad temper and her breath always smelled of beer. She poked the fire into life grudgingly and she put the pots on with a thump, angrily. The tuppence my mother gave her never satisfied her, and she looked at the coins in her hand as if she might want to throw them away and muttered something about 'rich Jews'.

'Batesky,' my mother said, after she had gone. It was the worst thing you could call a Christian. The male gender was bates.

But my mother had more important things to think about that particular Shabbos. Tomorrow was Saturday. It was the day we went to the synagogue, a converted brick

house on Chestergate right opposite the India Mill. We all
went, tramping down the street in our best clothes,
carrying the little velvet bags that contained our prayer
shawls and siddurs. On Sunday the Christians would be
marching down their side of the street to their churches, to
St Peter's, the Protestant church, or St Matthews, the
Catholic church, and they too would be wearing their best
Sunday clothes. But Saturday was our day and this
particular Saturday was to be a memorable one.

My mother would have longed to go to the synagogue
with us, to join the other women in the stuffy little
balcony and say a prayer to her own dead mother and
father. But she could not leave the house. Saturday was a
big day for her, a day of anxiety. It was the day my father
gave her the money for the week. Other fathers had already
done that, turning their entire pay over to their wives. But
my father would hang on to his until the very last moment,
after his long Saturday sleep, after he got dressed up for his
Saturday night and had had his dinner, and it would only
be a portion of his pay, and dealt out sullenly.

How much it was going to be my mother never knew. A
lot depended on his mood and how well he'd slept, and for
this reason she was shushing us constantly from the
moment we rose in the morning, putting her finger to her
lips and casting anxious looks upwards for sounds that
might indicate he had been awakened. In the meantime
she did not dare leave the house for fear he might get up
and go without giving her anything.

When we came home from the synagogue that day he
was still sleeping, and once again we had to tiptoe around
and speak in whispers. Then she pushed us out of the
house altogether, telling us to go and play with our friends.

Outside, the boys began a game of cricket on the backs

behind our row of houses. I was not able to swing the bat yet and I could never catch the ball, so I was not put on either side, but allowed to run for the ball when it travelled a great distance and bring it back to the bowler. But after an hour or two of running I grew tired of the game. Besides, it had become cloudy and began to drizzle. This did not stop them from playing, but I decided I'd had enough and went back into the house.

My mother was sitting by the fire when I came in, hands in her lap. Ordinarily, she'd have been sewing or doing some kind of work, but this was forbidden on the Sabbath, so all she could do was sit here and wait for her husband to get up, and worry over how much he was going to give her this week and whether it would be enough to carry her through. The fire was very low and the house was chilly, but she could not have afforded to send for Mrs Green again.

She started when she saw me and asked, 'Why did you come in so soon? Don't you like to play with the boys?'

I told her I didn't want to play any more. I wanted to be with her, and I don't think she minded. She was perhaps glad of a bit of company. She made me a butty – a slice of white bread spread with butter – and I ate it sitting close by her side. It was like that other night when I'd had her all to myself. She stroked my hair and we talked of this and that in very low voices, always mindful of my father sleeping upstairs, and somehow she began telling me of her childhood in Poland, and how she was a little girl when her parents died, one soon after the other, and how she was taken in by relatives and passed from one to the other, because none of them could really afford to keep her.

It was a sad story, but she did not cry as she told it to me. My mother cried sometimes, but never in front of us. I would see her on occasions, when she thought she was alone, with a handkerchief to her eyes, and would feel terrible about it and wish there were something I could do. I felt that way now, even though she was not crying, and I reached for her hand and held it, and she seemed to appreciate that and kissed me.

It was just then we heard the noise upstairs. He was getting up and dressing. His feet were thumping about.

My mother sprang up from her chair. ''arry, go out and play,' she whispered. 'Go on and join the others.'

But I didn't want to. Somehow, I wanted more than ever to be with her, even if he was there, and no amount of whispered urging on her part could make me budge. And then it was too late.

He came clumping down the stairs and into the room, his face as dark and forbidding as ever. He was dressed for his Saturday night all right. He wore his best suit, with a stiff white collar and tie, and he'd had his weekly shave. He ignored the two of us and sat down at the table with his back towards us, and my mother hurried to serve him his dinner, the biggest part of the scrawny little chicken she'd bought for the Shabbos, saved for him after sharing meagre portions among us, none for herself.

He ate with his head bent low over his plate and with animal sounds, grunts and champing of jaws, and he ate rapidly and was soon done, and pushed back his chair with a scraping sound, rose and seemed almost ready to leave. My mother was frightened. She went up to him as if to block his way.

No, he had not forgotten her. His hand dug into his trouser pocket and he brought out the money, a small roll of banknotes. He peeled one off, and after a moment's hesitation another, then he dug his hand into his pocket again and brought out some change. He handed this to her.

My mother looked at it in her hand and said in a low voice, 'Is that all you can give me?'

'What more do you want?' It came out of him in a snarl and his face grew blacker still.

'I owe money to the butcher,' she said, 'and the Levines, and I've got to buy shoes for 'arry. He'll be going to school next month, and I need to buy food for the house . . .' Her voice trembled.

He did not answer immediately. He rushed for his raincoat hanging on the back of the scullery door, started to put it on and, as he was struggling to find the other sleeve and already on his way out, said savagely, 'You and your bastards can go to hell.' Then he left, the empty sleeve still dangling behind him, and we heard his footsteps in the lobby and the lobby door slam shut.

It was silent after that. My mother did not move. She stood there with the bit of money in her hand. Her head was bent. I heard the clock ticking on the mantelpiece. The clouds had gathered outside and the room was very dim. From the distance I heard the sound of the cricket game still going on, the shouts of the players. All at once my mother roused herself. She raised her head and strode to the scullery. I watched her, wondering. It was as if she had reached a sudden decision about something.

She came out wearing her coat and putting on her hat, a big, broad-brimmed hat with a feather in it, which she was fastening to her hair with a long hatpin. She had also brought two straw shopping bags from the scullery. ''arry,' she said, 'I'm going to the market. Do you want to come with me?'

'Yis.' I spoke with alacrity. I always enjoyed going to the market. It was colourful and lively, as good almost as going to a picture show.

As we went through the lobby she did a rather strange thing. She paused at the door to the front room that was supposed to be our parlour. The room was empty save for the boxes and cartons that Rose used as the furniture for her fancy drawing room. One of the larger boxes was the throne on which she sat like a queen and haughtily issued commands to her servants. I thought perhaps my mother was looking for her and said, 'Rose is next door at the Finklesteins playing with Doris.'

'That's all right,' she murmured. It was not Rose she was looking for. It was something else that she was thinking of that I would know about later.

We both went out. It was still drizzling slightly. My mother walked swiftly and I had to trot to keep up with her. I had been to the market with her before, but I had never seen her in such a hurry to get there. By the time we reached the market it was already dark. Flares had been lit at the stalls, and their flickering light fell over the faces of the shoppers and the vendors as they bawled lustily through cupped hands, 'Cheap, cheap, buy, buy.' There were all kind of goods displayed and all kind of foods and smells, cheeses, black puddings steaming in a huge pot, sausages dangling down in a long string, huge fish with blood dripping from their gills and big eyes staring, pink bloomers and dresses and coats and trousers, the smell of roasting peanuts and chestnuts, the sweet smell of chocolates, and vendors shouting in your ears, 'Cheap, cheap, buy, buy. Come on, lady, buy, buy.'

I would have loved to dally among them, to stare closer at the array of all kinds of chocolates, to pause to look at the snake charmer with the turban on his head. My mother usually did this, and she shopped slowly and carefully among the stalls, looking for the best bargains. But this time she did none of that. She was still in a great hurry, as if she had some destination.

Well, she did. It was the big fruit and vegetable stand at the end of the market, where she often picked up some good bargains. There were several helpers here shouting their wares: 'Pomegranates, bananas, apples, oranges, 'taters, cheap, cheap. What'll you 'ave, lady?' But she was not interested in buying from them. She was looking for the owner. He was over in a corner, wearing a long white coat, a large, red-bearded man, too important a person to be doing any shouting himself. He did a wholesale business, too, and had a bit of an office at the back of the stand.

My mother told me to stay where I was and not move until she came back. I watched as she went over to the red-bearded man, whose name I was to learn later was Mr Pollit. She spoke to him for several moments, then turned away and to my utter amazement I saw her crawl under the stand.

The helpers were startled too and they looked enquiringly at the boss, but he did not satisfy their curiosity and told them roughly to get on with their work, which they did, resuming their shouting.

I stood there waiting for her to come out, petrified by what I had seen, and growing more and more fearful as time passed and still she did not emerge. I think I was about to burst into tears when finally, to my relief, she came crawling out. The two straw bags she had brought, one held in each hand, were bulging to capacity with fruit. She put them down to straighten out her hat and to wipe mush off her face with a handkerchief.

I ran up to her and she laughed. 'Were you afraid I wasn't coming back?' she asked.

'Yis.' I nodded, tears still in my eyes, and clung to her with both hands.

'Well, you didn't have to be. I'm back and I won't go away again.'

She seemed strangely excited and triumphant. Her cheeks were flushed. The owner approached us, hands clasped behind his back, and said, 'Well, how'd you do?'

'Fine,' she said. 'There's a lot of good stuff under there that shouldn't be thrown away. How much do you want for these two bagfuls?'

He shrugged. 'Take 'em,' he said. 'Go on, take 'em.'

'No.' She spoke firmly. 'I don't want them for nothing. I want to pay a fair price.'

'You're an 'ard woman to deal with,' he said. 'How's about sixpence?'

'That's cheap,' she said, and fumbled in her purse and gave him the sixpence.

We walked away hurriedly, my mother heavily burdened with the two bags. Just the same, she managed to set a fast pace and I had a difficult time keeping up with her. Meanwhile, I was fairly consumed with curiosity. 'Mam,' I said, 'what are you going to do with all that fruit? Can I have an apple? Can I have one now?'

'No, not now,' she said 'You'll have to wait till we get home. And then you'll see what I'm going to do with it all.'

'What are you going to do, Mam?'

'You'll see.'

There was something secretive and excited about her. A little smile played at the corners of her lips. And she hurried, despite the weight she was carrying, and I trotted faster, just as eager as she was to get home. It began to rain and this spurred us on still more. We were lucky. The downpour did not really begin until we had reached the house and we were able to hurry in without getting too wet.

The house was dark and empty. My mother looked around and I think she was relieved to find my brothers and sisters still not home. 'They must be at their friends' houses,' she murmured, and began hurriedly taking off her hat and coat. Then she carried the two bags into the scullery, and I followed her and watched with widening eyes as she poured the contents of the bags into the sink. I had never seen such an assortment of fruit, plums, apples, pears, oranges, peaches, fruit of all kinds, and most of it soft and spoiled, though there were some really good ones among them.

She turned on the tap and began washing them, and I kept on chattering and plying her with questions. 'What are you doing that for, Mam? Why are you washing them?'

'To get them clean.'

She found a plum that was in good condition and handed it to me, and that stopped my chattering for a while, but I was more amazed than ever when I saw her take a knife and start to cut out the bad parts of the various different kinds of fruit. 'Why are you doing that, Mam? What are you cutting them for?' I asked.

'To make them look nice.'

But now, having finished this part of the job, she began putting the fruit back into the bags, and took several plates off the shelf and put these under her arm while she lugged the bags out of the room. She seemed more excited than ever and so was I. I followed her back through the kitchen and into the lobby, then she entered the front room.

And now, for the first time in all the years that I could remember, she struck a match and lit the gas in the front room. It had never before been lit and had been used only during the day as a playroom, and it seemed to me, as I looked around, bewildered, that I was seeing it for the first time. It was a square little room and the walls were papered with some sort of green flowered pattern. It had a fireplace that I had scarcely noticed before and had probably never been lit either. Under the revealing greenish gaslight from the mantle above, it seemed even more bare and empty than during the day, completely bereft of any kind of furniture, save for the packing boxes that were used for our play.

My mother took these packing boxes now and placed them at the window. They were tall enough to come up to the height of the sill. Then, as I watched, completely mystified, she began to fill her plates with fruit from the baskets, and set them on top of the packing boxes. When she had filled all her plates, she drew back a little to examine her handiwork, much as an artist might his canvas. And then, apparently not satisfied, she started to rearrange some of the fruit, turning it round so that the bad parts she had cut out did not show at the window. Finally she was done and turned to me. Her eyes were shining. Her hands were clasped in front of her. She seemed almost intoxicated with joy. ''arry,' she said, 'we now have a shop.'

I was a bit incredulous. 'A shop?' I asked.

'Yes, a shop. Just like the Levines, and the Turnbulls and the Gordons. We have a shop too, only ours is a fruit and vegetable shop.'

'Why?' was all I could think of saying. 'Why do we have a shop?'

'So we can make a lot of money,' she answered. 'And I can buy your shoes, and clothes for your brothers and sisters, and pay all the money I owe and have lots of food in the house. A business of our own!' she added, echoing the words of Mr Levine that had been spoken some time before this but must have stuck in her mind.

But just then the front door crashed open, and in tumbled my brothers and sisters. The four of them had arrived together by coincidence, having been at different places, Lily at the library. She was carrying books as she came in first, the others behind her as they paused at the unexpected sight of the front room being lit.

They blinked in the light, taking in the strange sight at the window that met their eyes. They were all wet from the rain, their clothes soaked, their hair plastered against their foreheads and dripping.

'What's that for?' Lily asked, indicating the plates of fruit with a nod of her head.

'That's our shop,' my mother said proudly. 'We have a shop now.' She was smiling – she was probably anticipating their own joy.

But there was nothing like it on their faces. They were all silent for a moment, staring at the display of faded fruit in the window.

Then Joe spoke: 'I thought we were going to have a parlour.'

'And a piano,' Saul squeaked.

'Well, you will,' my mother said, and she could sense their disappointment now and it threw a damper on her own spirits. 'Of course you'll have a parlour,' she reassured, 'and a piano and everything. Only we'll have to have the shop for a while so we can get these things. That's what the shop's for, so we can make some money from it to buy all the things we need, and as soon as we do I promise you we'll give up the shop and turn it into a parlour.'

'You're a liar!' It was Rose who spoke, her voice choked and trembling. She had been standing at the very back of the group, but had pushed her way forward and was standing right in front of my mother, half crouched in front of her, eyes blazing. It had been a crushing blow to her, much worse than for the others. It had taken away her duchy, her drawing room, her butler and retinue of servants. We were all staring at her, petrified, and my mother's face had gone white. Rose was beside herself with rage. 'You're a liar,' she repeated. 'You're never going to turn this into a parlour. It's always going to be a shop, because you're the shopkeeper type, a common Polish peasant woman. It was our room and you stole it from us. You're a thief and a witch, and I hate you, I hate you, I hate you.'

Then, before my mother could stop her, she had dashed forward and with both hands swept all the plates off the cartons. They went crashing to the floor, spilling their contents all over, the plums, the apples, the oranges, and they rolled in corners, around our feet, everywhere, and having done this Rose ran out of the room, weeping.

In the shocked silence that followed I saw my mother glance around her, bewildered, at the ruins of her shop on the floor; then she put her face in her hands and wept brokenly.

Chapter Three

The rest of the summer slipped by rapidly and the autumn weather began, chill and rainy for the most part, with an occasional good day when the sun broke through the clouds and shone with a hard brilliance. But it was a grey, cloudy day when school started.

I awoke early, tense and excited. It was far too early to get up yet. It was barely daylight and people were going to work, and I could hear the sound of their clogs marching rhythmically down the street, and the very sound increased my excitement because it made me think of my clogs that I was going to wear for the first time that day.

I lay back in bed, chafing with impatience. School was less important to me than the wearing of these clogs. I had been up half the night thinking of them and it had been that way ever since my mother had taken me back to Hamer's to be fitted for a pair. She'd given up the idea of shoes; she'd had to. Mr Hamer had been tactful; he hadn't mentioned them, as if she'd come in for the first time, and he'd gone about fitting me with a pair swiftly and efficiently. But he'd stuck up for me when I wanted to go out of the shop wearing them.

'You don't want 'im to put these things on again, do you?' he said, holding up my torn shoes between two fingers with something like disgust.

'He'll have to,' my mother said firmly. 'I want him to keep the clogs for school. At least they'll be new when he goes there.'

There was no talking her out of it, and I had to content myself with just stealing glimpses of them in the box between then and now. I couldn't wait. I felt imprisoned lying in bed. And yet there was nothing I could do but wait. I listened for other sounds once the march of the clogs had died down, and the whistles had given their final blast.

It was still dark; I would have to wait what would seem endless hours before the awakening began in our house. Actually, it would only be an hour or so before the Jewish tailoring workers began their tramp to the workshops, and it would be dawn. I watched it come. Then I pricked up my ears at a faint stirring in the room next to ours. It was my mother, always the first to rise; it had to be her. . . .

Yes, it was, for next I heard her tiptoeing softly out of the room and along the landing. She paused and there was a faint clanking sound as she picked up the bucket. It would be full to the brim and she would carry it carefully down the stairs. I listened. I heard her walking through the kitchen and opening the back door and going into the yard to the water closet. The door of the closet creaked as it opened and there was a splashing sound, followed by a snorting and flushing as the chain was pulled.

She was returning to the house and was cracking wood over her knee for the fire. I had seen her do this often and had always marvelled at the strength she showed. It would not take her long to get the fire going, and to put the kettle on and to prepare breakfast. And now, with all this done, I heard him come out of the bedroom. Unlike my mother, he did not walk on tiptoe, but clumped heavily down the stairs.

I did not have to worry about his voice in the morning. He hardly ever spoke then. He ate and left, the door banging shut after him.

Now it was our turn. My mother's voice called up the stairs, waking us, and I answered first, jumping out of bed and shouting, 'I'm coming, Mam.'

'Not you, 'arry,' she called back. 'I want you to stay in bed until I'm ready for you.'

I was terribly disappointed. 'Can't I come down, Mam?' I begged. 'Can't I?' I wanted so much to rush downstairs to my clogs. If she was not ready yet to help me put them on I could at least hold them in my hands. 'I'll not be in the way,' I promised.

But it was no use. 'Stay where you are,' she commanded.

The next half-hour or so was agony for me. There was a great tumult of shouting and rushing about going on downstairs. I listened to it, chafing. My mother's voice rose constantly, ordering them to hurry. Lily was the only one of them, really, who was anxious to get to school quickly. The other three were delaying as long as possible, fearful of St Peter's, fearful even of the long walk there, and Lily, thinking only of her scholarship exam, and preparing for it, shrieked at them too. They all had to walk together; this was something my mother insisted on.

At last they were going. My mother was shepherding them to the door. She would stand there and watch them go, clinging close to one another, joining the noisy throng of children going from our street and from other streets. At last the door closed and my mother's voice came softly up the stairs. 'All right, 'arry, you can come downstairs now.'

I flew. I was down in a second and there was a little smile

on my mother's lips. She knew how I felt. But she herself was excited. I could sense that as she served me my breakfast. Her hands were trembling a little, and there was that tell-tale flush on her cheeks. It was an important day for her too, a big day in her life. It was the first big step up for her children. We wasted little time on breakfast and the dressing began. The clogs would come last, after I had put on my new suit.

Her hands trembled even more as she took the suit out of the drawer. She had spent weeks making it. At first, she had thought of using one of my brothers' old suits and cutting it down a bit, but then had decided on something very special, something that would truly make the head-master's eyes light up with interest. She had taken her best purple velvet dress, the only good dress she really had, and had cut it up into a suit for me. It was a great sacrifice on her part – she would never have another dress like it – and it had entailed a lot of work on top of all the work she already had with us and with her shop.

But the sacrifice was nothing at all to her. She was tremulous with excitement now as she put it on me. It was a Little Lord Fauntleroy suit, with short pants, a jacket, complete with a large white lace collar.

'Oh, you look beautiful, so beautiful,' she exclaimed, standing a little distance away from me and viewing her handiwork with hands clasped under her chin, her eyes shining.

But I was scarcely interested in the suit. 'Can I put me clogs on now?' I pleaded.

'Yes.'

She was ready at last, and now it was I who was trembling as she went to the cupboard and took out the white box stored there and brought out the clogs. She let me touch them first before she fitted them on to my feet, smiling a little as she saw me fondle them. Perhaps there was a touch of regret in her smile. How she had resisted until the very last, hoping still there would be enough money for shoes. But her new shop, resurrected from that terrible first day, had disappointed her, bringing in enough for clogs, but not for shoes.

But they were better than nothing, because my old shoes, Mr Hamer had told her, were falling off my feet and were fit for nothing but throwing in the midden, and my mother had agreed with him.

Still, I think, my happiness made up for a great deal in her mind and her smile also contained a little of my own feelings. 'You'll just have to walk very quiet and respectful when you go in the school,' she said, as she put the clogs on my feet, kneeling in front of me on the floor. 'If you don't draw attention to your clogs, maybe the headmaster won't notice them.'

I wasn't listening. I was fairly quivering with impatience to try out the clogs. As soon as she had snapped the buckles on tight I sprang off the chair and began to stamp about like a young colt. But the real test would come when we were outside. Again I chafed while my mother got herself ready. She had put on her own best clothes and had brushed her coat carefully before putting that on, and finally the hat with the feather. She also took an umbrella in case it rained.

As soon as we got outside I began scraping my feet against the pavement. Nothing happened, and I broke free from my mother's hand and ran out into the street and tried it against the cobbles. This time sparks shot up and I screamed, 'Look, Mam, look!'

'Yes, I see,' she said, smiling, 'but we've got to go, and I don't want you to wear your clogs out before you get there.'

We went up the street, but our progress was slowed by my trying to raise sparks every few feet. Then there were further delays as women came to their doors, curious about my outfit, and my mother had to explain to them what it was about. At the top of the street we crossed over to the other side. Mrs Turnbull was just bringing her husband outside, and seating him in his chair. She turned at the sight of us, and exclaimed, 'Well, look at him! A regular bloody little toff! And where's he going all dressed up like that? To the King's ball?'

'No, I'm taking him to school, the one up the park,' my mother said.

'St Peter's isn't good enough for him?' Mrs Turnbull said. 'I can't say it surprises me, though. He's been acting like a rich gentleman's son all summer long, buying sweets nearly every day.'

'Has he?' said my mother.

'Been in and out, in and out, nearly every day, bothering the life out of me, tapping on that glass counter with his penny. Hasn't given me a minute's rest. It'll be a good thing for him to be off at school. Wish I could do the same thing with me 'usband. Between those two I'm a wreck. Well, at least I'll be done with one of 'em.'

'I'm sorry about 'arry bothering you,' my mother said. 'Maybe he won't now that he's going to be at school all day.'

'We can only live in 'ope,' said Mrs Turnbull.

My mother pulled me by the hand and we went on. After we had gone a distance, she said, 'Does Sarah send you every day for ginger beer?'

'Yis,' I said.

'And do you always spend your penny on sweets in Mrs Turnbull's shop?'

I nodded.

'I think it's time you stopped buying so many sweets,' she said. 'Perhaps you should start saving up your pennies for something you need, like shoes. If I'd had just a few more pennies I could have bought you shoes.'

'I like clogs,' I said.

'Well, it isn't good to eat so many sweets,' she said. 'And I don't think it's good for Sarah to be drinking so much ginger beer. I'll have to talk to her mother about it.'

We didn't say any more and I was glad, because for some reason the subject always made me feel uncomfortable. There was still something secretive about it when Sarah sent me on the errand and if Florrie was in the shop she always gave me a glowering look. And Mrs Green, too, started muttering when I passed her house going to or from the grocery.

We began to climb the steep hill that ran alongside the park. In winter it was used as a toboggan run during the few times that it snowed and in summer courting couples holding hands made their way up the hill to the entrance of the park. The trees, I recall, had just begun to turn yellow and red, and some of the leaves had already fallen off and had filtered through the iron rail fence on to the ground. When we reached the top of the hill, we paused, both of us out of breath. We turned to look back. There was a view of the whole town beneath us, the streets slanting down to the mills and the river behind them, the rows of houses staggered one below the other, with the slate roofs shining from the damp, and curls of smoke coming out of the short, stubby chimneys. A yellowish pall hung over the scene and the tall, slender stacks of the mills were half buried in its density.

I tried to make out our street and our house, but they were all so much alike it was impossible to do so, and at last, rested, we continued on our way. And now the ground flattened out and it was easier walking, and soon we had entered into a new world. There were no more rows of houses, but individual homes with little fenced-in gardens around them, and each one different from the other. I looked at them in awe, and my mother looked too.

'Some day,' she said, 'we'll have a home like these. Would you like that?'

'Oh, yis,' I said and asked, 'When will we have one?'

'Soon, I hope,' she said. 'Very soon if the shop is a success.'

She still believed in her shop, despite the fact that she was struggling with it. But that day her hopes were high. A slight drizzle had begun, and she opened the umbrella and we both walked under it, briskly, and once again I became conscious of my clogs and exulted in the sound they made as the iron rims on the soles struck the paving. I would look back at the sparks that shot up from them occasionally and laugh with joy, and sometimes my mother would laugh with me and her hand holding mine would squeeze tightly.

'There it is,' she said suddenly. 'There's your school.'

There it was before us, a red-brick building with a rhododendron garden in front, and a large play yard at the side, with goalposts. We both became silent and a little frightened too, I think. The entrance door was big and wide and imposing, with large black hinges and an arch over it. It must have been very heavy, because my mother had some difficulty pulling it open and then we stepped into a wide hall with a shiny wood floor.

My mother had been here once before and she knew where to go. The headmaster's office was at the very end of this hall. There were classrooms on either side of us, and through the glass panes in the doors we could see children seated at their desks and teachers standing up in front of blackboards. Except for the faint murmur of voices that came through the door it was very quiet. But as soon as we began to walk down this hall the quiet was shattered by the clumping of my clogs. My mother had forgotten her own warning and quickly put a finger to her lips. But it was too late now. The faces of teachers were staring at us through the glass in the doors.

Then suddenly a door at the end of the hall flew open, and out burst a short, pot-bellied man with a shiny bald head. The head was bent down slightly and he came charging towards us like a mad bull. 'What's this?' he shouted as he came closer to us. 'What's all this noise about? Clogs?' His eyes had caught my feet. They lifted up with fury in them. 'Clogs in my school, scratching my floors? Never! Out with you. Out this minute!'

My mother was terrified. She stood there trembling. 'But you promised,' she said. 'You promised you would take him if he was nicely dressed. Look at him. Look how nicely dressed he is.'

'I'm looking, madam, and all I see is clogs. I don't care if he's wearing the mantle of a prince. Clogs aren't permitted in this school. Never! I take a few Hebrews, but never once have I taken one with clogs. It costs me far too much to have my floors polished to have some young Hebrew scratch them up with clogs. So out you go. Come, madam, don't waste any more of my time.'

He literally pushed us towards the door, using both hands, and out we went into the rain. It was coming down quite heavily now, but my mother forgot to put up the umbrella. She was walking swiftly and hardly seemed aware even of my presence beside her. I trotted to keep up with her and looked up anxiously at her face. I wasn't too sure I knew what had happened in there, but I knew my mother had been badly hurt and I saw the signs of it on her face. I could tell she was struggling to keep back the tears. She was looking straight ahead and her lips were tightly compressed, and the rain fell on the brim of her hat with a little drumming sound, and some of it struck her eyes and mine too.

So I went to St Peter's after all, and the neighbours agreed it was perhaps best for me and there was no use trying to keep up with the swanks up the park. My mother said nothing. She packed my velvet suit away and put my ordinary clothes on me, and got me up in the morning with all the others and struggled to get us dressed and breakfasted, and stood in the doorway watching us go.

She would be there waiting for us, too, when we came home. She was forever filled with anxiety over us, and perhaps there was good reason for it. My brothers had often come home with bloody noses and black eyes and torn clothes. The trip itself was dangerous. You never could tell when one of the ragamuffins who went to St Peter's might turn on you.

We clung close together, with Lily always urging us to go faster. She was in a permanent hurry to get to school and was far less afraid of the batesemas than we were. The first morning I went she held my hand, on the orders of my mother, and she kept pulling me along at a fast pace and we were all forced to keep up with her.

There were other children from our street trailing behind, and then we noticed Arthur Forshaw striding ahead of us with his books under his arm. At sight of him Lily increased her pace still more and my two brothers complained. Rose sneered, 'She's trying to catch up with Arthur Forshaw because she's in love with him.'

Lily halted and whirled on her furiously. 'You keep your big mouth shut,' she said.

'She is,' said Rose, ignoring her and continuing to address Joe and Saul. 'She's always talking about him.'

Lily lifted a hand to smack her, then changed her mind and walked on, but noticeably lessening her speed. Arthur, with his long stride, was soon far ahead of us. He disappeared from sight altogether when we reached the Devil's Steps, climbing up them and then, I suppose, on to Wellington Road and up that street about a mile to the Grammar School.

We walked on, past Mersey Square and up the hill where the cab stand was, and here you had to be careful. I was instructed to walk close to the wall, as far away from them as possible. Though they seemed oblivious to your presence, and were sitting high on their perches looking innocently ahead and swinging their whips idly to and fro, they would sometimes manage to catch you with a little flick of the whip on the tip of your ear, and it would sting for hours afterwards.

We went safely past them without any mishap that morning and we passed the soot-blackened statue of St Peter set in the middle of the busy roadway called St Petersgate. A short distance ahead was St Peter's Church and the vicarage, and next to it the school, a low, red-brick building. The boys' play yard was in front and it swarmed with children, and echoed with the screams and shouts of their voices.

Both Joe and Saul paled as we approached the gate that led into the yard and held back a little. I would soon understand why. In the meantime Lily led me into the school to be registered by the headmaster. His office was simply a high desk in a corner of the standard seven classroom. He sat there now, long and thin, with an enormous pair of red ears that I discovered later he could wiggle freely back and forth. He was busy writing in a ledger book and he paused to look down at me as we came up to the desk. 'So this is another one of the Woodenlegs,' he said. For some reason he always called our family the Woodenlegs. We never knew why, but it seemed to be used affectionately.

'Yes, sir,' said Lily.

'And he's the last one of the lot?'

'Yes, sir.'

'The best or the worst?'

'I don't know, sir. I suppose you'll soon find that out for yourself.' She was smiling. She was not afraid of him. In fact, she was his favourite, and she liked him too and had often spoken of him at home.

'I suppose I will.' He was smiling a bit himself. Yes, he liked her and had made her his ink monitor, the highest honour anyone could achieve at the school. He was also tutoring her for the scholarship exam. But his attention was concentrated on me at the moment. A severe look came over his long, thin face as he looked down at me and a frown appeared on his forehead. 'You just behave yourself and you'll be all right,' he said. 'Because if you don't, you know what'll happen, don't you?'

I nodded.

'What?'

I stared stupidly up at him. I didn't know the answer.

'This,' he said, opened a drawer in his desk and took out a stick. It was a thick one. 'Hold out your hand,' he said.

I hesitated. I'd heard of canings. Tears began to come to my eyes.

'Go on, 'arry,' said Lily. 'Don't be afraid.'

I hesitated a little longer, then fearfully half raised it with my palm up. The stick swished in the air and I could almost feel it as it came down, expertly missing the tips of my fingers by a fraction of an inch.

'I missed you that time,' said the headmaster. 'But I won't the next. So you just behave.'

Lily was smiling. She hadn't been deceived by the act, one that he practised on all new pupils. She gave him the information about me that he needed and he wrote it in his ledger. Then she was about to lead me back into the yard when he stopped her. 'Lily,' he said, 'I've got a piece of paper here that I was going to give you later. But you can take it now. It's the permit slip for the scholarship exam that you'll be taking soon. You've got to have your father sign it.'

'Yes, sir,' said Lily, taking it from him and I noticed a strange look on her face as she did so.

'Be sure you get him to sign it as soon as possible. Otherwise you won't be able to take the exam. Remember that.'

'Yes, sir,' said Lily.

She took me back into the yard, searched for Joe and Saul, and left me with them. They were standing with their backs against the wall that separated the vicarage from the schoolyard, trying to keep out of the way of the raga-muffins, some of them in bare feet, racing madly about the yard at various games or fighting or chasing one another. I pressed against the wall with them and began to feel fear too. What we did not notice was the gang of boys balancing on the parapet of the wall a short distance away and approaching us with grins on their faces. Suddenly, a heavy weight fell on my shoulders and I was knocked to the ground. Simultaneously, I heard yells from Saul and Joe. All three of us were on the ground being pummelled by the gang.

It was a whistle that saved us. They sprang off quickly at the sound and disappeared into the crowd, while the three of us got to our feet and dusted ourselves off, more frightened and bewildered than hurt.

Our rescuer was Cocky Rawlings, the standard five teacher. Only you didn't call him Cocky to his face. It was a nickname given him by the school because of his choleric temper and fierce manner. He was a rather short, stocky man with a dark complexion and dark curly hair, and rimless glasses that flashed threatening looks in every direction. He carried a stick in one hand, a whistle in the other, and as soon as he came out into the yard and blew the whistle there was quick obedience from everyone.

The screaming, the shouting, the mad racing about ceased. The yard grew strangely quiet. Everyone lined up in rows, each with his own class. I was told where to stand among the youngest of the boys, the little ones like myself who were in the 'baby' class. Cocky stood, jaws tight, one hand clenching the stick, the rimless glasses fixed upon us, daring anyone to utter a sound. Then, in a military command voice, he barked, 'Forward march!'

We marched like soldiers, bodies held erect, knees lifted, and woe to anyone who put the wrong foot forward. One by one the lines entered the building, winding their way through the cloakroom, where those who possessed hats and coats could hang them up. And now into the school proper and to our respective classrooms. The girls joined us from the back part of the building.

In the morning, the folding partitions that separated the different classrooms were pushed back so that the school became all one large room. We were not allowed to sit yet. We remained standing. Facing us was the headmaster, tall, thin, grim-faced. He too held his stick in one hand. Behind him, at the piano, sat a pale, blonde young woman, the standard six teacher, Miss Penn.

When the last one had marched in, the headmaster allowed a full minute to pass, during which complete silence reigned, and then, in a voice that was clearly audible throughout the school, he said, 'Everyone will rise.'

This might have been puzzling to us since we were already on our feet, and those of us in the 'baby' class hesitated until we heard the rustling sound sweep through the one big room and saw everyone mounting the low benches on which we sat at the desks. We followed suit and in that moment, as all of us rose to full view, all the sadness of the Lancashire poor was revealed in the rows of thin, scarecrow bodies, the pinched half-starved faces, the tattered clothing, the bare, dirt-blackened feet, the sores and scabs on knees and legs. How clearly and horribly all this showed and no wonder they sometimes called St Peter's the Ragged School.

'We will now say the Lord's Prayer,' said the headmaster.

They did not need prayer books. They knew the words well, by heart, and so would I afterwards, although the Jewish boys and girls were not required to say these prayers and remained silent with heads bowed a little, as if this would make us less conspicuous.

> Our Father who art in 'eaven,
> 'Allowed be thy name . . .

How well I remembered it afterwards, and some of the hymns that followed, with the headmaster and all the other teachers joining in, the headmaster beating time with his stick and Miss Penn thumping out an accompaniment on the piano.

Finally, and always with a sense of relief to the Jewish children, it was over, and we were able to get off the forms and sit on them. The partitions were pushed back into place by white-haired old Mr Bell, the janitor, and Cocky Rawlings, the only man teacher in the school other than the headmaster himself, who taught standard seven.

Once the prayers and hymns were over the headmaster seemed to relax, and on this first day of school he began to visit each classroom. He entered with a wink to the teacher and took over from her to quiz the class. It was the same performance each year.

'How many doughnuts in a dozen?' he would ask.

Hands shot up. One was chosen. The answer: 'Twelve, sir.'

'Correct.' This one was easy, but now came the hard one. First, he gave another wink to the teacher, who already had her handkerchief out to stuff into her mouth. Then he asked, 'How many thripenny doughnuts in a dozen?'

There was a lot of hesitation, foreheads creased, puzzled looks on faces, and invariably there was one pupil who answered, 'Four, sir.'

The headmaster made no reply. With still another wink to the teacher, who was already choking on her handkerchief, he turned and marched out stiffly, the wide ears sticking out at the sides of his head.

Eventually he came to the 'baby' class. He had saved this for the last, because our teacher was Miss Goddard, a pretty, dark-haired girl of perhaps no more than sixteen or seventeen, unmarried as yet. Even Cocky's rimless glasses strayed over in her direction through the glass panes in the top of the partitions from time to time. She had a lovely smile and a sweet, gentle way about her. She was less liked by the other women teachers, but unquestionably a favourite with the headmaster and his visits here were frequent.

That first morning he gave us a performance that was as much for her benefit as ours. Standing in front of us, he said nothing at first and then, as we looked at him, we saw his ears beginning to wiggle back and forth. Slowly at first, then with gathering momentum, until they actually seemed to be flapping back and forth like wings attached to the sides of his head. It drew gasps of wonder from us and even little cries of fright from some, so that Miss Goddard had to make him stop with a gentle little reprimand.

He was about forty then, and a bachelor, and his frequent visits to the 'baby' class did not go unnoticed. They were even talked about on our street. But there had been rumours before about him and the teachers, about Miss Penn particularly. Now it was Miss Goddard. There was also talk that he had once been a milkman and had done his schooling at night. In fact, he was supposed to have been our own milkman, the one who came rattling into our street with his pony and cart, ringing a bell and crying, 'Mee-ulk! Mee-ulk!' Like Mr Mellon, the one we had now, who stopped in the middle of the street right opposite our house, while everyone ran out with their jugs for a pennyworth of the fresh, frothy milk that he ladled out of the big can in his cart.

How true those rumours were about him I don't know. But I do know that he liked Miss Goddard a great deal, and his eyes always seemed to light up when he came into the classroom and looked at her. He also liked my sister Lily, though not in the same way, of course. It was he who had encouraged her to take the scholarship exam and put the notion into her head that she might some day become a schoolteacher. He had also given her some special coaching for the exam, and he had made her his ink monitor and kept her busy running errands. I saw how busy she was that first day at school. I caught glimpses of her flitting about, filling up inkwells, running to classrooms with notes from the headmaster, dashing down to the cellar to mix some more ink, and it was because of all these duties she had to perform that she was late getting out of school that first day I came and kept us waiting for her outside.

Dark, heavy clouds were gathering in the sky. Already lights were being turned on in the shops in St Petersgate, opposite the school. It looked as if a downpour might start any minute. Children were still swarming out of the schoolyard.

'Where the bloody 'ell is she?' muttered Joe.

His face was pale with worry and fear, and he could not stand still. It was not the threat of rain that bothered him, but rather the fact that all the other Jewish children had left. As a rule, they went home together, because this was the time when the batesemas, freed from the restraints of school, the sharp eyes of Cocky Rawlings and the head-master, went wild out in the streets and launched their worst attacks on the luckless Jewish children who were caught alone. In a group we were usually able to fend them off.

The other Jewish children had waited for a while, then had grown impatient and had gone off without us. There was still time to catch up with them if we hurried, and Joe was frantic with impatience and kept glancing at the school door and walking to the windows to peer inside.

Saul and Rose were fuming also, and Rose, never fond of her older sister, was saying unpleasant things about her and trying to get us to go on without her. Perhaps, if it hadn't been for the strict warning our mother always gave us to stay together, we might have done so.

At last she came hurrying through the door and the three of them began attacking her bitterly, accusing her of putting their lives in danger.

'Oh, shut up,' she said contemptuously. 'Nobody's going to hurt you. Just follow me.'

She took the lead, walking in front with me, holding my hand, her head held erect defiantly, with her long, silken hair flowing behind her, her pace brisk. The other three followed, casting fearful looks about them. The other Jewish children were not in sight and it was clear we were not going to catch up with them.

In our hurry we failed to keep our eyes open as we passed the cab stand, and Joe suddenly let out a howl and clutched his ear. One of the idly swinging whips had caught him on the edge of the ear. And then, to make matters worse, we heard jeering laughter behind us.

We swung our heads round and there they were, the same four who had pounced on us in the morning from the vicarage wall. They were walking behind us with arms linked, full of glee at Joe's mishap, and it was clear they were up to no good and probably had been waiting for us to leave the protection of the school.

'Don't pay any attention to them,' Lily hissed. 'Just keep walking and don't look back at them.'

I was frightened. I'd had less experience than they, but I was already familiar with these situations. I clung tightly to Lily's hand. The other three were walking so fast they were almost crowding on top of us. And the four batesemas were maintaining the same pace. They had begun their favourite verse:

> The rabbi, the rabbi, the king of the Jews,
> He bought his wife a pair of shoes.
> When the shoes began to wear,
> The rabbi, the rabbi began to swear.

Howls of laughter followed, hoots, jeers, cries, words: kikes; sheenies; yids; bloody Jews. Who killed Christ? They went through it all. And they were getting closer and closer.

'Don't run, don't run,' Lily hissed at my siblings over her shoulder. 'That's what they want you to do. Then they'll be on you. Just keep going.'

That was a lot easier said than done. She was almost running herself and I was too, terrified already by what I sensed was coming. It was as we reached Daw Bank and were approaching the Devil's Steps that my brothers and sister behind us broke ranks and ran, stumbling into us. Lily and I began to run too and, with wild yells of glee, they were on top of us. Just as I was going down, screaming, with someone on my back, I caught a flash of someone flying out of the Devil's Steps. The next moment, while I was being pummelled, I heard a voice yelling, 'Get off 'em, you bloody little sods.' There was a thumping sound, then the weight lifted off me and someone was helping me to my feet.

Tears streaming out of my eyes, I looked up at my rescuer. It was Arthur Forshaw.

'You're all right now, 'arry,' he said. 'They won't hurt you any more. The little buggers have gone.'

He also helped the others up, all of them crying and more frightened than hurt. He dusted off their clothes for them, then picked up his books. They were scattered over the ground and one of them, which he still held in his hand, had been used as a weapon on the heads of our attackers.

We helped him pick up the books, all of us grateful, Lily effusive in her thanks. 'You saved our lives,' she said.

Arthur grinned. 'I wouldn't go that far. I just bashed a few heads, that's all. Never knew books could be useful that way too.'

We began walking home, with Arthur and Lily walking in front and the rest of us following. Lily seemed to have forgotten altogether about me, and she and Arthur talked steadily and animatedly as they went along. I watched them from behind. They seemed to have so much to say to each other and they made quite an interesting picture, the two of them, Arthur tall and towering over her, and Lily looking up at him as she spoke or listened, her long, silken brown hair flowing down to her slender waist, bobbing with her quick, eager movements.

Rose was noticing them too and could not hide her jealousy. 'Just look at her,' she muttered, 'look at the way she's sucking up to him. You'd think he was a prince or something, or a lord or a duke, instead of just a common bates from our street.'

'He saved our lives,' Joe reminded her, echoing Lily's words. 'And he goes to the Grammar School.'

'Anybody can go to the Grammar School,' Rose said contemptuously. 'It's not like Eton or Rugby. Those are the real high-class schools. He's just a bates and she's in love with him. Anybody can tell that and I'm going to tell her.'

By 'her' she meant my mother. Ever since she had lost her imaginary drawing room to the shop she had refused to talk to my mother, and she referred to her always as 'her', just as we referred to our father as 'he'. And this jealousy of Lily was nothing new; it had been that way from birth, almost, and it would always be that way; and this, together with her new attitude towards my mother, would continue well into adulthood and would be a source of constant pain to my mother.

My mother was waiting for us outside on the corner as we approached our street along Brook Street. She was searching anxiously in the distance, with one hand cupped over her eyes, even though there was no sun out. In fact, it had begun to rain and she was holding an umbrella over her head. She had started worrying ever since she saw the other children come home without us and had been about to set out in search of us.

Joe, Saul and I ran up to her and excitedly poured out the story of the attack. She listened in horror. She put an arm tightly round me. 'That this should have happened on his first day,' I heard her mutter. 'Why didn't you come home with the others?' she asked.

Joe, our spokesman, said, 'We couldn't. Lily had to do something for the headmaster and she kept us waiting.'

'Where is she now?' She was a little bewildered too. Rose had walked straight past her and gone into the house – that was to be expected. But somehow, with her attention focused on us, she had not noticed Lily walk by with Arthur.

'She's over there,' Joe said, pointing.

Lily and Arthur had come to a halt in the middle of our street and they were both still talking in the same animated fashion. The rain was coming down quite heavily by now, but I doubt if either of them noticed it. Our eyes swung over to them and in my mother's eyes there appeared a different sort of expression. She was about to call out to Lily, but Joe interrupted.

'Arthur saved us from the batesemas,' he said. 'He saved our lives.' And he went into detail, explaining the rescue.

It made my mother hesitate. 'That was wonderful,' she said. 'I'm going to have to thank him for what he did.' But aside from that it made no difference and she called out, 'Lily!'

Lily, interrupted, turned her head. 'Yes?' she called back.

'It's raining hard. You'd better come in.'

'I will in a minute,' Lily said impatiently.

'No, I want you in now.'

She said something to Arthur and they separated, he going towards his house, Lily to hers. We followed Lily inside. She was excited. 'Oh, Mam,' she burst out, 'guess what. I was just talking to Arthur Forshaw and I told him how I planned to take the scholarship exam this winter, and he said he would help me prepare for it. He's still got the books he used to study for the exams and he's going to let me have them, and he said I can come into his house after school and he'll go over the studies with me. Isn't that wonderful? I'm bound to win now.'

'Yes, it's very nice of him,' my mother said slowly. 'But I don't think . . .'

Before she could finish, Lily had remembered something. 'Oh, Mam, the headmaster gave me this paper that he has to sign. It's for the exam. The headmaster says it should be done as soon as possible and unless he signs it I won't be able to take the exam.'

She had been fishing in the pocket of her pinafore, and she brought out the paper and handed it to my mother. I could see the uncertainty with which my mother took it from her and the unhappiness on her face. 'Can't I sign it?' she asked.

'The headmaster said he has to sign it.' Then she asked, 'Mam, can I go over to the Forshaws' house now?'

'No.'

'Why not?'

'I don't want you going into a Christian's house.'

'Oh, Mam,' she wailed, 'Mam, Mam, what's wrong with it? Why can't I go into a Christian's house?'

'Because you're Jewish, that's why.'

'Well then, can he come in here? He said he would if I wanted to.'

'No, he can't come in here. I don't want a Christian in my house.'

'But you let Mrs Green come in. And Annie, too. And you have Christians coming into the shop.'

'That's different. I don't want Arthur to come in here.'

'But if he can't come in here, and I can't go into his house, then how is he going to be able to help me? Don't you realise what this means to me? If Arthur helps me I'm bound to pass the exam, and I'll get the scholarship and I'll be able to go to the Grammar School, and then maybe I can become a teacher and I won't have to go into the tailoring shop . . .' She was desperate, pleading, and suddenly she remembered. 'Mam, do you know what Arthur did for us today? When we were coming home from school there was a bunch of batesemas and he . . .'

'Yes, I know,' my mother interrupted. 'Joe already told me. I'm very grateful to Arthur. I think it was a wonderful thing that he did and I'm going to make up a basket of fruit for him. But he's a Christian and I don't want him in the house, and I don't want you in his house.'

Lily let out a cry of anguish. 'Oh, you.' she spluttered, 'you're just what Rose says, you're, you're . . .' She could not say it, and she burst into tears and dashed upstairs.

Chapter 4

Well, now, the autumn days had gone by before you knew it and winter came on with the cold weather that brought us to school shivering. We had coats, some of us, and we hung them in the cloakroom with our caps, hoping they would still be there when we left, for there was a good deal of stealing at St Peter's and you guarded your lunch, too, very carefully, the slices of bread and butter that our mother wrapped for us in newspaper.

It rained a lot still and sometimes the cloakroom would smell like a laundry with all the damp clothes drying. The lights were on all day in school because the rain and the perpetual clouds brought early darkness. Sometimes, too, heavy fogs rolled in, covering the streets like grey shrouds, so dense you could not see an inch in front of you. The headmaster would send us home early when this happened and we would grope our way homewards like blind people, and now and then we'd be guided by the red bobbing lanterns on the back of some clop-clopping cart in front of us.

It was a relief to get home, to burst into the house, all of us simultaneously, to rush to the fire in the kitchen and thrust our hands towards the red-hot coals. And then to

stand there letting our clothes dry and eat the slices of
bread and jam that our mother had prepared for us.

The days were much shorter now. You no longer saw the
people when they came home from the mills: the women
in their striped petticoats and shawls and little bits of
white fluff stuck in their hair; the men carrying their
dinner pails wrapped in big red and white spotted
handkerchiefs. Darkness came on early and yellow lights
showed in all the houses when they were coming home,
and you simply heard the hurried clattering of their clogs,
and the doors opening and closing, and a bit after that the
smell of frying fish and chips and bacon and lard.

I was busy all the time, it seemed. Soon after tea was over
I was on my way to cheder with my two brothers and all
the other Jewish lads from our street. We had to go every
day after school. We were taught Jewish history and the
Hebrew language, together with religion. We went in a
noisy, chattering group, carrying our little black Hebrew
books that we were supposed to have studied. We loitered
a lot along the way, peering in shop windows, kicking
some empty can we'd found back and forth among us, and
invariably Sam Roseman would treat us to his famous
performance: 'One, two, three!' As he counted, his right
arm moved back and forth like the piston of a locomotive,
his right knee was cocked upwards, and at the last word he
let go with a series of loud farts that made us double up
with laughter.

There was still another delay as we came on to
Chestergate Avenue. The mill itself was dark and silent,
but from the grating in its pavement there came a muted
roaring sound accompanied by flashes of light. We could
never resist going across to look down. We were gazing at
the boiler room of the mill and the furnace that was kept

going all night. A big, brawny man, naked to the waist, face blackened, was shovelling coal. He paused to look up at us and grin, the flames dancing behind him. He waved and his lips moved, but we could not hear the words. We waved back and stood watching, fascinated, until someone remembered it was time to go.

At last, we came trooping into the cheder, guilty, blinking in the strong light.

The rabbi stood waiting for us, warming his back against the fireplace, angry and impatient, the long cigarette holder in his hand with the cigarette almost burned down to the end. 'So here you are, finally,' he burst out. 'Where have you been? Playing a little footer, perhaps? Smashing people's windows? Well, let's see how much Hebrew you know. Sit down.' And he added contemptuously, 'Scholars!'

We scrambled for our seats, glad this was all the reprimand we got. The benches were arranged in rows before the fireplace. This room might well have once been the fancy drawing room my sister Rose always dreamed about. It was a large room, airy and light during the day, with high ceiling and a wide, ornate moulding round the borders. There were bow windows looking out on to what had once been a garden, with wooden seats in front of them. The marble fireplace took up almost one entire wall and had a large mantelpiece. The floors, now dark and stained and worn, were probably the original oak floors.

It was redolent of an elegance that belonged to the Victorian era and the aristocracy over which Rose always fantasised. It had given way to the musty smell of siddurs and was filled these nights with the voices of a dozen or so young Jewish boys chanting Hebrew words, and the bellowing voice of a rabbi trying to drum knowledge of an ancient past into their heads.

Our lesson lasted about an hour and during that time the poor rabbi must have aged far beyond his forty or so years. We tormented him endlessly, with the strange noises that Sam Roseman made, sending us into fits of suppressed laughter, with the spit balls that he and his friends threw at one another, but mostly with the mistakes that we made in our Hebrew. The rabbi moved among the benches with the cigarette holder in his hand and the cigarette smouldering, raging, shouting, pointing with a yellow tobacco-stained finger at some spot in the siddur, and sometimes boxing an ear when his rage became uncontrollable.

It must have been a tremendous relief to him when the hour of instruction was over. 'Go home,' he said, his voice hoarse from shouting. 'Go to your mothers and tell them I have done all I can, but I do not know how to perform miracles. Tell them only God can do that.'

And I recall that as we rushed out he wiped his forehead with a handkerchief and muttered slightly to himself. He had other troubles besides us. He had a son who was refusing to go to the synagogue.

Sooner or later that winter we all came down with a cold, sometimes two or three together, so that there was a constant sneezing and blowing of noses, and my mother was forever busy tearing up old sheets and turning them into handkerchiefs, or snot-rags, as we called them.

My turn came and mine was a bad one, with a burning fever that kept me in bed and then, best of all, home from school for another few days after I got out of bed. I was not sorry. By this time I shared my brothers' fear and hatred of St Peter's. I was glad to be home and it was like the old days that I remembered so fondly, being with my mother all day, sitting on the floor near her playing with my few broken toys.

She was always busy and bustling about, especially now that she had her shop, and her long skirt with the apron over it would make a rustling sound as she hurried to answer a knock on the door that meant a customer.

I usually followed her around and sometimes went to the door with her when a knock came. I had learned by now that most of her customers came in during the early part of the afternoon, and they came less to buy than to sit and gossip. It had become a sort of clubroom for them, and some of them would buy a glass of the sour milk that my mother had begun to make and sell, and they would sip as they talked, and in this fashion they would while away a pleasant afternoon.

I think my mother loved these afternoons and looked forward to them. It was an escape from some of the unhappiness of her life and, watching her as I always did, finding a corner for myself when the women began to come in and seeing the flush on her cheeks as she sat behind the counter with all her customers around her, some sipping their sour milk and the room buzzing with talk, I sensed that she was in her element and that she had found something in the shop that was even more important to her perhaps than the little money she made out of it.

There she sat behind that counter, like a queen on her throne, with all her ladies-in-waiting gathered about her. She also made sour cream and potted cheese, and sold these too in addition to the faded fruits and vegetables, and she'd had shelves built along the walls, and if it had not been for the Levines, she would have turned it into a Jewish grocery. But she would never have done that to the Levines, to whom she would always be grateful.

Nevertheless, she had accomplished a great deal and these afternoons were perhaps her biggest reward, the high spot of her day, of her whole sad life.

This particular day was bleak and cloudy. A sharp wind was blowing and the women came in one by one, huddled in their shawls and shivering. To their relief, my mother had built a fire in the shop. She didn't always do this – coal cost too much – but today was exceptionally cold, so she had splurged a little with her meagre supply of coal and the glow of the fire in the dimness of the room added to the cosiness of the gathering.

I watched from my corner, hidden by a sack of potatoes on one side and a sack of onions on the other. Fanny Cohen, who was my mother's closest friend and who had been the first to arrive, was sitting on an upturned orange crate near the counter, a thin, bedraggled woman with hair hanging over her eyes, rocking her baby back and forth to keep it from crying and interfering with the talk that was going on.

They were jabbering away in a strange mixture of English with a Lancashire accent and Yiddish, with an occasional Russian or Polish word thrown in. I scarcely listened. The topics did not interest me. Since this was Thursday, the day Mrs Zarembar went into the country for her chickens, there was much speculation as to the kind of chickens she would bring back, and then it was the high prices the kosher butcher was charging for his meat, and from there they went on to the trouble the rabbi was having with his son who would not attend the synagogue, and then a rumour that one of the Harris girls was going out with a boy from Manchester.

And right after this someone mentioned a name that made me prick up my ears.

'What about Sarah?' asked Mrs Mittleman, a loud-voiced, aggressive woman who lived at the lower end of the street. 'What's doing with her?'

I listened now.

'Yes,' somebody else asked. 'Is she better?'

The questions may well have been directed at Mrs Jacobs, a one-eyed woman who lived with her little hump-backed husband and retarded son Rafael in the house next to the Harrises, the one usually best informed on this subject.

At first she shrugged, as if to say why should she know more than anyone else? The fact that the walls separating our houses were paper thin and you could hear everything that went on in the house next to you didn't mean that she was listening. She made this clear. 'How should I know?' she said. 'I see Sarah sometimes, and what else do I know?'

'Is she still sick or not?' insisted Mrs Mittleman. 'I hear she's sick and I hear she isn't sick. So what's the true story?'

'I've seen her walking outside already,' volunteered Fanny Cohen, shaking her baby up and down this time instead of from side to side. 'I saw her even today.'

The eyes turned questioningly on Mrs Jacobs again and still she said nothing, and Mrs Mittleman exclaimed, 'Today? In this weather? So how can she be sick?'

'And if she isn't sick, why isn't she going to work?' one other woman wanted to know.

It was puzzling and it was up to Mrs Jacobs to explain the matter, and after a moment she burst out, 'Why should she go to work? Why should she not go to work? Is she sick? Is she not sick? You think I have nothing to do all day except listen to them argue?'

'They argue?' said Mrs Mittleman, her voice probing,
demanding. 'About what?'

'How should I know?' said Mrs Jacobs irritably. 'Who
cares? Let them argue. So the father wants her back in the
shop. The mother says no, she is not well enough yet.
Sarah herself, all she wants to do is go out and get fresh
air. The mother says the air is not good for her, she
must lie on the sofa in the parlour. Sarah says this, the
mother says that, the father says another thing. So it goes.
You think they know what's best? I know. A long time
ago I told them. Sarah needs a husband, not fresh air or
a sofa in the parlour. But my Rafael is not good enough
for them.'

An uncomfortable silence fell among them for a moment
and eyes glanced surreptitiously at one another. This
situation was an old one and they understood the bitterness that had crept into Mrs Jacobs's tone. She could never
see her son as others did, a gawky boy who said foolish
things and whose mouth dribbled like an old man's. Her
attempts to make a match between him and Sarah had
been going on for a long time.

'My son is a good religious boy,' she said, pursuing the
matter still further. 'He was barmitzvahed like any other
boy on the street, he goes to shul every Saturday and he
makes a living. So he doesn't operate a machine. He sweeps
up and carries bundles on to the lorries, but he works
steady and he brings home his pay every week and what
more can a girl want? You tell me.'

But no one said anything. No one wanted to get involved
in her problem. The uncomfortable silence lasted a
moment longer until, to their relief, one woman whose
eyes had strayed to the window cried out, 'Ah, here comes
the Zarembar woman.'

All eyes instantly went to the window, mine too. Yes, there she was, the fat little woman waddling her way up the street, struggling with her two bulging, squirming straw bags. Everyone noticed too how fast she seemed to be trying to walk.

'She must be in a hurry to get home,' someone murmured.

But they were all getting ready to follow her into her house. Those who had been drinking sour milk put their glasses down on the counter and they all began pulling shawls over their heads. In another few moments the shop would be empty, but to their surprise, instead of continuing up the street, she turned in at our house

We heard the front door open, then close after her. She had never done this before and everyone looked at one another with a puzzled expression. In a moment she appeared in the doorway. She must have deposited her two bags of chickens in the lobby, because her hands were free and we could hear the faint cluckings behind her. She stood there surveying us all, turning her head from this side to that and murmuring faint greetings. Her cheeks were fiery red from the wind and cold, and she was rubbing her two hands together, perhaps from the same thing, or was it from a certain suppressed excitement that seemed to emanate from her?

They all sensed it and were looking at her curiously. Certainly, this had nothing to do with chickens.

'Come in,' my mother said. 'Come to the fire and warm yourself.'

She walked slowly up to the fire, with all eyes on her. There was not much of the fire left, but embers still glowed and she held out her hands towards them. In the meantime an impatient Mrs Mittleman called out, 'So how are the chickens today? Did you bring any good ones?'

'Yes, I have some very good ones. The best.' She threw this over her shoulder at Mrs Mittleman, but absently, as if her mind were on something else.

The others had noticed it. They waited, their curiosity growing. The fat little woman did not seem in a hurry. She held out her hands towards the fire. Yet there was every indication that she held some sort of secret within her. After another moment she turned her head and glanced around the room once more, and asked my mother, 'Mrs Harris is not here?'

My mother looked at her in surprise. Couldn't she have seen for herself that she was not here? 'Not unless she's hiding under the counter,' she said mischievously and glanced under it herself.

No one laughed and my mother added, 'You want to see her?'

'No,' said Mrs Zarembar.

'Then why do you ask for her?'

The others wanted to know that too. But now the fat little woman was glancing around yet again and this time her eyes lit on me. 'He understands Yiddish?' she asked my mother in a low voice.

'My children speak only English,' said my mother and there might have been a touch of regret in her voice, because it was not the way she had wanted. But it was the way it had turned out.

However, her words seemed to reassure Mrs Zarembar, and she turned round completely to face them and began to speak, her voice so low at first that they had to come closer to listen; and soon they were all gathered round the counter in a tight little knot, while I remained seated in my corner. The clouds outside had grown menacing and could be seen through the window hanging low over the chimneys and rooftops of the row of houses opposite us in thick black masses, and the room had darkened still more and the embers in the fire were like tiny red eyes.

The voices whispered. They were all speaking now and there were gasps of horror, little cries of incredulity intermingled. I did not understand then what it was about, but I had the feeling that something terrible had happened, a catastrophe worse than anything that had ever befallen our street.

I heard Mrs Jacobs give a shout of triumph. 'And my Rafael was not good enough for them!' she cried, lifting both arms up to heaven, to God, in a gesture of gratitude.

'Are you sure?' my mother asked, her voice trembling with emotion. 'Are you absolutely sure?'

'I swear!' cried Mrs Zarembar. 'On the graves of my father and mother, they should rest in peace, I swear.'

There was a hubbub of voices. Clearly, this was the most sensational bit of gossip ever to come out of my mother's shop. Mrs Mittleman's voice rose, dominating all the others, demanding, 'This I must hear once more. Tell me again. Start from the beginning. I want to know everything that happened.'

By this time they had forgotten my presence completely and had begun to use English with their Yiddish, and as a result I was able to understand much of what Mrs Zarembar repeated to them – repeated, I must say, with much relish.

Mrs Zarembar's forages into the country for chickens – good fat ones at low prices – usually followed the same route, taking her across the moor and past the peat bog where we sometimes dug for the chunks of peat that became our fuel when we could not afford coal; and then out into Cheadle where the farms began in those days. The tram would have taken her out there much faster and more easily, but a tram cost money and what else did she have to do with her time?

Besides, she enjoyed her walk, even though she had difficulty walking with legs that were thick and short and old. But her awkward footsteps took her through woods and fields, and past trickling brooks that sparkled in the sun like jewels. In the summer the fields would be covered with glowing buttercups and daisies and bluebells that gave off a rich, perfumed smell. But even in the winter, with harsh winds blowing like today, it was enjoyable and her cheeks tingled with health. She had made her stop at the farm where she purchased her chickens and, after much haggling, had concluded her business and was on her way home, weighed down on either side by a squirming bag, refreshed by the cup of tea that the farmer's wife always gave her.

She was walking through a huge grove of old oak and beech trees, whose bare branches swayed in the wind and gave off a soughing sound that was like a deep sigh. Her feet trod softly on the carpet of dead, rotted leaves that lay on the ground and a loamy smell rose up from the earth. She was alone, it seemed, with peace and quiet all around her, when suddenly she saw two people walking some distance ahead of her, moving very slowly and in dreamlike fashion, a young man and a girl, with their arms linked round one another's waists. They were lovers, evidently, and every so often they paused to kiss.

'They kissed?' Mrs Mittleman interrupted breathlessly.

'Yes.' Mrs Zarembar frowned, obviously annoyed at the interruption.

Yes, they kissed several times, long, passionate kisses, enfolded tightly in one another's arms. Then they would go on. Mrs Zarembar, following them slowly, smiled to herself. How well she remembered her own romantic days. Perhaps she would have deviated from her story and gone into an account of those days if there hadn't been mutters of complaint from the other women.

She continued. They were walking very slowly ahead of her and she deliberately slowed down her own footsteps so that she would not catch up with them, because it was such a pleasure to watch them. She did not want to spoil it with her presence and the clucking of her chickens. Then gradually something began to dawn on her. She saw them only from behind, but she was beginning to realise there was something familiar about them. They stopped for another kiss and now it came to her. Of course! How could she have been mistaken?

The heads drew closer as she came to this part, because her voice was lower. I was not able to catch the words she spoke, but again came the same gasps of horror, and once again Mrs Jacobs triumphantly cast her one good eye and both arms up to heaven and shouted, 'And my Rafael was not good enough for them!' Only this time she added, 'Now it becomes a question, is she good enough for my son?'

No one paid any attention to her, for Mrs Mittleman was demanding to know what she did then, and Mrs Zarembar was shrugging and saying, 'What could I do? What should I do? I nearly fainted from the shock. But after all, I am not the girl's mother. It was not for me to say or do anything. I turned round and went home another way. I couldn't bear to look at them any longer.'

'If it was me,' declared Mrs Mittleman viciously, 'I would have struck her. I would have pulled her hair out. I don't care if she was my daughter or not. She's a Jewish girl and she has no right to be going out with a goy, and kissing him, no less, and God knows what else she might have been doing.'

'No, no,' my mother intervened. 'She did the right thing. It's for the mother to decide what to do and the mother has to be told.'

'Who will tell her?' murmured Fanny Cohen. Her baby, quiet for a while, had begun to cry again and she was jouncing it up and down.

'What the mother should do,' said my mother, not answering the question, 'is send her off to America.' It was her panacea for all our ills: America, the answer to everyone's problems, including her own, and if she herself could not go it would have given her satisfaction to see someone else go at least.

But Mrs Mittleman shook her head stubbornly. 'No, a good hiding would be the best thing, a beating that she'd never forget.'

And then, suddenly, someone said, 'Sshh!'

All the heads turned and there, standing in the doorway, was Mrs Harris. She had come in so softly that no one had noticed and it was hard to say how long she had been standing there, or how much she had heard. She was huddled in her shawl, her little hen's eyes peering suspiciously at them from beneath the wig.

I had been so immersed in the talk going on, aware that it was about Sarah and Freddy, that I had not noticed her come in either and I felt the same shock as they did. A long, awkward silence followed, broken finally by my mother, who spoke nervously. 'Good afternoon, Mrs Harris,' she said. 'Why don't you come in and warm yourself by the fire.'

The fire had long since gone out and there was only grey ash left in the grate. But Mrs Harris had ignored her invitation, and without a word had begun to examine the bushels and boxes of vegetables, feeling and pinching and sniffing. Mrs Zarembar was the first among them to decide that it was time for her to leave and she said her goodbyes with invitations to all of them to come and see her chickens, invitations that were accepted with alacrity, for they began instantly pulling their shawls over their heads and hurrying out. Fanny, whose baby was bawling lustily by now, followed suit and she was the last to go.

A deep silence settled over the shop. My mother sat watching Mrs Harris as she went silently among the vegetables still huddled in her shawl, still poking and sniffing here and there. My mother looked troubled and I knew what was going through her mind. She was wondering how to tell her the dreadful bit of news that had been passed to her over the counter.

She waited. Mrs Harris didn't seem satisfied with any of the things she saw, she found fault with everything, this too soft, this no good, the tomatoes too ripe. My mother didn't argue with her. It was becoming clear that the woman had come in less to buy than to talk. She herself looked troubled and unhappy, and there was no telling how much she might have heard, standing in the doorway.

But regardless of that there was much for her to be troubled about, with four daughters and a son unmarried. Yet there was one bright spot in all this and my mother ventured to say, 'I hear that Leah is going out with a boy from Manchester. Is it time yet to say mazeltov?'

Mrs Harris gave a bitter little laugh and a shrug. 'What is he? A presser in a shop. He hardly makes a living for himself, let alone a wife.'

'But he goes to shul?' said my mother.

Again she shrugged. 'He goes to shul, yes, but he smokes on Shabbos, so what kind of Jew can he be?'

My mother sighed. There was no bright spot after all. Any boy who smoked on Shabbos would automatically be disqualified from marrying one of the Harris girls. But there was much worse for them to discover, my mother must have reflected, and she edged closer to what she had to do, saying, 'And Sarah? I hear she is much better now and goes for walks.'

'Yes, walks,' replied Mrs Harris, not looking at her, still examining the baskets of vegetables and fruits. There had been something bitter in her tone and it could have meant that she knew something.

My mother watched her closely and I saw how her hands were clenched together. How difficult all this must have been for her, whether Mrs Harris knew or not. But she couldn't have known. Such a monstrous thing couldn't have been kept within her so quietly. No, my mother must have decided she had to get it over with quickly before it destroyed her too. 'Mrs Harris,' she said in a low voice 'I have something to tell you.'

'Tell me?' She looked up at her from a basket, her little eyes inquisitive.

'Yes, I must tell you. It is very important.' She glanced at me, and Mrs Harris saw the glance and realised that it was something confidential that I should not hear, even though they were talking in Yiddish.

She shuffled up to the counter, and my mother leaned across to her and began to whisper, and I saw what seemed like an electric shock go through the old woman's body. I saw her clutch the shawl at her neck and heard her own hoarse whisper, 'No, no, no. It is not true. It is a lie. The Zarembar woman lies.'

'I wish that she did,' said my mother, her voice trembling. 'But she has sworn on the graves of her mother and father, and she has told the story twice, and we have questioned her and she does not change a word.'

'No, it can't be true,' insisted Mrs Harris, and it was clear she had known nothing until now and was in a terrible state of shock. 'How could she have even known the shaigets? She has been in bed all summer.'

There was more whispering between them, with their heads close together and both leaning over the counter. I saw my mother glance towards me several times and Mrs Harris also looked back at me, and then my mother said, 'You will see. He knows.' She called, ''arry, come here.'

I got up off the floor and walked over to the counter. I felt a little afraid. I did not know why I was being brought into all this.

''arry,' my mother said, 'has Sarah been sending you to Gordon's for ginger beer?'

'Yis,' I replied.

'And does she always ask you to give the empty bottle to Freddy, and to make sure he waits on you?'

'Yis,' I replied.

'And 'arry,' said my mother, 'did Sarah give you a note to give to Freddy also?'

'No,' I said, 'she put the note in the ginger beer bottle, and Freddy put his in the bottle too.'

'You see?' said my mother, turning to Mrs Harris triumphantly. 'That's how it was done.'

But Mrs Harris was still shaking her head vigorously and saying, 'No, no, no.' Then she demanded, 'Can he say emes to all this?'

''arry,' said my mother, 'has the rabbi taught you what emes is?'

'Yis,' I answered. 'Emes Adonai.'

'It means truth to God,' said my mother. 'And if you say it and are telling a lie you can die. Do you know that?'

'Yis. The rabbi told us.'

'Then can you say it now?'

I nodded.

'Say it then.'

'Emes Adonai,' I said.

And no sooner had I spoken these two words than Mrs Harris let out an anguished cry, and clapped her hands to her face and instantly ran out of the shop, startling both of us. We remained as we were, my mother and I, not moving or saying anything, with the shop growing darker as still heavier clouds gathered outside. We heard the door close behind her and we saw her pass the window, almost doubled over in her shawl and running. Then rain began to spatter lightly against the window.

My mother roused herself with a sigh and said, 'They'll be coming home from school soon. I'd better go out to meet them with an umbrella.'

This was not her usual practice, for we were accustomed to getting wet in the rain. But now there was a deeper anxiety than ever. She was afraid, terribly afraid. I watched her as she hurried to get an umbrella and went out. I was alone in the shop and it was very dark, almost like night. The rain drove harder against the window and there was a little whistling sound from the wind.

The truth was, ever since that day of the attack, Arthur had been our escort a good part of the way to and from school. He would go as far as the Devil's Steps with us in the morning, and he would be waiting for us there in the afternoon and walk us home; and my mother had not been able to do anything about that, nor had she tried; nor had she really wanted to because of the protection Arthur gave us.

I am sure, though, she must have had many doubts as the winter went on and spent sleepless nights worrying over it, and when we came in from school she cast anxious looks at Lily, as if to see if there was any change in her.

Well, all she saw was that Lily looked bright and animated, her cheeks flushed with elation. Arthur, who was fully aware of the situation and accepted it good-naturedly, tutored Lily as they went along the streets coming to and from school. They walked ahead of us, Arthur towering over Lily and Lily's long hair bobbing at the back of her waist, her face turned eagerly up to him as they talked.

Sometimes they read from one of his books as they walked and their heads would come close together, and Rose would give a sarcastic laugh and say, 'I'll bet they're going to start kissing soon. Won't she smart when I tell her about it.'

But my mother, to whom she was referring, never did get to hear about this part of it, because Rose hardly ever spoke to her and once we came home it was all forgotten anyway. Except perhaps by Lily, who was in seventh heaven these days.

She was quite sure now that she was going to pass her exam and win a scholarship – and if she did, could her mother object to her walking to the Grammar School with Arthur every day? One of my mother's fears when Lily had first broached the subject of a scholarship and going to the Grammar School was her having to walk all that distance alone. Well, there would be nothing to fear now. I had never seen Lily so happy and confident as she was in those days. She studied most of the time, burying herself in her books at the kitchen table, oblivious of the noises we made; but when there were things to be done around the house for my mother, like washing the windows or polishing the brass candlesticks for Friday, she sang over her work, and she had a lovely, sweet voice and my mother would smile over her happiness.

There was one cloud hanging over them both constantly. Almost every day before she set out for school, Lily would ask, 'Did you speak to him about it?'

My mother's forehead would crease and the worried look would come to her face. 'Not yet,' she'd murmur. 'I didn't get the chance.'

'Oh, you never get the chance,' Lily would cry. 'What am I to tell the headmaster? He keeps asking me for the slip.'

'I'll speak to him tonight,' my mother would promise.

But it was not tonight. Nor the night after. My mother simply lacked the courage. Could anyone blame her? During the day he came and went swiftly. He ate his meal with his head bent low over the plate, shovelling the food into his mouth with noises and grunts, and no one dared speak to him then. As soon as he was done he was up with a scraping sound of the chair, and soon putting on his coat, and leaving with one sleeve dangling behind him and his arm groping for it. Then at night, while she was busy mending and darning under the gaslight, he came home, and who could tell what condition he was in and what might result if she broached the matter?

So she kept putting it off, day after day, night after night, and the little white slip of paper the headmaster had given Lily remained tucked away under the oilcloth on the mantelpiece, where my mother kept her valuable things, still neatly folded, unsigned.

And time was slipping by. It was now December. God knows, there were other more important matters to think about. The war was now well under way. Battles had been fought and men killed. Our street was emptying of its men. One after another they were being called up. My father's turn would soon come. Perhaps this was on his mind. Maybe this was another reason why my mother hesitated to approach him about signing the slip of paper for the exam. Yet it could not be forgotten. The exam would take place early in the month of January, a week or so after Boxing Day.

And now there was something else to contend with, this one coming on that dark, rainy day, a catastrophe that overshadowed everything else. For the time being, that day, all my mother could think of was to run out with an umbrella and meet us coming home from school.

We all heard the cries, the slaps, the screams, the voice roaring, the other voice pleading for mercy. It was late evening. It was after supper. We were sitting round the fire reading, our heads buried in books, magazines, mine in a comic paper.

At first, we thought it was the Finklesteins, who often fought among themselves. They were our next-door neighbours and almost every night the sounds of their fighting came through the paper-thin wall, and once, I remember, Jane the oldest one came running into our house with her arm bleeding where her mother had stabbed her. My mother had cleaned the wound and bandaged it, and kept her there with us until she got up enough courage to go back.

But it was not the Finklesteins this time. We had lifted our heads from our books and magazines to listen. No, it came from further up the street, from of all places the

Harris house, the one place where there was always order and quiet, along with strict religious observance.

Others had heard it. All up and down the street, on both sides, doors were opening and people came out in the dark to listen. They did not exchange comments among themselves, as they sometimes did when the Finklesteins fought. They knew where it was coming from, and after standing out there for a few moments they went inside and closed their doors quietly.

In our house we said nothing either. We knew by now what it was all about. So did everyone, for that matter. The news about Sarah and Freddy had spread like wildfire on both sides. Mr Harris had come home late from his workshop. He had plodded home with his son, Sam, and barely had the two entered the house than Mrs Harris, still weeping, had told them. Mr Harris had not even waited to remove his bowler hat, but in the wild rage that swept through him as he went into swift, immediate action, the hat fell off and he finished the terrible hiding he gave Sarah with his yarmulke bobbing on his feverish head.

Eventually, it was over, and the cries and shouts and screams subsided, and in our house we all drew in a deep breath of relief. But it was not quite over for us yet. My mother was trembling, as if she herself might have received the punishment. She stood facing us, with her hands clasped under her chin, and said, 'You see what happens when a girl like Sarah goes out with a shaigets. Do you know what a shaigets is?'

'A goy,' mumbled Joe.

'Yes. And do you know what would happen if a Jewish girl married a goy?'

No one answered her question at first. We were all staring at her.

'What?' asked Joe.

Her eyes seemed to be fixed especially on Lily as she answered. 'She dies,' she said and then, seeing the horror that came into our eyes, she relented a little and went on, 'I don't mean she actually dies. But as far as the parents and all her family are concerned she is dead and they sit shiveh for her.'

'What's shiveh?' Joe asked.

'Shiveh is mourning for the dead. The family has to sit for seven days in their stockinged feet. That is what they have to do when a daughter or a son marries a Christian.'

She was still looking steadily at Lily as she spoke, and Lily was pretending not to notice, but after a moment she got up and said, 'I think I'll go to bed.'

'Yes, I think you all should,' my mother said.

No one argued that night. We followed Lily up the stairs quietly.

And now, soon afterwards, Sarah was leaving us. All the street watched. They stood on their doorsteps on both sides and watched as Sarah walked down the street with her father on one side of her carrying a satchel and Sam on the other carrying a trunk on his shoulder. Sarah was smiling a little, and she looked very pretty and grown-up in her dark coat that did not completely cover the dress that encircled her ankles and a large broad-brimmed hat with a bunch of cherries on one side.

They paused briefly at almost every doorstep on our side so that Sarah could say goodbye to the families gathered there. No one ever went away anywhere on our street without saying goodbye. Even when you went to Manchester, a distance of just about eight miles by tram, it was the custom to go from door to door to say goodbye. And Sarah was going much further.

To Australia. My mother would rather she had gone to America, but the Harrises had relatives in Australia, so that was why she was going there and, as far as my mother was concerned, while Australia was not as good as America, it was better than nothing. She was satisfied, just as Mrs Mittleman was satisfied that her advice had been carried out too. A good hiding such as her father gave her that night would teach her a lesson she would never forget. She expressed herself clearly on that subject later in the shop and all the others agreed.

That day, watching her go, I could almost see the envy on my mother's face. How she wished she and her family were going off to Liverpool to board a ship. Sarah came up to us finally. We were the last ones she would say goodbye to, since they had to turn on Brook Street to go to the railway station.

My mother clasped Sarah in her arms and wept a little, as all the other women had done, while Sarah's father and brother stood waiting impatiently, Mr Harris's bearded face glowering under his bowler hat, Sam perspiring a little under the weight of the trunk on his shoulder.

'You must write to us,' my mother said. 'You mustn't forget.'

'Yes, of course,' Sarah said. She was smiling, but she spoke absently and I am sure her mind was on something else, and even then she was casting glances down the street towards the Gordons' shop on the other side.

But when she kissed me her manner was less absent and she hugged me for quite a while, and I caught the last scent of lavender from her. 'Goodbye, 'arry,' she whispered. 'I won't forget you and you mustn't forget me. And thank you so much for fetching the ginger beer.'

Then she was all done and ready to go. She straightened up and took a last look around her at the street, and once again, for the last time, her eyes strayed down towards the lower corner on the other side. And there was Freddy, who had come out of his shop in his long white apron, standing looking up at her.

They both looked at one another for a little while, then Sarah walked on between her father and Sam, and I stood watching them go along Brook Street. In the distance you could see the viaduct. Trains crossed it and they were heading for the station about two miles away in Edgeley. I watched until they had disappeared from sight, but I remained standing there until a train ran across the viaduct and I pictured Sarah sitting on it looking through a window, watching the town disappear with that sweet smile on her face.

It was all in vain. The Harrises might well have saved themselves all the trouble they went through with Sarah, not to speak of the dangers of the ship crossing to Australia with the German U-boats sinking ships. For it was not long afterwards that Freddy joined the army and went off to France to fight in the war, and Florrie was left alone finally, which she had always dreaded, with less chance than ever of marrying that fellow from Birmingham.

Chapter Five

It snowed once that winter. It began to fall from a yellowish sky one afternoon and the snow looked dark coming down, almost as if it were flakes of soot rather than snow. But when it struck the rooftops and the ground and the windowsills it was white, and we almost went mad with joy. We ran up and down the street, trying to catch the flakes in our hands, and tilting up our faces so that we could catch them in our wide-open mouths too, with our tongues sticking out.

The snow came down steadily all afternoon, and covered the rooftops except for the chimneys and the base of the chimneys where the heat from the fires kept it from sticking. Then soon there was enough snow on the ground to make toboggan slides.

It was a Sunday afternoon and everybody was home, and the Christian men and boys were still wearing their best black Sunday suits that they went to church in, and most of them didn't bother to change. Stanley Jackson and Johnny Melrose and Willie Humberstone and the other Christian lads opposite us began to make a slide on their side, and Zalmon Roseman and Philly Cohen and my brothers Joe and Saul and all the other Jewish lads on our side began to make one for us too, so pretty soon you had a Jewish slide and a Christian slide, and all the men and women came out on the doorsteps to watch, or if it was too cold for them they watched from the windows.

I tried it myself and I was scared at first. You started at the top, out on the street near the Harrises' house, and the slide ran all the way down to Wood Street, at the very bottom, and the further down you went on the incline the faster and faster you went. I fell several times before I got the knack of it; then I was like all the others, yelling and screaming as I raced down, and balancing myself with my arms spread out.

After a while the surface of the two slides became glassy, and warnings began to be shouted from doorsteps. Several accidents had taken place, and children had dropped out with bruised knees and cut faces, and I was one of them. I had taken a bad fall and scraped a hand. But still I refused to go inside the house and stayed out watching.

Now, some of the men had joined in the activity. Johnny Melrose's father had taken a run down, surprising everyone with his agility and skill, and by being able to keep his pipe in his mouth all the time. A quiet, stocky man, who tramped to and from the mill daily with his head cast down a little, the pipe always in his mouth, he hardly looked the kind who'd be tobogganing down a slide. But he was a regular daredevil at it, racing swiftly, balancing himself with ease and landing at the bottom on both feet.

And now, soon, the women were sliding down with the men, clinging to their waists, screaming and probably less frightened than they seemed. I saw Freddy Gordon come out of the shop with his long white apron on and march up the street, obviously on his way to the top of the slide. He stopped halfway up the row. Mrs Green was standing outside her door and I could see Annie behind her in the doorway, holding the baby.

I heard Freddy say, 'Come on and take the slide with me, Annie.'

'Oh no, I couldn't,' said Annie and you could see she was flustered by the invitation.

'Go on,' her mother urged. 'Go on and give yourself a bit of fun.'

'No, I couldn't,' Annie repeated. 'I'm afeard and I've got to mind the baby.'

'I'll mind 'im for you,' Mrs Green shouted. 'Go on, you bloody fool. You might never get the chance again.'

She almost pulled the baby out of Annie's arms and pushed her straight at Freddy. He caught her and led her up the hill. Everybody was looking at them, and Annie knew it and looked embarrassed. Freddy himself didn't seem to mind the eyes staring at them.

Later on it would be discussed in our shop and there'd be much shaking of heads over what they had seen, with someone saying with a laugh, 'Well, if things work out right Mrs Green will get all the beer she wants for nothing. There was a lot of agreement on this and a lot of unpleasant things were said about Freddy. And someone muttered, 'Please God, she shouldn't have another baby.' There was a long silence after that.

That day they all watched as Freddy and Annie started down the incline, arms round one another's waists, Annie obviously frightened and clinging tightly to Freddy. Down they went. Freddy was expert at it. He waved the free arm cheerfully as they picked up speed, then raced past the houses and the staring people, past the grinning, cackling, delighted Mrs Green, coming to a safe stop right in front of the Gordon shop, where Florrie stood, grim and tight-lipped, hands on hips, furious. 'You bloody fool,' she shouted, unable to contain herself any longer. 'You're at it again.'

The slides melted during the night, and most of the snow had disappeared when we got up and stared, disappointed, through the window. Here and there a patch of dirty white remained, but it was nothing. We went to school as usual. This time Arthur did not accompany us. It was forbidden. He walked ahead of us with his long stride and his books under his arm, and Lily pretended not to see him. She walked with me in front, holding my hand, and her head bent a little, and her long, silken hair bobbing behind her, silent all the way. She was terribly unhappy about not being allowed to speak to Arthur any more and bitter too. She hardly ever spoke to my mother either these days. But she studied harder than ever, poring over her books at night and, whenever there was an opportunity, during the day.

At school she was busy with her monitor duties, rushing down to the basement to mix ink, rushing back up again to fill inkwells, rushing with notes from the headmaster to the teachers, always rushing, with her long hair swinging about. But we were all being kept busy learning Christmas carols. The Christmas holidays were approaching and a religious fervour had swept over the headmaster, and now at any time during the day it could be expected that classes would be interrupted, the partitions pushed back and all of us ordered to stand on the forms to sing carols: 'Good King Wenceslas looked out . . .' I think this must have been his favourite, because it was sung over and over again, with Miss Penn thumping out the accompaniment on the piano, and the headmaster beating time with his stick and bouncing up and down on the balls of his feet, his large red ears sticking out like two wings on either side of his head, and they were a deeper blood-red than ever as the religious passion flowed through his veins.

Outside, the skies remained grey and overcast, and the days were shorter than ever. By the time we left school, lights were on in the shops and on the motor lorries, and lanterns bobbed at the back of carts. Curiously, although Arthur was not allowed to walk with us or speak to Lily any more, he always happened to be at the Devil's Steps as we came along, and he managed to stay in sight just a short distance ahead of us as we walked the rest of the way home, and it was always a comfort to us to know that he was there.

Lily came home from school with us, bitter and almost in tears one day. The headmaster had spoken to her again about the permit slip and warned that if she did not get it in before the Christmas holidays, signed by her father, she would not be allowed to take the exam.

'I'll try to talk to him tonight,' my mother said nervously.

'You're always saying that,' Lily burst out. 'It's always tonight and you never do it. I don't think you want me to take the exam. You don't want me to go to the Grammar School. You want me to go into the tailoring shop – with him, work with him, be with him all day. I'd rather die than do that,' she added passionately, the tears starting to come to her eyes.

'You mustn't talk that way,' my mother said. 'Of course I want you to take the exam. And of course I want you to go to the Grammar School and become a teacher. I want nothing else. But you've got to be patient. If I ask your father at the wrong time that would be the end of it.'

'It's always the wrong time,' Lily said. 'I don't think

there's ever going to be a right time. If you don't ask him, then I will.'

'No!' my mother cried. 'You mustn't do that.'

'Why? Why can't I ask him?'

'You mustn't, that's why.'

That was the end of the discussion and I really think my mother was determined to speak to him when he came home that night. She was in a highly nervous state when she said goodnight to us. Lily gave her a long look before we went upstairs and my mother nodded as if to let her know she understood its meaning. Yes, there was every indication that she was going to do it, no matter what. She even had the permit slip on top of the mantelpiece ready to show him and that in itself showed how determined she was.

Yet in spite of that she failed once again and it was hardly her fault. Nobody could have predicted that for the first time my father would not come home alone.

We saw him fast asleep on the torn black leather sofa in the kitchen that was also the living room when we came downstairs next morning. A strange man stretched out on the only comfortable place there was to sit in the entire house, occupying the room where we ate and read our books in front of the fire, and which we lived in. His face showed on the pillow, a rather pale, flabby face and his feet were sticking out of the blanket. He was snoring heavily and frequently coughing in his sleep.

My mother put a finger to her lips and said 'Sshh' as we entered.

Who was he? we all wanted to know in whispers. She explained in whispers too: he was our boarder. A friend of our father's, or at least an acquaintance he had struck up in the pub, a Jewish man from Leeds who had just come into our town and was looking for lodgings.

There was an immediate outcry from all of us. From
Rose especially. This was even more shocking than the
shop: a boarder, and to make matters worse a pal of his and
another one like him undoubtedly.

Rose burst into a torrent of abuse. 'Oh, isn't it like her, to
do this to us? She doesn't care about us. All she cares about
is herself and the money she can make. Money, money,
money. That's all she can think of. It's a wonder she doesn't
turn us out of our own beds to put this tramp up.'

Little did she know that was more or less what would
have to be done. But my mother wisely refrained from
mentioning it then. She answered Rose gently, saying,
'You'll get used to it and it won't be as bad as you think.
He's not a tramp. He's a hard-working Jewish man, who
doesn't have a home of his own, and yes, I can use the
money. There's nothing terrible about that.'

'Nothing's terrible for you,' Rose sneered.

My mother did not say anything to this. Nor did she
mention that taking care of a boarder would add more work
to all the other things she had to do, her shop that was
enough in itself to keep her busy, and then all the other
chores of the household. Although she may have been
thinking of it.

Nor did Lily speak. She had been silent through it all.
Her mind was on one thing only. The moment she had
come downstairs her eyes had gone to the mantelpiece.
The permit slip was still there unsigned. 'You did nothing
about it,' she burst out suddenly.

Attacked from this other side, my mother drew a deep
breath. 'No, I couldn't,' she said. 'I was going to but then he
came home with this man and I couldn't speak in front of
him.'

'You wouldn't have anyway,' said Lily bitterly, beginning to cry. 'You're just finding excuses.'

She sounded now like Rose and my mother must have had difficulty holding back her temper. But just then our attention was drawn to the man on the sofa. He had awakened and was half sitting up listening to the quarrel. 'Good morning,' he said cheerfully.

'Oh, I'm sorry,' my mother said, embarrassed. 'We didn't mean to wake you up.'

'That's all right,' he said, and coughed and looked about for some place to spit, and finding none must have swallowed what he had in his mouth. 'That's all right,' he repeated. 'I'm the one should say sorry. I shouldn't be lying here in your kitchen. Where's Jack?'

'He's at work,' my mother said.

'It's that late?' He sat up fully, smiled at us and said, 'Hello, kiddies.'

We said nothing and my mother put in hastily, 'They're off to school. Go on,' she said to us, 'you'd better hurry.'

We left and Rose, thinking she had found a new ally in Lily, walked beside her at the front, still spitting venom about her mother. 'Oh, it's nothing more than spite,' she said. 'All she wants to do is drag us down to her level. She's real low class. I don't know about you, but one of these days I'm going to pack my things and just leave. That tramp is just about the last straw for me. After this I don't know how I can face the neighbours.'

Lily said nothing. Nor did we. Our hearts were pretty heavy that day, thinking of the unwanted stranger who'd been brought into our midst. With Rose chattering her spite, we walked to school in silence. And perhaps Lily was the unhappiest of all of us. She tried to avoid talking to the headmaster that day and he, probably sensing the hopelessness of it, said nothing to her. He knew about my father – everybody, in fact, did – and he must have guessed the situation.

The first thing we did when we came home, bursting into the house in our usual fashion, was glance at the sofa, as if expecting to find him still there. And seeing it empty, its old familiar self again, the bedclothes gone, the white wadding sticking out of the torn parts, hope rose in all of us. But the first words our mother spoke dashed that hope.

She had seen where our eyes had gone and knew what we were thinking, and she said, 'He'll be back tonight with your father. He went to work in the tailoring shop. But you mustn't worry. He's a very nice man. I had a long talk with him after you left this morning. He's been all over the world. He's worked on ships and he's been everywhere, even to America. He has no home of his own, and no relatives, nobody at all.' Her voice had softened and taken on a sympathetic note. Of course she would feel that way about someone who was alone in the world, as she had once been. She went on, 'He promised not to be a bother. So you must try to be nice to him. He might not stay long – I don't know – he never stays long in one place.'

And then, almost as if she had forgotten something, she added, 'Oh yes, I should tell you this and you must try not to be upset. We can't let him sleep on the sofa. It wouldn't be right. So I gave him the girls' room, and the girls will sleep in the boys' room. You'll have your own bed, of course, and I managed to borrow a cot from Fanny Cohen for him in the little room.'

There was a shocked silence after she spoke. Then a scream. It came from Rose. 'I told you,' she cried. 'I told you she'd do this. She'll do anything for money, even turn her own children out of their beds.'

'I'm not turning you out of your bed,' my mother said. 'You're going to have your own bed to sleep in.'

'Oh, you witch!' Rose went on screaming. 'You're just an old witch and I'm not going to stay in this house a minute longer. I'm getting out of here.'

She ran out of the room and we heard her clattering up the stairs. We all stood there looking at each other.

'She'll be all right,' my mother said. 'She'll get over it.'

Then Lily noticed something. Her eyes had gone to the mantelpiece. 'Where's the permit slip?' she asked.

My mother smiled. 'I gave it to Larry,' she said.

'Who?'

'That's our boarder's name,' she explained. 'I told him all about the exam you want to take, and how it's necessary to have the slip signed and the trouble I'm having asking your father to sign it, so he offered to ask him for me and I gave it to him.'

Lily looked worried and uncertain. 'What makes you think he'll be able to do it any more than you?'

'Your father seems to like him. It isn't often your father likes anybody or has a friend, but he seems to have taken to Larry, so maybe he'll be able to get him to do it. At least he can try.'

Just then we heard Rose coming down the stairs. She was walking very rapidly. She did not come into the room, but passed the door and seemed to be heading for the front. My mother quickly ran to intercept her and we followed. 'Rose, where are you going?'

She stopped at the door. She was carrying a small bundle wrapped in an old shawl that my mother had given her once and had been used as an ermine cloak in her duchess roles. She spoke curtly over her shoulder. 'I'm leaving home,' she said.

My mother went up to her and put an arm round her shoulders. 'Now stop being silly,' she said. 'Come back in the kitchen and I'll give you a nice cup of cocoa and a biscuit.'

Rose shrugged her arm off and snapped, 'I don't want your cocoa and your biscuit. I hate you.' She went out, slamming the door after her.

Joe said worriedly, 'You'd better go after her, or she might really leave.'

'She won't leave,' my mother said confidently.

But as the afternoon passed and it grew dark and time for supper, she began to look worried. It was raining outside and Rose was still not back. After setting the table, she suddenly put on her shawl and picked up an umbrella. 'I'll soon be back,' she said.

'Can I go, Mam?' I begged.

She didn't answer, so I went along with her, walking close to her so that I could share the umbrella. The rain was coming down heavily and it drummed over our heads. My mother seemed to know exactly where to go. We climbed the brew that ran alongside the iron rail of the park, then turned into the park itself: as close as Rose could get to her dreams, I suppose . . . up the park.

And there she was, sitting forlornly on a bench in the rain, with the little bundle beside her. She did not resist when my mother pulled her up and firmly led her away, holding her hand on one side, mine on the other. She was soaked and shivering with cold, and obviously had been crying.

Not a word was spoken on the way home by any of us, and not a word again after Rose had changed her clothes and joined us at the table.

*

He coughed all night. He coughed and spat. My mother had taken the precaution of spreading newspaper on the floor beside the bed, and from then on it would be a daily routine for one of us to pick up those newspapers and take them out to the midden. Afterwards, we didn't mind so much.

But we did at first, and we minded his coughing at night and especially his spitting, and we minded being in the same room, the two girls in one bed, the three boys in the other, all of us so terribly close together, while he occupied that other room.

The change began not more than three or four days after he had come to live with us, the night we came home from cheder, Joe, Saul and I hurrying into the house and pausing, shocked, when we heard a man singing. It came from the kitchen, and we went through the lobby cautiously and stopped again in the doorway leading to the kitchen.

A strange sight met our eyes. We had never heard a man singing in our house before, but much less we had never seen a man at it sitting before the fire with Rose sitting opposite him and actually laughing, and Lily laughing too with her books in front of her at the table, and my mother opposite her with her sewing, laughing.

The song was one of many comic songs that Larry would sing for us on those winter nights and I have never forgotten it:

> Me father bought some cheese,
> Me mother began to sneeze,
> The cat had a fit in the cellar,
> The dog had the same disease . . .

It went on, verse after verse, Larry singing lustily in a hoarse, cracked voice, with a smile on his pasty face, a cigarette in his hand, a cough interrupting now and then, a spit into the fire making the red-hot coals hiss.

Seeing us standing there he halted and cried out, 'Well, well, here's the men of the family. Come in, lads, and join the fun.'

We did. We soon learned the song and sang with him. We all did. We sang and laughed, and whatever hostility we had felt towards him before this vanished that night. Even Lily took time off from her books to join in and Rose – all her coldness had gone and her thin, pinched face was alive with happiness.

But Lily, especially – her eyes were shining, and she seemed almost intoxicated. I found out why when the evening came to an end, and we were all ready to go upstairs to bed and were saying goodnight to Larry. Lily flung her arms round his neck, kissed him and said, 'Thank you so much, Larry. Thank you.'

My mother was smiling. Rose knew already but we didn't and, seeing that by the puzzled looks on our faces, she said, 'Larry got your father to sign Lily's permit for the exam. So you see, he isn't such a bad fellow after all.'

Yes, it was done at last, thanks to this man who had brought new life into our house. After that night we couldn't wait to see him again. We hurried home from cheder, hoping this would be one of the nights when he preferred to stay at home with us to going out to the pub with our father, and we could sit by the fire with him and sing his comic songs, or listen to him tell us about his travels to Australia, India, America, all over the world.

I think, if he'd had his way, he would have stayed with us every night and indeed, as time went on, it was almost every night. Larry had brought a lot of joy into our lives, but we had given him something too. We were the closest thing to a family he'd ever had, and he clung to us as much as possible, and I suppose my father began to resent it.

It was a strange thing, his feelings towards Larry. I don't think he'd ever had a friend before. He was a loner, a man completely isolated from everybody else, shunned by the Jewish men on our street because of his drinking and violent temper, and not too welcome by the Christians in the pubs that he frequented. His accidental meeting with Larry in a pub one night had brought him the only man he ever knew who would tolerate him, and talk to him and even seem to like him.

Larry told us about this meeting one night. It wasn't easy, he said. He saw him sitting alone at a table, and went over and introduced himself as a fellow Jew.

'Bugger off,' my father growled.

Larry laughed, telling us the story. 'I didn't bugger off. It was the first time anyone had ever said that to me and I decided I was going to see this through. So I stuck it out.'

And by persisting he gradually got around my father, and after a few drinks they were pals and my father began to talk.

'He told me the story,' Larry said to my mother. He said this in a low voice, thinking perhaps we weren't supposed to know.

My mother understood and said calmly, 'They know.'

For that matter, a lot of the people on our street knew the story. They would have had to, because they were living on the street at that time. We ourselves had heard it from our mother and she had told it to us in the hope, perhaps, that we would understand him a little better, and perhaps be more tolerant and kinder towards him.

It began in Poland, where my father was born, the oldest in a family of ten noisy, unruly children. I still have a picture of them all taken after they came to England. It is one of those old sepia photos on hard backing that has endured throughout the years without fading, a credit to early photography. It shows them in three formal rows, my father at the far end in the back row with a sullen look on his face. My grandparents are in the centre, my grandfather looking very distinguished with a van Dyck beard, wing collar and Ascot tie, silk top hat, clasping a silver-knobbed cane between his knees, my grandmother big and thick-lipped and bosomy and much bejewelled, with bracelets and necklaces and earrings dangling.

My grandmother was the matriarch of the family. My grandfather, for all his distinguished looks, made his living as a roofer, and he was known to sing while he worked, and quite well too, often with an appreciative audience below. My grandmother ran the household with an iron fist, her loud, harsh voice commanding, along with her blows, and usually gaining obedience from all except my father.

He was the unmanageable one. He had been sent out to work at five and had worked long hours at the various jobs he'd had, and he had been beaten and kicked by his various masters, and it had left him sullen and embittered and violent and difficult to get along with. At twelve he was already a heavy drinker, coming home often blind drunk at night, and when he was drunk he terrorised the family. My grandmother was at her wits' end. Her husband was of little help to her. She had to solve the problem herself and she finally hit on the solution.

So my father came home from work late one night and found them all gone, the house stripped of furniture. They had abandoned him, gone to England, leaving him to shift for himself. He may have gone mad then. He roared and raged. He beat his head against the wall until he collapsed senseless and terrified neighbours called the police, who carted him off to a hospital.

After he had recovered and was released from the hospital, he set out in search of his family, determined to find them and insist on his place among them whether they liked it or not. It would be his way of wreaking vengeance. Slowly, bit by bit, working his way across Europe to finance his passage, he made his way to England. In London, he learned of the new, big, growing Jewish colony in Manchester. He went there, but arrived too late. They had only recently moved to the smoky little mill town a few miles away. But he had their exact address now.

It was late at night when he arrived at our street. My grandparents and their family were living in the very same house that we were to inherit later. My father, tired and worn – he had walked all the way from Manchester – knocked loudly on the door. He knocked several more times before my grandmother's head appeared at the window above.

'Who's there?' she called down.

'It's your son,' he shouted back. 'Let me in.'

A pause. Her heart must have stopped beating then. After a moment she said, 'Go away. You are not my son. Go away or I'll call the police.'

'Old witch,' he shouted back. 'Open this door or I'll break it down.'

By this time the whole street had awakened. Heads were popping out of windows. Lights were being turned on. Voices murmured.

Desperate, unable to make up her mind what to do, my grandmother acted on impulse. She did what only she could have done. She went to the landing and picked up the bucket that had been well used through the night. It was almost full to the brim. She carried it to the window and poured its contents down on the head of the intruder.

He let out a yell and shook himself like a wet dog, and cursed and pounded on the door so hard that finally it had to be opened for him.

There are many people who have considered the story to be apocryphal, but its truth has been confirmed by my mother and the aunts and uncles who were roused from their beds that night and saw and heard what went on.

Furthermore, that wasn't the end of the story by any means. The vengeance that my father had sworn to take came down hard on their heads. Now, more than ever, he terrorised them with his drinking, his cursing, his fists. Those who lived on our street in those early days remembered the constant bedlam that went on in the corner house, the shouting and shrieking and fighting, worse than anything that happened in the Finklestein house.

So once again my grandmother had to think up ways of getting rid of him. And it was unfortunate – for my mother, for all of us – that my mother should have turned up on the scene just then, a young, sweet, innocent sixteen-year-old girl just arrived from Poland, without friends or relatives, and that she should have boarded in the house of a woman in Manchester who was a close friend of my grandmother's, and that my grandmother came there to visit one day.

The moment she set eyes on the young girl she knew she had her solution. It must have flashed over her at once and it was not hard to inveigle the girl into a match that was to bring her nothing but misery for the rest of her life. No sooner had the marriage taken place than my grandmother announced with suspicious generosity that she was giving over her house to the newly married couple. She herself was taking her family off to America.

This time it could not be called abandonment, yet I don't think my father was deceived. His face always turned black whenever there was talk of the relatives in Chicago, and although my mother kept up a steady correspondence with them through the years, he himself never mentioned them.

And with this extra bitterness inside him it was little wonder that he turned away from the world and remained sullen and hostile, a hard man to get along with. Larry understood that and knew that he was an exception to my father, perhaps the only friend he'd ever had, and his conscience must have bothered him a great deal on the nights that he refused to go out with my father and stayed by the fireside with us.

My father did not take it too well – that much was clear. His face darkened when Larry said he was staying home and he stormed out with a heavier bang than usual of the front door, and with the sleeve still dangling all the way up the street. Nor was he pleased when he came home and found Larry sitting up with my mother, talking with her while she mended our clothes. He ignored Larry's greeting and stumbled out into the back yard to use the water closet there, and Larry, after exchanging a glance with my mother and saying goodnight, would quickly make his way upstairs to the little room, where the newspapers were spread out on the floor beside his bed for him.

We knew very little of this ourselves. It was all told to us later. But we did know that we revelled in Larry's presence, and that he brought a joy into our lives that we'd never had before. Almost every night through that winter we sat with him, singing and listening to his stories, and it was wonderful, having said goodnight and getting into bed, to hear the murmur of his voice and my mother's. Perhaps it gave us a taste of what it was like to have a father – maybe that is what made us all, even Rose, feel so happy that winter.

Then there was that last night and the climax to which it had all been building. It was the end of the night of songs and the final song of the evening was the one we liked best, with all of us, my mother included, singing at the tops of our voices. It was a sailor's song, one that Larry had brought back from the sea, and it went something like this:

> 'earts of oak are our ships,
> Jolly tars for our men,
> We always are ready,
> Steady, boys, steady,
> We'll fight and we'll conquer,
> Again and again.

These last three words were roared and were accompanied by a thumping of fists on the table, round which we had been sitting, drinking our last cup of cocoa and with much laughter from everybody, before the goodnights were said.

But on this night, we were just bellowing out the end of the song and were thumping on the table, making the cups jiggle, when everybody halted and all our eyes went towards the door. We had not heard him come in, much earlier than usual, but there he was, standing in the doorway, with his cap pulled low over his brow, his face dark, his lower lip drooping the way it always did when he was in one of his savage moods.

He was standing there, just glaring and saying nothing, and it was obvious to us that he was drunk. We could smell the liquor, and it was hard liquor not beer, and hard liquor always made him ugly. He seemed to be swaying a little as he stood there.

Then it burst from him. 'What the bloody 'ell is this, a public 'ouse?' He was looking at Larry as he spoke and his glaring eyes were inflamed. 'You bloody sod, you. I got you a job, I gave you a home, and you turn my home into a bleeding pub and you sit up nights with my wife and maybe you think she goes with the deal. Come on, you stinking rotten sod. Come on and show me what kind of man you are.'

He put up his fists in fighting position and we all shrank with fear. My mother's face had turned white.

Larry, however, remained calm. He put his smouldering cigarette down on the saucer that served as an ashtray and got to his feet. 'Come on, Jack,' he said smoothly, 'come on and let's go outside for a bit and talk this over.'

He went up to him and put an arm round his shoulders and my father struck him with a fist straight in the mouth. I'm sure it hurt, there was blood coming from the lip, but it was as if it was nothing to Larry and he went on trying to calm my father. 'That's no good, Jack,' he said. 'We're friends and we don't want to fight.'

'You're no friend of mine,' roared my father, still keeping up his fists. 'No friend tries to steal another man's wife and children. You're a bloody sod, that's what you are, and you're getting out of my house. You're getting out now or I'll put you in the hospital.'

He swung again, but this time Larry caught the hand and held it in a firm grip. 'All right, Jack,' he said. 'I'll get out. But let's go out for a bit in the yard. I think you need it.'

This time my father let him lead him into the yard and we heard him vomiting. We ourselves went upstairs and got into bed, shivering. A bit later we heard Larry helping my father up to his room, their feet mounting the steps clumsily.

Larry left the next day while we were at school.

Chapter Six

Without Larry the house was dead again and there were long silences at night in front of the fire, broken only by the rustling of the pages of our books or magazines, and the occasional outbursts of fighting that went on in the Finklesteins' house next door. And my mother sat up alone with her sewing after we had gone to bed.

We missed him, we missed him terribly, and Rose grew sour again and abusive to my mother with her sarcastic remarks, and Lily was buried completely in her books, studying for the exam, and she became irritable when my mother asked her to do something around the house and would want to know why Rose couldn't do it. Then Rose would attack her with some vicious comment that would show her jealousy and hatred, and then the two would fight bitterly, and my mother would have to intervene and do the work herself.

It was in the early part of January that the exam was to take place at the Grammar School and it was unfortunate that it should have to be on a Saturday. My mother was not sure if she could let her go and break the Sabbath law about writing on this holy day. Lily was furious; she screamed that she didn't give a damn about the Sabbath law, and for once my mother grew furious herself and, the first time I had ever seen her do it, she lashed out with the back of her hand and caught Lily on the mouth. Lily herself was stunned. She stared at my mother for a moment with a hand across the struck mouth, then she let out a wild cry and ran out of the house.

For a while it looked as if Lily would not be able to take the exam after all. My mother had consulted Mrs Harris, an authority on Jewish law, and the old woman had shaken her head and muttered that it would be a sin. She reminded my mother of how she herself had once been tempted to break the Sabbath law and how she had resisted. It was a story that everyone knew, how coming home from the synagogue one Saturday afternoon, she had taken it into her head to go for a walk through the park – as if the devil had directed her there. The park was empty and as she strolled along she suddenly spotted an umbrella on a bench. It was a beautiful new umbrella, one that she would have loved to have. But one did not dare carry an umbrella on the Sabbath. She knew that well enough and yet she was tempted, and she paced up and down in front of the bench several times, eyeing the umbrella.

God saved her from sin, she said simply. God rescued her from the devil and sent her home without the umbrella. All day she could not rest, thinking of that umbrella lying there on the bench, just waiting for someone to pick it up and take it home. Oh, how she prayed that the park would remain empty until sunset, when she could return and claim her prize. And as soon as the sun had set, and the last prayer was said in the synagogue, Mrs Harris rushed back to the park. But alas, the umbrella had gone.

She had never forgotten it. She sometimes even to this day, years after the incident had taken place, dreamed of that umbrella. 'But I am not sorry,' she told my mother. 'I did not sin.'

Hearing this story again from the very lips of the woman who was involved, my mother was almost convinced that she could not permit Lily to take the exam on a Saturday.

'Perhaps,' she said to Lily, 'we could ask them to let you take the exam on another day.'

'No, no, no,' cried Lily, thinking no doubt what she did not dare say, that she would only be calling attention to the fact that she was a Jew and thus make it harder still for her to get into the Grammar School.

'Couldn't you at least talk to the headmaster about it?' my mother asked, 'If he's so anxious for you to take the exam, perhaps he'll do something. All you have to do is tell him that on Shabbos we're not allowed to write.'

'No,' Lily cried again, 'I can't do that. I can't tell him that.'

'Why?' asked my mother, bewildered, 'why?'

'Because I can't, I can't, I can't.'

There was no doubt of it, Lily could not be made to do this no matter how much was at stake for her; and my mother brooded for a while over the possibility of going herself and talking to the headmaster, but instead decided to go to the rabbi and discuss it with him.

And it was this that saved Lily's life – because she'd sworn once that if she couldn't take the exam she would kill herself. My mother came back from her talk with the rabbi smiling. He had given dispensation. Under the circumstances, he had said, since her entire future depended upon it, and especially since she had threatened to take her own life if she could not take the exam, it was permissible.

I saw Lily close her eyes and draw in a deep breath when my mother told her this. And her hand went to her heart, as if there had been a pain there. How much it had meant to her we could scarcely realise. We watched her from the door as she went off on a Saturday morning to take the exam. All the other people on our street were going to the synagogue at that time, all marching down the street behind one another carrying the little velvet bags that contained their siddurs and tallithes. She turned on to Brook Street and we watched her walk swiftly forward, her long silken hair swaying behind her back.

I noticed that Arthur Forshaw had come out on to his doorstep and was watching her too.

Then, late in the afternoon she came home looking pale and worn, and not very happy. My mother looked at her anxiously and asked, 'Well?'

'I failed,' Lily said simply.

A shocked look came on to my mother's face. 'You failed? They told you already?'

'They didn't have to tell me. The results won't be in for a while yet. But I know I failed.'

Relief showed now on my mother's face. She knew her well. She always thought she had failed after a test at school. And she always passed, and passed well. 'You'll pass,' she said confidently.

'No, I won't.'

She went upstairs, and she slept all through the day and the evening, and through the night and part of the next day. She mustn't have slept properly for weeks and she was making up for it.

The days slowly grew longer, the weather warmer. It rained, and the sun shone intermittently through the clouds, and a long curved rainbow formed behind the square brick tower of the India Mill. The sparrows were busy in the gutters of our houses and you could hear their chirping in the early morning, and see them during the day, picking up bits of old dry manure from the horse droppings and flying back with them to the gutters to build their nests.

At St Peter's they were preparing for holy week. Once again the partitions were being pushed back during the day, and they stood on the forms to sing Easter songs. At cheder, at night, we were learning about our own holy week, Passover, and we were studying the Haggadah, and the story of how Moses led the Hebrews out of Egypt and away from the wrath of the Pharaoh, and we were learning to recite the four questions and sing the songs that we would have to know at the seder, the feast that was held in every Jewish home on the first two nights of Passover to commemorate the release of the Jews from slavery. The rabbi sang well in the fine, deep, rolling voice that we'd heard often in the synagogue and we sang with him.

We came trooping in one night, as late as usual, perhaps a bit later because it was a warm night and we had loitered even more than ever gazing down through the mill grating at the stoker, feeling guilty and prepared for a good hard scolding from the rabbi, only to find him in extraordinarily good humour.

He was standing in front of the fire, which was blazing less heartily than in the winter but was lit nevertheless, his back towards it, the long cigarette holder in his hand. He was actually smiling and did not make his usual sarcastic remarks, but seemed only anxious for us to take our seats.

Once we had seated ourselves he said, 'I have a surprise for you tonight, an announcement to make. We are going to be honoured by the presence of a brilliant young Hebrew scholar, who will speak to you about Passover and its meaning to the Jewish people. He is a young man whom I have known since the day he was born.' He smiled and paused, and puffed on his cigarette and continued, 'As you know, I am not only a rabbi and your teacher. I am a father too and the young man of whom I speak is my son. If I sound boastful you must forgive me, but I am no different from all fathers; I am inclined to feel that my children are superior beings endowed only with the greatest of qualities. However, it is common knowledge that when my son was ten years old he could read the chomish from beginning to end. He also studied the Talmud. He speaks and writes perfect Hebrew . . .'

All this was already familiar to us and the rabbi had good reason to be proud of his son, but there were other things that he did not mention and that we'd heard; rumours that there was trouble between the rabbi and his son, that the boy no longer attended the synagogue, that he did nothing, in fact, except sit in the library on St Petersgate and read.

It was as if all this was over and forgotten, and the rabbi awaited his son's arrival that night with anticipation and excitement. He was in a joyful mood; instead of boxing ears, he pinched them and patted heads as he went among us correcting our mistakes; and he frequently consulted his watch that he kept tucked in a waistcoat pocket, and he would also look towards the doorway. Then at last we heard the front door open, and footsteps sound along the hall.

Quickly, the rabbi halted the lesson and we all glanced towards the door, waiting. He appeared in a moment and stood hesitating in the doorway. He was of rather short stature, slim, with a pale, ascetic face, and shiny glasses sitting on the bridge of an aquiline nose, and dark, curly hair. He resembled the mother a great deal. He was about sixteen then, the older of the rabbi's two children, the other being a girl.

He did not seem to want to come in, and the rabbi went towards him, put an arm round his shoulders and urged, 'Come in, Max, come in. What are you afraid of?'

He did seem a bit afraid. He hung back a moment longer before he let his father lead him in and then a little argument ensued between them in low voices. Sitting in the front row with the smaller children, I was able to hear some of what was being said. Obviously, Max had not wanted to come, but had been talked into it by his father and now regretted it. He did not want to give us the talk that he had promised.

'But why,' I heard the rabbi say, 'why don't you want to speak to them? They have been looking forward to it all evening.'

'Father,' he said, 'I might not say the right things.'

'What are the right things?'

'The things you want me to say.'

'But I want you to say what you want to say, not what I want you to say.'

'You might be sorry, Father.'

'Then, Max, I'll be sorry.'

He must have had infinite confidence in his son to have said that. He must also have known very little about him and the wanderings his mind had taken in the past year or so. All he could think, perhaps, was that he had brought the boy back to the cheder and the rest God would take care of.

He retreated back to the fire and stood with the long cigarette holder in his hand, a new cigarette just fitted into it and lit, smiling and proud as Max stood in front of us.

There was a pause, a brief silence broken by a slight tittering in the back row where Zalmon and his friends sat, quickly shushed by a look from the rabbi, then Max began to speak.

His voice was not very strong, nothing like his father's. It was weak and shaky at first, though it gathered some strength as he went along.

'Not too long ago,' he said, 'I sat like you on those rows of benches, learning my Hebrew and, at this time of the year, the Haggadah in preparation for the seder, and listening to my father tell us about the ancient Hebrews and their flight from Egypt. And like you, my heart was warmed by this tale, and I felt new pride in being a Jew and belonging to a religion that has endured thousands of years of suffering and persecution . . .'

I could not help glancing at his father while he was saying this. The rabbi's face was glowing and he was standing erect with the cigarette holder in his hand and a small cloud of blue smoke in front of him, a large, strong man and quite a contrast to the slight, thin figure of his son. He was drinking in every word that the boy was saying.

I too turned my attention back to the speaker. He was talking now of the seder.

'There was nothing I loved more than the seder. The table decked out in its finest white tablecloth, the candles bright and shining, the wineglasses filled with red sweet wine into which we would dip a finger for each of the plagues that were visited upon the cruel Egyptians, the bitter herbs, symbols of our suffering, in their little saucers, to be nibbled at when the appropriate time came, the plate of matzohs covered with a cloth, the door open for the angel to come in, with all of us gathered around, heads buried in the Haggadahs, following the story as my father, clad in his white robe, intoned the long tale of the flight from Egypt . . . and the house smelling of chicken soup.

'There was magic and wonder in it all,' he continued. 'I looked forward to it all year long. I could hardly wait for the service at the synagogue to be over so that I could go home and sit with my father and mother and sister at the table and listen to this ancient story of the Jews' suffering and flight, and the miracle that permitted the Red Sea to open and give them escape, and all the plagues that God visited upon the Egyptians for their cruelty.' He smiled. 'This particular bit of vengeance always pleased me,' he said. 'God was more just than ever in that moment. But perhaps what I liked best of all was my own participation in the seder, when I rose to ask the four questions. It was the duty of the son of the household to do this and I was the son. You all know the questions. I am sure my father has taught them to you. "Why is this night different from all other nights?" They begin with that one and I always spoke loudly and firmly, and my father gave me the answers to each one. But then, that night, the night that is so important to me, when I was about . . . fourteen, just a year after my barmitzvah, there was a fifth question.'

He paused and I happened to glance at the rabbi just then. He was holding the long cigarette holder upwards in his hand, smoke curling from the cigarette, and his mouth was open a little, the round red cherry-like lips pursed as if in surprise. Then Max went on and I swung my eyes back to him.

'I must say this,' Max said. 'I must be quite honest. My question did not emanate from within my soul, as if it were a miracle, so to speak. I had been doing a great deal of reading. Well, I have always read a great deal. My father

will testify to that. But in the early part of my life, until my
thirteenth birthday, my reading was confined to the
Talmud, the early Hebrew scholars, the ancient Greek
philosophers, the British, French and German classics. But
then in the library I had stumbled on other books, writers
of a different sort, with views that were strange to me at
first, strange and disturbing. Gibbon, Smith, Seligman,
Engels – and yes, Marx. They mean nothing to you now.
Perhaps they will some day, Marx especially.'

And now, glancing at the rabbi, I saw a distinctly
shocked expression on his face. It no longer glowed with
pride. I thought for a moment that he was about to say
something, but he checked himself while Max continued
to speak.

'So perhaps I was already primed for this question.
Perhaps it had been there gnawing inside me for some time
before. But I did not dare ask it that night. I would have
upset the seder completely and hurt my parents, and I did
not want to do that. I kept it inside me, and it is there still,
gnawing away, troubling me. I have tried, for my father's
sake, for my mother's sake, to eradicate it, but I cannot. It
persists constantly, that fifth question, and especially now
that another seder is near. I think constantly of all the
suffering that is going on in the world and all the injustices
that are taking place. I think of the cruelties that man has
inflicted upon man throughout the centuries, long before
the Jews fled from Egypt to escape the wrath of the
Pharaoh, long after that. I think of the slaughters that have
taken place in the wars throughout history, the one that is
being fought now in France, and I ask myself, why does
God countenance all this? If God is our creator, the
supreme, kind and benevolent being whom we all worship,
why does he permit us to destroy one another? And why,

too, does he permit one religion to persecute another when both are his children? And so there came that terrible question – supposing, supposing it is all fantasy – is there really a God?'

'No!'

The cry burst from the rabbi. There was an agonised look on his face. We all stared at him and Max turned round to face him, a sorrowful look on his face. 'I warned you, Father,' he murmured. 'I said you were not going to like it.'

'It is the devil talking. It is not you. Get out of here. Go home and cleanse your mouth.'

Max did not say any more. He turned and walked out of the room, and we heard his feet marching through the corridor and the door closing after him. The rabbi was pacing up and down before the fire, his head bent, an expression on his face that was bitter and filled with pain. He seemed completely oblivious of our presence. But after a moment he roused himself sufficiently to wave a hand and say, 'Go home.'

We quickly sprang up from our seats and hurried out, chattering excitedly among ourselves over the strange thing we'd witnessed that night, not quite understanding it, not at all sure what it was Max had said that angered his father so much, but aware that it must have been something of great significance.

It created a good deal of talk on the street, in my mother's shop. They all knew about it from us. But they knew more than we did. Their heads were close together as they bent over the counter towards my mother and their voices whispered excitedly. I heard some of it. I heard them say that he was a revolutionist, and that he was involved with anarchists and Socialists and even, God help him, with the Russian Bolsheviks. They clasped their hands and shook their heads back and forth and moaned, as if they were in the synagogue saying prayers for the dead.

Soon, however, everyone was busy with other things, with preparations chiefly for the coming Passover holiday. Special dishes were being prepared in advance and the house smelled of fermenting beets that would become rossel, the red juice we would drink all through Passover, and another kind of smell from the mead my mother was brewing in the cellar, and still another from the chicken fat that was being rendered, and that would be spread on the matzohs.

Now the matzohs themselves arrived and this always created a lot of excitement on the street, on both sides, with the Christians curious onlookers as Levine's horse and cart came clattering round the corner and drew up at our kerb. It was piled with boxes of matzohs, all ordered in advance by the families on the street. We clustered around eagerly, while Mr Levine, his pasty face sweating with exertion, handed out the boxes to us, calling out the names as he did so, 'Jacobs, Mittleman, Cohen, Finklestein, Berger, Zarembar, Blank . . .' Hands reached for them, boys carried them into the houses, where they were stored carefully to await the first day.

And finally, after the house had been cleaned from top to bottom, the last of the forbidden bread removed from sight, given usually to some Christian family across the street, the remaining crumbs – the chomets – were swept up, placed in a bag and taken out into the street to be burned. And all the Christians stared at us in something like horror at what must have seemed to them a pagan rite, smoke coming from all the bags, flames flaring upwards, and the women murmuring prayers.

But then at last it was the first night of Passover. We dressed in our best clothes. That year, thanks to the shop, all of us had shoes and new suits, all three of us, and we walked proudly to the synagogue, Joe carrying the little purple velvet bag that contained the one siddur we shared and our tallithes. It was clear, warm weather. Everybody strode briskly in front and behind us. New shoes squeaked as we marched through the streets, and mill workers coming home just then stared at us, then bent their heads and continued their clattering in the opposite direction.

But one of them, a man, managed to call out, 'Bloody Jews. Who killed Christ?'

There was some laughter from a few, but for the most part they said nothing and continued on their way. We too said nothing, pretending not to have heard. The sun was setting behind the square brick tower of the India Mill. The sky would be red while we were in the synagogue.

Korer the treasurer, tall, thinner than ever, his face almost skeleton-like, stood in the doorway, silent and grim, greeting no one as the congregation entered. His eyes fell a bit sharply on my brothers and me, then turned away as he remembered that our dues had been paid.

The synagogue was filled to capacity. Every seat was taken. Blood-red sunset showed at the stained-glass windows. It grew darker gradually. A Christian woman came in and lit the gas lights, moving swiftly from one to the other with a taper in her hand, seeming almost afraid and anxious to get this over with; then, having done the last one, scurrying out quickly.

A silence fell after she had gone. Now all eyes were on the door and through the door came the rabbi, swathed in his huge striped tallith, and then a gasp went up. For right behind him, wearing a smaller tallith that came just over his shoulders, was the rabbi's son Max, the godless one, the revolutionist.

There were whispers, heads put together, and from the balcony over our heads we heard the gabble of voices. Then there was silence once more and the service began.

That Passover was a strange one altogether, for not only had the rabbi's son shown up at the synagogue for the first time in months, and right after his talk at the cheder, but we too had an unexpected guest at the seder. It was our father. He was seated there at the table when we came home from the synagogue, his head bent a little, the same glower on his face. My mother's face showed some of her feelings. It glowed with happiness, but she hardly dared talk. And none of us did. We whispered to one another. We took our places at the table and, lifting up our glasses of wine, we began the seder with the blessing.

It was Joe who recited from the Haggadah. My father did not know any Hebrew, and even if he had I doubt if he would have conducted the seder and we did not expect him to. It was enough that he was there. He had never attended our seders before this; for that matter, we could not remember any occasion when he had sat down at the table with us before this. Why now so suddenly? It was a bit of a mystery and yet I have the feeling that it had something to do with Larry and the fight he'd had with him, and perhaps other things connected with our boarder.

There was something about that night that was definitely different from all other nights, and these words that we spoke later from the Haggadah had a double meaning for us. There was a softness and a gentleness in our home that we had never experienced before. He said nothing to us all through the ceremony, and he ate in silence too, afterwards, his head bent low over his plate.

But he was there with us and we felt an odd sort of happiness; and later, lying in bed, the sweet warmth of the wine I had drunk lulling me gradually to sleep, the house very still, a sense of peace came over me and I must have been smiling as I fell asleep.

But for my sister Lily there was no peace and no rest that night or any of the other nights. The worry showed on her face and in the shadows round her eyes. She had probably not slept for weeks, ever since she had taken the exam. Throughout the day there was a strained look on her face. In school she went about her duties silently. She and the headmaster scarcely looked at one another. She had no news for him, he had none for her. The notification was to come to both places, the school and the home. As soon as Lily got home, dashing into the house, her eyes went to the mantelpiece where the letter would be.

My mother, coming out of the shop where she had been serving a customer, shook her head. 'Not yet,' she said, then added cheerfully, 'Oh, it'll soon come and then you'll see, you'll have passed.'

'No, I won't,' Lily said mournfully. 'If I'd passed they would have let me know already.'

'How do you know that?' my mother asked. 'Has somebody told you that?'

She looked at Lily suspiciously. Had Arthur been talking to her, was what she meant? But Lily refused to walk into the trap. She shook her head, though in a way they had been talking. On the way to and from school they had exchanged looks, with Arthur's questioning and Lily shaking her head slightly, barely perceptibly. No, she had not received the notification, was what she said. There was constant gloom and anxiety on her face, and she was irritable with everyone; and Rose, taking advantage of the situation, deliberately taunted and sneered and goaded her into a fight.

It meant so much to Lily. For one thing it would save her from having to go to work in the tailoring shop – and be with him all day long. That fear must have haunted her more than anything else. It would have kept any of us awake nights and we were all in sympathy with Lily – except perhaps Rose, whose perennial jealousy was at its height since the time Lily had been picked to take the exam. But the rest of us wanted her to pass and go on to the Grammar School, and we kept our eyes peeled for the postman just as much as Lily did, and dashed into the house when we came home from school along with her and searched the mantelpiece.

Once, as we were coming home, Joe cried out, 'There's the postman.'

He was late in making his rounds. He had usually delivered to our street before we came home. But there he was now, and he was stopping at our house. We raced madly towards him. Even Rose tore along with us, caught up in the excitement. Our mother was at the door, taking the letter from the postman when we arrived, and the expression on her face showed her own excitement.

She could not read. Lily tore the letter from her and immediately disappointment showed in her face. She handed it back to my mother, saying, 'It's from America.'

Ordinarily, this would have been reason enough for the excitement to continue. Well, it did in my mother. She did not get letters from America as often as she would have liked to and no matter how many disappointments there had been in the past, each one made her tremble with new hope. I saw the flush suffuse her cheeks and her hand shake as she gave the letter to Joe to read.

I felt some of the hope rise in myself. I had caught the fever from my mother. I too wanted to go to America. Lily, uninterested, too disappointed to care, turned away. But the rest of us clustered around Joe as he tore the envelope open. Was this to be the letter that said they were sending for us? Lily was forgotten.

This one proved to be from Uncle Abe and it was ecstatic. But it had nothing to do with us. It was about himself. He had just got married. I have never forgotten this letter. 'Yes, I have just got married,' he wrote, 'I am working and making good money, and I have a nice home and a beautiful wife with electric lights and a bathtub . . .'

At least my mother was able to laugh. She had a good sense of humour that was not always shared by the women in her shop. She read the letter to several of them, remembering the words from Joe, and they stared at her puzzled as she choked with her laughter. They could not seem to understand what was so funny in the letter and my mother, wiping her eyes, folded it and gave up trying to explain. She changed the subject, becoming serious again.

Then, late one afternoon while we were in the midst of lessons at St Peter's, a wave of excitement seemed to sweep through the school. There was much whispering among the teachers, signalling to one another through the glass sections of the partitions and going into one another's classrooms. The headmaster was striding back and forth, visibly excited, his ears very red. Then he went into a consultation with Cocky and a few moments later they were pushing the partitions back, and old Mr Bell came trotting in to lend a hand.

We were mystified. It was not prayer or hymn time, and there was no holiday coming that we had to prepare for. But the excitement had communicated itself to us, and we twisted in our seats and chattered loudly, and teachers began shouting at us to be quiet. Silence fell as the headmaster stood before us, stick in hand, face grim.

Then he spoke. 'Duffers, dullards, blockheads, thick-skulled, unwashed ones, lend me your ears . . .' A wink to the teachers and faint laughter among them, then in a more serious tone the headmaster went on: 'Today is an important day in the life of this school. For the first time in the history of St Peter's a girl has won a scholarship to the Grammar School. Two years ago a boy from this school won a scholarship. But never did we think a girl could win one. About the only thing girls in this school have ever done well is skip rope and sit in their seats in such a fashion that you could see their next week's washing . . .' A little scream of laughter from Miss DuRose, the standard four teacher. Ignoring her, the headmaster continued, 'The good Lord had pity on us this time. He gave us a girl with brains. Most of you wouldn't know what brains are. Well, they're the stuff you haven't got, the stuff that helps you think. This girl has 'em. She not only won her scholarship, but she passed her exam top of the list. She beat not only all the other girls who took that exam, but all the boys too. I suppose you all know who this girl is. She's been ink monitor here for the past year and I know we'll never get another one like her, and so we're all going to give her three cheers. Come up here, Lily . . .'

They had to push Lily up to the front. She didn't want to go. She was petrified. She clung to her seat until the others near her began pushing, then Miss Penn and Miss DuRose had to go up to her and take her hands and lead her to the headmaster. He put an arm round her shoulders. Her head was bent and she was crying. I thought Miss Penn and some of the other teachers were crying a little too.

The headmaster also seemed to be affected. He had to clear his throat before he spoke again, then he said, 'All right, you duffers and dullards, let's have it good and loud. Hip, hip . . .'

It was good and loud all right. Everybody, children and teachers, joined in with three cheers, even though many of the children in the younger classes didn't know what it was all about and cheered because the others did. It was a triumphant march home. The other kids clustered around Lily and chattered noisily. Not only the Jewish kids, but Christians as well. There was no danger of our being attacked on this trip. Everyone, even the worst of the ragamuffins, regarded Lily with awe. Who in our school had ever been given three cheers led by the headmaster himself? Even the cabbies, sitting aloft on their perches, sensed something different that day and did not flick their whips over our heads as we went by.

Then, as we reached the Devil's Steps, there was Arthur leaning up against a wall reading a book, waiting for us. As soon as he saw us he closed his book with a snap and sprang towards us. In his own excitement he had forgotten all about the ban and so did Lily. He knew, of course. He had seen the list posted on the bulletin in the school.

He explained this to Lily as they walked on together. He explained also that she would have to appear at the Grammar School for an interview very shortly. But there was nothing to worry about in that; it was merely a formality, especially in her case, being top of the list . . . 'Oh, it's just tremendous,' he said, his voice elated, his eyes dancing. 'I let out a yell when I saw your name right up there on top. I threw my cap up in the air. People thought I was dotty. Well, I was for a while. I came nowhere near top when I took the exam and I was proud just to be on the list – somewhere in the middle, I think. Nothing at all like you.'

He kept this up all the way home, ignoring the ban, forgetting about it completely probably in his excitement, and Lily forgetting it also, looking up at him as they walked along, hardly saying anything else, her eyes shining with her joy, not merely at the tremendous victory she had won, but at the praise that flowed ceaselessly out of him. It was a triumphant march home, with all of us tagging behind these two and jabbering among ourselves over the happening that day.

And when we had turned on to Brook Street and had marched down it some distance, we saw our mother standing on the corner, shading her eyes with a hand as she scanned the street for us. She was holding something in her other hand, and as we got close and began to run up to her we saw that it was a letter. Yes, it was the letter that Lily had been waiting for all this time. There was scarcely any need to open it, but Lily did while we poured out the news to my mother, all of us speaking at one time.

Lily read the letter as we stood there. It confirmed everything we all knew, but there were other details in it. 'You're right,' she said to Arthur. 'They want me to come down for an interview. Next Wednesday.'

Arthur nodded, grinning, then he turned to my mother and said reassuringly, 'That's one thing she won't have to worry about. She'll pass the interview with flying colours, like she did the exam . . .'

But then the words faltered on his lips and the grin died off his face as he saw my mother's expression. She was looking straight at him steadily and she made no attempt to answer his remark. It was clear what her expression was saying and Arthur, after an awkward moment, turned and walked away from us, and crossed the street to his house.

We were delayed going into our own house. People ran out of their houses to congratulate Lily. They'd all heard by now. A huge knot gathered round us and it included even a few from across the street. Arthur's mother came over, smiling, holding out a hand to Lily and telling her how wonderful it was, and saying to my mother, 'Now that makes two from the street.' My mother gave a little embarrassed nod, but didn't say anything. Then Mrs Humberstone came walking across with her rolling, sailor-like gait, a large, heavy woman, and when she reached Lily she gave her a resounding whack with the palm of her hand on her back, and shouted out congratulations. And Mrs Green, too, together with Annie carrying her baby, Annie quiet and smiling and proffering a hand, Mrs Green cackling and showing her broken yellow teeth, and saying maliciously, 'Well, now, and who said ye weren't the chosen ones? Ye got everything, ye 'ave.'

It was quite some time before we were able to go in. My mother's face was flushed and she was in seventh heaven with all the praise and envy and the wonder of what had happened. She must have seen herself once more close to her goal, a few steps more up the ladder. But Lily was silent, and as soon as the door had closed after us she turned on my mother and said savagely, 'Why did you do that to him?'

My mother's mouth opened. She looked at Lily bewildered, all her joy crumbling. 'Do what? To who?'

'To Arthur.'

'What did I say to him? What did I do?'

'That's just it. You said nothing. He spoke to you and you ignored him, as if he didn't exist. And the way you looked at him!'

'How did I look? Oh, what are you talking about?'

'You know what I'm talking about. You treated him as if he weren't a human being, just because he's a Christian.'

Then she burst into tears and ran upstairs, and my mother simply stood there looking down at the floor, an expression of sheer misery on her face, almost on the verge of tears herself.

But all that was forgotten and peace once more restored between them as my mother began to make a new dress for Lily to wear at the interview. It was the first new dress Lily had had in a long time and it added an extra bit of joy to the whole event. My mother had gone to the market and bought some soft white material and some remnants of lace, and she sat up still longer at night sewing. There were fittings and arguments between them over this or that about the dress, things I didn't quite understand. But the excitement had communicated itself to all of us, all, that is, except Rose, who sneered and scoffed, and was bitterly jealous of all the attention being paid to Lily.

The neighbours continued to come in to congratulate Lily and to help or make suggestions about the new dress. It was still being talked of throughout the whole street, and Rose's resentment rose ever higher. She wore a perpetual sullen expression on her thin, pale face. More than anything else she was angry over the dress. It seemed to strike deeper even than the glory that surrounded Lily over her winning of the scholarship. I saw her look balefully at it as my mother sewed at the table, and once while we were having our bedtime cocoa, and reading our books and magazines at the same time, Rose, accidentally or not, spilled some of her cocoa, and my mother and Lily screamed as it ran over the table towards the dress.

My mother was not quite quick enough snatching the dress away and the edge was stained. Lily began to cry and in a fit of rage she lashed out at Rose and caught her on the face. Rose sprang up screaming and struck back, and there was bedlam for a moment until my mother separated them.

'She did it on purpose,' Lily cried, still weeping.

'No, she didn't,' my mother, defended, though she may have suspected otherwise. 'It was an accident.'

'It wasn't an accident. She wanted to ruin my dress.'

'She's a liar,' shouted Rose. 'She always lies. She lied to you about not talking to Arthur Forshaw. She always talks to him. Every day when she sees him she talks to him. She's in love with him and that's the only reason she wants to go to the Grammar School. So she can walk to school with him every day and be with him all the time.'

'She's a dirty liar,' screamed Lily. 'It's not true. It's not true. It's not true.'

And she would have dashed at Rose again if my mother hadn't interfered and seized her hands, and pushed Rose away, Rose only too ready to engage in more battle.

'Now stop this,' my mother shouted. 'I've had enough.'

'She's not telling the truth,' Lily insisted. 'I haven't been talking to Arthur. Only that day when you saw us. But I wasn't talking to him before then and I haven't since, and it's not on account of him that I want to go to the Grammar School. She's just jealous. That's why she's saying these things and that's why she ruined my dress.'

'I know it's not true,' my mother reassured. 'And she hasn't ruined your dress. There's just a little cocoa spilled on it, and I can wash that out easily. Now go on up to bed, all of you, and no more fighting.'

We trooped upstairs silently and there was less gaiety than usual over the ritual of throwing our clothes down on her, both on our part and hers too.

But even that episode vanished from our minds as the day of the interview grew closer. We were all excited. The whole street, in fact, was excited over it, and when the women came into the shop there was little else they talked about, that and the future that lay in store for Lily, a future vastly different from that of the other boys and girls who would be leaving St Peter's this year, all of them doomed to work in the mills or the tailoring shops.

My mother glowed with pride and quiet joy, although perhaps occasionally I saw a troubled expression on her face. It would appear at different times, when she was alone usually, and I could observe her from a distance. She seemed to brood for a moment, then would rouse herself and go about her work quickly, as if determined not to think about whatever it was had been bothering her.

Lily herself was clearly nervous as the day approached and with her usual pessimism was quite sure that she would fail the interview. Over and over my mother had to assure her that this couldn't possibly happen, until finally she grew exasperated with her insistence and burst out, 'If you keep on like this you'll talk yourself into it, and them too, and you will fail.'

Lily burst into tears. 'That's what you want me to do.'

My mother looked at her in astonishment. 'Why should I want that?'

'Oh, you've got reasons.'

'What reasons? What reasons could I possibly have for wanting you to fail the interview?'

'You're not too anxious for me to go to the Grammar School.'

'Why? Why?'

But Lily refused to answer. She ran away from my mother. She would not explain and my mother did not press her, but brooded a great deal over the strange accusation.

Then finally the day came. For the first time we were to go to school without Lily. But she would walk with us as far as the Devil's Steps. We hurried downstairs in a state of suppressed excitement. Lily, taking more time today in getting ready because of the new white dress, would follow later. But as we burst into the kitchen we came to an abrupt halt. He was there, sitting at the table, still eating his breakfast, head bent low.

We glanced at our mother for explanation, and she replied with her eyes, telling us to be silent, to seat ourselves at the table, to say nothing. We did so, Rose too. Not a word was being spoken and the only sounds came from the smacking of his lips. Why was he here? He was usually gone to his workshop long before this. Nor did he seem to be hurrying, as if he had all the time in the world. We ate feeling uncomfortable, wanting to leave as soon as possible. Already we could hear the sounds of other children out in the street going to school. But we couldn't go without Lily, and without seeing her in the new dress.

At last we heard her footsteps on the stairs. My mother looked eagerly towards the doorway and the rest of us looked too, and in a moment Lily appeared clad in her new white dress. It was long and came down to her ankles, with lace ruffles and lace cuffs and bodice, and her long dark silky hair flowing behind her. She looked beautiful and very grown-up, her figure long and slender, a slight flush that was excitement on her cheeks. I think even my father must have looked up for a brief moment and I believe that what he saw may have startled him, though he gave no indication of it and bent his head again over his plate almost immediately.

My mother clasped her hands together with delight and could not take her eyes off Lily. 'Oh, you're so beautiful,' she said. 'So very beautiful. And you look like a proper woman.'

Lily was obviously embarrassed. 'Do you like it?' she asked, meaning her dress.

'I love it,' my mother said and there was delight in her voice, and something made her turn towards my father then and ask, 'What do you think of your daughter today? Doesn't she look lovely? Aren't you proud of her?'

They were questions she would never have asked before. Never would she have dared draw him into the family picture. But her enthusiasm was so great she could not help it. And he in turn – we all looked at him to see his reaction, a bit amazed ourselves at our mother's daring – well, he did this: he wiped his mouth with the back of his hand, swung round in his chair and said, without looking at Lily, 'Where's she going? To a ball?'

'No, she's going to the Grammar School for an interview. You know she passed the exam. She came out at the top of the list . . .' He must have known all this. It would have been impossible for him not to have known with all the excitement her victory had created on the street. Surely it had been talked about in the tailoring shop too, as everywhere else. Surely he must have heard, and wasn't it altogether possible that one of the bolder men had ventured to break through his sullen barrier and mention it to him?

Yes, it's very likely that he knew and that this could have explained his presence among us this morning. But he was feigning ignorance. 'She's going to the Grammar School? Then she's finished with St Peter's?'

'Yes,' my mother said and for the first time a bit of uncertainty came into her voice.

'Then', my father said, crossing one leg over the other, 'her schooldays are over. She doesn't need any Grammar School.'

A stunned look appeared on my mother's face. On Lily's too. On all our faces. There was a brief silence, then my mother burst out, 'What are you saying? Do you realise the honour she's won, top of the list, the best of all of them, and now a chance to go to the Grammar School without any cost, and to become a teacher.'

He cleared his throat. It was a habit of his that usually preceded an outburst, and we all tensed and drew together for comfort. 'It's time she started earning a living, never mind becoming a teacher. I was earning a living when I was five years old. They sent me out to work in a slaughter-house. I cleaned up the blood and entrails of the animals and the shit and the hair and the eyes that rolled out of the heads.' His voice was rising and beginning to choke with rage. 'Five years old, I was. Did I have an education? Did I go to school? She's been going all her life. She's twelve years old. Girls younger than her are working already and making money. It's time she started helping out in this house.'

'But she's got this chance. It's her one big chance. She'll never have it again.'

My mother was pleading and begging, but it was no use. He got up suddenly from the table, pushing the chair away from himself with that familiar scraping sound, and reaching out a hand to Lily, said, 'Come on. Let's go. I'll give you a new kind of education.'

Lily shrank away from him and said, 'No, I won't go.'

'You'll go,' he roared. 'You'll go, or I'll drag you there.'

He grabbed hold of her and Lily screamed, 'Mama, don't let him take me.'

My mother tried to stop him, and he pushed her away so savagely that she fell and we all rushed to help her. He paid no attention and grabbed hold of Lily's arm again, then with the other hand he twisted her beautiful hair into a rope and pulled it, now with both hands, and Lily, screaming and still trying to resist, was pulled along.

My mother, on her feet now and sobbing, rushed after them and we followed, sobbing too. He dragged Lily out of the house and I could see people standing outside, staring. Some of the children on their way to school stopped to stare. I saw Arthur among them. He had probably been waiting for Lily to come out, hoping that this time my mother wouldn't mind if he walked with Lily to the Grammar School. He was standing in the middle of the street, his eyes wide with horror.

My mother, sobbing hysterically, stood in the doorway with her hands over her eyes and we around her crying too. And for a long time we could hear Lily's screams as she was dragged through the streets by the rope of her hair, and her voice coming to us clearly, screaming, 'I won't go. I won't go.'

Part II

Chapter Seven

'My dear mother-in-law, father-in-law, brother-in-law, sisters-in-law and all the children, just a few lines to let you know that we are well and hoping to hear the same from you . . .' It began that way, as did all her letters to America. My mother paused in her dictation, while my pen scratched a little longer to catch up with the words she had just said. I was seven years old, and had learned to read and write quickly, and to spell. I was quite definitely the letter writer of the family. The job had been passed on from Lily to Rose, and then to Joe and Saul, and now to me.

It was a summer evening and we were alone in the kitchen. I could hear the sounds of children playing in the street, and perhaps I was a little envious and wished I could be out with them. But I did not mind too much. I liked writing to America. I had come to feel much as my mother did about wanting to go there and a letter always seemed to put me a step closer to them.

As I waited, while my mother gave still more thought to what she was going to say next, I dipped my pen into the little blue inkpot, trying to be careful, remembering the shouts of my standard three teacher, Miss Daniels, and

the way she went among us scolding and rapping knuckles
with a ruler if you got too much ink on the nib and made
blots on the paper. I was perhaps one of the worst in the
class. My handwriting was an illegible scrawl slanting
across the notepaper and full of blots, and usually I came
away from the lesson with ink on my hands and face, and
my knuckles sore from Miss Daniel's rapping.

It would be that way now by the time the letter was
done. Already, as soon as I lifted the pen out of the inkpot,
a huge drop fell on to the paper, and I had to sop it up with
the blotter before my mother could continue. At last we
were ready.

'I only hope', she dictated, 'that this letter will reach you
safely. With this terrible war on, and the Germans sinking
our ships one after another, you never can tell. But with
God's help let us hope it will find its way to you. I would
not want to lose touch with you, for you are the only
relatives I have and you are all very dear to me . . .' The
thought made her start to cry a little and I had to wait
uncomfortably while she dabbed at her eyes with a handkerchief. However, she soon continued. 'And I know you
will want to hear the latest news of the old street. Much
has happened since I last wrote to you. The war has
changed a lot of things. For one thing, Mrs Turnbull no
longer has her boarders to drink beer with. They have all
gone off to fight, so we don't have to worry any more about
their getting drunk on Saturday nights and shouting bloody
Jews across the street at us. And I suppose her poor
husband doesn't mind their going too because now she
remembers to take him in at night.

'And I suppose the Harrises feel better about their being
gone too, though they have another sorrow. The army took
Sam. He was half blind, you know, but they took him

anyway. Last month he came home on leave and the shul gave a party for him. It was the night before he was to go back. The poor boy got up to make a speech but he couldn't, because he started to cry and everybody cried with him. He didn't want to go back, but of course he had to.

'Well, I'll tell you of one man on our street who really wanted to go. That's Mr Finklestein, our next-door neighbour. You remember how they always used to fight, and the terrible things that went on in their house. Well, it was never Mr Finklestein's fault. He was really a very nice man. He used to come into my shop many times just to get away from his wife – the "Little Thripenny Bit", we used to call her, because she's so small. And a real madwoman. Well, I suppose he's a bit wrong in the head too, but in a nice sort of way. When he came into the shop he'd ask me to make him a sponge cake and herring sandwich. I'd cut up a herring and put slices in between two pieces of sponge cake, and he'd eat it with a lot of sighing, and the juice dripping down his sleeve, and he'd say, "Ah, this is the life," as though he were in heaven.'

My mother laughed and I laughed too, remembering it, and she went on, wiping her eyes again, but this time from laughter, and my pen scratched again as she said, 'I really miss him. But they fight just as much as ever next door, and the Little Thripenny Bit is as mad as ever, and maybe even more so. But there has been a change in her too. Remember how proud she used to be of being English born and stuck her little nose up in the air when she passed us, and sometimes used to call us "those Russian Jews"? Even when you were here she was like that. Well, now, she talks to everybody, and all she talks about is her husband and how he is leading the men in battle and capturing Germans and winning medals. Everybody knows that Mr Finklestein is just a cook behind the lines, but we don't say anything and just wink at one another. One of these days they're going to carry her off to Macclesfield and put her away.

'Oh, yes, there's another one went off to fight. That's Freddy Gordon. I wrote to you about him before, and that terrible time when he and Sarah Harris got caught walking together out in the country, and how lucky the Harrises were they caught it in time and were able to send Sarah off to Australia. Thank God she's getting along fine there, and just before the war broke out we understood she was engaged to a well-to-do man who owned a general store in Melbourne. She might have to wait until the war's over to get married, but at least she's safe. Annie Green was not so lucky. She's the one who lives across the street and had that baby, and everybody believed Freddy was the father. He was no good, that boy. As soon as Sarah left, he took up with Annie again and I suppose he made a lot of promises that he never kept. Anyway, he's off to war now and poor Annie is all alone again, and her mother is gnashing what's left of her teeth. She feels as if she's been cheated, because what she really wanted was for Annie to marry Freddy so that she'd have free beer whenever she wanted it. She claims the shaigets broke his promise . . .'

'How do you spell shaigets?' I interrupted.

'You're asking me?' my mother asked, amazed. 'How should I know?'

'Well, I don't know how to spell it. What shall I do? Shall I ask Lily?'

My mother hesitated. There was no one else in the house except Lily. The others – Rose, Joe and Saul – were outside with their friends. But Lily was upstairs in her bed, too tired and too ill to be bothered.

After a moment she shook her head and said, 'Put something else. Can you spell goy?'

'Yis.'

'Then put goy.'

I wrote this word and we continued with the letter. 'Now I have some really sad news to tell you,' my mother dictated. 'It's about our rabbi and his son Max. The boy ran away. First, he was supposed to go into the army, but he didn't register, so the police came looking for him. It was a terrible disgrace for the rabbi. He's a very patriotic man. He's always told us that without England taking us in we could have all been lost. He always ends the services with "And God bless our King and Queen". And now his son had refused to serve and was being sought by the police.

'But you'll never guess where he ran to. This is the worst part of it. To Russia. They got a letter from him finally. He begged their forgiveness, but he said it was something he had to do. He could no longer go on pretending to be something that he was not. And he couldn't serve in a war that would only create more misery in the world, no matter who won. He was going to fight to end misery, he said. For the revolution. He was going to fight with the Bolsheviks. That's what he wrote and you can imagine how the poor rabbi felt. It almost killed him . . .'

There was an interruption just then, a timid knocking at the front door that meant a customer, some child, probably, for the women knocked louder or simply walked in. My mother rose and went to answer it and I sat with my pen in my hand waiting for her to come back.

From outside there still came faintly the shouts and shrieks of children playing, and from somewhere in the background the Forshaws' gramophone playing a war song: 'Pack up your troubles in your old kit bag and smile, smile,

smile,' the voice sang. But I was thinking of what I had just written for my mother, and remembering the rabbi's haggard face and his absent-mindedness, and how we had taken advantage of all this to torment him still further . . . how Zalmon had secreted himself in the cupboard that contained the doorbell mechanism and kept making the bell ring, and how the rabbi used to jump each time and spring towards the door, thinking probably it was someone come about his son, some more bad news, and how we had choked with laughter and almost fallen out of our seats.

My mother came back from the shop smiling. 'It was a little batesky from Back Brook Street,' she said, 'a little ragged girl. She was so frightened she couldn't talk at first. She just stood there shivering and staring at me with big wide eyes. You see, it was the first time she had ever been in a Jewish house . . .' My mother laughed. She would tell this to Fanny Cohen later and they would both huddle together with their shoulders shaking. But she was keeping her laughter in as she told it to me then and there was something almost like tenderness in her voice. 'Then, finally, when she could talk she wanted to know if we had any pig's knuckles. I told her we didn't carry such things and she'd better go to Gordon's. And then . . .' She was having a bit of difficulty now controlling her laughter. 'She was so frightened she just peed in her drawers and ran out, leaving a puddle on the floor . . .'

I laughed too, but then my mother grew serious and said, 'Where did I leave off?'

I had to read the last sentence to her, rereading my own handwriting with a great deal of difficulty. My mother then continued, 'I don't think the rabbi will ever recover from the shock and the loss of his son. It shows in the way he conducts the services. He stumbles over words and loses his place, and Mr Harris has to stand by him all the time and show him where to read. There is some grumbling among people in the congregation and some talk about maybe we ought to get a new rabbi. But most of us won't hear of it and we plan to stick by him . . .'

She paused a moment and finally went on, 'I have told you most of the sad news about the street, but now I must tell you some more sad news about ourselves. I said at the beginning of the letter that we are all well, but that isn't quite true and I am very unhappy about what is happening. I suppose I should thank God that we are making a living. Even Rose is working now and all done with school. Lucky for her she didn't have to go into the tailoring shop with her father. She got herself a job in a fancy dressmaking shop, is learning the trade and is quite stuck up over it. She hardly ever talks to any of us. She goes about with her nose up in the air, just like Mrs Finklestein. Almost all the people who come into the dress shop are rich people, and she has begun to think she is one of them. Sometimes I don't know whether to laugh or cry. But there are worse things, believe me. There is poor Lily, stuck in that shop with her father. She never got over it. She was so close to becoming something and then he had to drag her into the shop.'

It was getting difficult for my mother to speak and she began fumbling for her handkerchief. I waited uncomfortably, my pen poised over the paper, and a large drop fell off the nib on to the last line I had written. I hastily blotted it, while my mother began to speak again, her voice slightly broken, at the same time dabbing at her eyes. 'I don't know how a man can be so cruel. But I suppose he can't help it. He has had such a hard life himself. I only hope that Lily will understand this some day. But right now she is in a bad way. He shouts at her a lot in the shop when she does something wrong, and she sits at the sewing machine crying and everybody there feels sorry for her. And when she comes home at night so tired she can hardly eat her supper. My heart just breaks . . .'

I had to wait again until my mother was able to proceed. It was not a happy letter. I thought too of my sister Lily and the situation she had fallen into. When I took the tea to the workshop I carried two cans, one for her and one for my father. As I entered the shop, I saw her from the distance bent over her machine, sewing, and I saw the misery on her face. She must have hated every moment of her life then.

My arrival gave her a brief respite. A look of gladness came over her when she saw me and she reached for the tea can greedily. My father, still bent over his machine, continuing to treadle, glowered and said savagely without looking up, 'Don't take all day. This isn't a Sunday picnic.'

The workshops had never been so busy. They were making uniforms mostly for the soldiers, and the material was rough and heavy and hard to sew. When Lily came home at night she walked very slowly, and it was just as my mother said, she was often too tired to eat. She went up to bed right away.

She was there now, asleep I suppose. My father had come home before her – the two never walked together, she always behind him, dragging herself home wearily. He was gone by now, off to his pub.

But I had begun writing again. 'I wish there was something I could do. But what can I do? I sometimes lie awake thinking of it, remembering the wonderful chance she had and what a better life there could have been for her if only she had been allowed to go to the Grammar School. I was in such agony I often wanted to speak to the rabbi about it, but he had his own sorrows, poor man. If this war was not on I would go down on my bended knees and ask you to send for her. Just her. Never mind us. But even if you were to say yes and send the ticket I would not let her go with the German submarines sinking so many ships these days.

'In the meantime she is going to suffer. If at least there were some nice Jewish boys around for her to meet. But they have all been taken by the army. Benny Mendelsohn went. Do you remember him? And of course Sam Harris, and a few others. They took the boys across the street too. Stanley Jackson and Johnny Melrose – his mother used to light your fires on Shabbes, remember? – and Arthur Forshaw. You know, the boy I once wrote to you about, the one I was afraid Lily was taking a fancy to. He's in the army too and is over in France. He writes to Lily sometimes and she writes to him. I haven't tried to stop that, although I don't like it too much. But I don't have the heart to say anything. After all, this is wartime and he's in France, and God knows what could happen to him there . . .'

No sooner had she dictated this, and while my pen was still scratching, there came a strange cry from upstairs. The girls' bedroom was directly above us, so it could only have come from Lily. My mother sprang to her feet in alarm, and I stopped writing and quickly soft footsteps came rushing down the stairs. She would have gone past us and straight through the lobby if my mother hadn't stopped her, crying, 'Lily!'

Lily was wearing a thin wrap over her nightgown and had slippers on her feet. She was clutching the wrap to her to keep it from opening, and her face was very white and her hair hung behind her in a wild, uncombed, unbrushed mass. Her eyes seemed very big and dark.

'It's Emily,' she said in a whisper.

My mother was puzzled at first. 'Emily?'

'The telegram girl,' Lily said almost impatiently, anxious obviously to get to the door. 'I saw her from the window riding her bike on Brook Street coming towards us.'

Now my mother understood. Emily Goff, a tiny girl whose parents ran a stationery shop on King Street, had been conspicuous at St Peter's because of her dwarf-like figure. The headmaster had often made jokes about her, but in a kindly way, because he had liked her, as everyone else had. She was not a particularly bright girl, not too good at her lessons, but perennially cheerful and laughing, and she could whistle like a boy. She could whistle almost any song, sweetly and beautifully, and the headmaster often made her stand up in front of the school assemblage to perform for us. The canary, he used to call her.

Emily still whistled merrily as she rode daily on her rounds, with the package of black-bordered envelopes sticking out of the leather pouch strapped to her waist. Since the war broke out, and since leaving St Peter's, she had become the telegram girl. Still very tiny, with feet that could barely reach the pedals of her bicycle, making her ride almost standing up, she went whistling from street to street, from door to door, delivering her messages from the War Office, seemingly unaware of their tragic content.

It was the whistling that Lily must have heard to begin with and that had sent her flying out of bed to the window. It was the sound that always heralded the girl's arrival and brought people to their doors with white faces and hands clutching hearts in dread. We heard it now as Lily was speaking and we rushed to the door with her. The letter remained unfinished, forgotten on the table, with its several pages of ink-smeared scrawl.

Yes, there she was, coming round our corner, standing up on her pedals, whistling brightly. A war song: 'Mademoiselle from Armentières, parlez vous . . .'

It was one of those lovely, soft summer evenings. The sun had already set behind the square brick tower of the India Mill and streaks of violent red remained in the sky. The street, which had been ringing before with the shouts and cries of kids at play, had suddenly grown quiet. The children had stopped in the midst of play to stare at Emily and to get ready to rush after her to whatever door she was going. Those who were sitting outside remained seated, glued to their chairs, with eyes also fastened on the little dwarf-like messenger girl. Others inside had come to the doors. Hands were on hearts. Whose house would it be? It had happened before on the street. It had become a guessing game, a terrible, terrorising game.

Certainly, she would not stop at our house. In fact, she rode right past it. My father had gone to Chester with other men to be examined by the army doctors and had come home drunk, with a strange leer on his face, as if to say he would not oblige us by going off to war and getting killed.

We said nothing, although I know my mother cried with relief.

Yes, Emily rode right past our house, the first one she came to, in fact, and then since the Forshaws' house was almost directly opposite ours, she went past theirs too. The Forshaws had turned off their gramophone, and both of them had risen to their feet and had been watching the girl, and I noticed how Lily's eyes remained fixed on her during this time, and when Emily had ridden on Lily gave a little sigh.

It was quite audible, and my mother's eyes went to her sharply and then across the street. You could almost hear the same sigh coming from the two over there. They didn't settle back into their seats, however. Nor did the others whose houses Emily went past. Now they had to know whose house it would be. All the way to the top of the street she rode, whistling her song, and Mrs Turnbull came out of her sweet shop to get ready. It had happened to her once already. The boarders gave her name as next of kin and there had been this one casualty before.

It hadn't affected her too much and she wasn't in any great fear now as she stood waiting for the telegram girl to stop at her place. But it was not there, on this side that Emily stopped and got off her bike with a slight, nimble hop.

I heard my mother let out a little gasp. All eyes on the street were rooted to the spot, necks craning to see better. The next thing I remember was Mrs Harris running out into the middle of the street, screaming and tearing at her clothes and face. Her wig fell off, revealing white hair that she tore at with both hands. Her husband had run after her and was struggling to restrain her, and his bowler hat fell off, showing the little black yarmulke beneath.

Almost immediately people were running to the spot and I noticed a rather peculiar thing. They came from the Christian side too. Mrs Humberstone had lumbered over there quickly, with other women, including even Mrs Turnbull, who was generally the most distant and hostile of them all. Even in that bewildering, chaotic moment, as we all converged on the hysterical woman, it struck me as odd.

My mother was there among them, and she fought to get to Mrs Harris and halt what she was doing. The rending of the clothes was a ritual that the orthodox went through in mourning for the dead, but so great was the woman's grief that she would have destroyed herself too had not my mother and these other women pinned her hands to her sides and dragged her back into her house, some of the Christian women entering along with my mother and other Jewish women, Mrs Humberstone carrying Mrs Harris's wig in one hand and the bowler hat in the other.

It was all over finally and people went back into their houses. A few children resumed playing, but most of us, Christian children as well as Jewish, hung around the Harrises' house chatting excitedly over the event that had taken place and the knowledge that Sam had been killed.

There was all sorts of wild speculation as to how it had happened and voices, high-pitched, yelled at one another.

'He was blown to bits by a shell . . .'

'No, 'e wasn't. 'E got it in the 'ead with a bullet . . .'

'Yer barmy idiot. A German stabbed 'im in th' belly with a bayonet . . .'

My mother remained inside the house with Mrs Harris for some time, long after the other women had left, and with the group in front beginning to disperse, I went back to our own house and was startled to find Mrs Forshaw there talking with Lily, and Lily's face for once looked flushed and animated.

Mrs Forshaw smiled at me as I came up to them. 'Hello, 'arry,' she said quietly.

'Hello,' I mumbled and hung my head. I was not used to it yet, to seeing Christian women on our side, especially at our house.

'Well, I must be getting back,' Mrs Forshaw said to Lily. 'I'll let you know when I get another letter from Arthur and I'd appreciate it if you would let me know when you get one. That way we'll be doubly sure he's safe.'

'Yes, it's a very good idea,' Lily said. 'I'll be glad to do it.'

'Thank you. Ta-ta then.'

'Ta-ta.'

'Ta-ta, 'arry.'

I didn't answer and continued to hang my head, and Lily said sharply, 'Say ta-ta to Mrs Forshaw, 'arry.'

'Ta-ta,' I mumbled.

Mrs Forshaw smiled again and went back across the street, striding swiftly, her tall, slender body very erect. And Lily stood watching her, her eyes shining.

'She came over to ask if I'd had a letter from Arthur lately,' she said, and I suppose she thought she had to explain why Mrs Forshaw had been there talking to her, and I suppose too she was so happy over the event she wanted to talk about it. But not to my mother.

She must have thought about that as we went in, because she stopped abruptly and spoke to me over her shoulder. 'You don't have to tell Mam that I was talking to Mrs Forshaw,' she said.

'Why?' I asked.

'She might not like it. You won't tell, will you? Promise?'

I nodded.

It wouldn't be the last time she'd ask me that and most of the times I kept my word.

We were in the third year of the war then and things were going badly for us. The German zeppelins were bombing London and fear hung over us constantly. At night the streets were pitch-black and no lights showed at windows, and in the houses we trembled at every little noise and waited tensely for the church bells that would warn us to rush down to our cellars.

The women still gathered in my mother's shop, even though it had dwindled to almost nothing. Food was being rationed, and even spoiled fruits and vegetables were hard to get. Nor was there any milk, so that my mother could no longer make sour milk for the women to refresh themselves with while they gossiped. But the talk was no longer the same either. Very little time was wasted on the petty little goings-on of the street; now it was about the war, and they talked of 'retreats' and 'advances' and 'flank attacks', using the words as freely as though they had spoken them all their lives.

And sometimes the 'Little Thripenny Bit', our next-door neighbour, joined them too. This in itself was a remarkable change, for she had always disdained my mother's shop, had turned her tiny nose up in the air as she went past and said aloud for everyone to hear, 'I don't know what the street is coming to.' Or, 'All these Russian Jews can think of is making money.'

But now she had become part of the daily afternoon gathering in the shop, thrusting her way in and dominating the conversation with her high-pitched voice to tell of her husband's valour at the front. 'He led the charge,' I remember hearing her say once. 'He went over the top first man with his bayonet fixed, and they all followed him, and they captured two hundred and twenty-five Germans. My husband took charge of them, and General Haig clapped him on the back and said, "Well done, my man, well done."'

The women said nothing, but they winked at one another and those in the back tapped their foreheads.

At St Peter's, the headmaster paced constantly up and down in front of his desk, head bent, hands clasped behind his back, his large ears redder than ever, his long, bony features cast in gloom. Sometimes, he would pause, and whirl suddenly on the class and shout, 'What about the war loan?'

A deathly silence followed. No one dared speak and eventually he resumed his pacing. The war weighed heavily on him. Cocky had gone off to war to become an officer in the tank corps, but they had refused to take the headmaster for some unknown reason. It was rumoured on our street that he had an undescended testicle and this was the reason. Someone who had known him when he was a milkman claimed that the headmaster had confided it to him once.

Regardless of what it was, the headmaster was a very troubled man. Every report of new casualties, surrenders or retreats increased his disturbance and he could no longer think of school matters. Sometimes he would halt his pacing to order the partitions pushed back and everybody on their feet to sing patriotic songs:

> Rule Britannia,
> Britannia rule the waves,
> Britons never never never shall be slaves . . .

How many times did we sing that song, and 'God save our noble king . . .' and others like them, with the headmaster roaring along with us and the women teachers belting it out too in high sopranos, until our faces grew blue and our voices hoarse?

And yet the battles raged on and little Emily was busier than ever on her bike, pedalling faster to keep up with the stack of black-bordered envelopes in her leather pouch, whistling as she rode. And the wounded, the lucky ones, the blighties, were pouring in all over England, filling all the hospitals, filling the infirmary in our town until they were lined up in the corridors with no more ward space.

More wounded were being brought in on stretchers, their bodies, their legs, their faces swathed in white bandages, until one day even the corridors at the infirmary were filled, and there was no more space for them. Then the authorities took drastic action and the swanks were turned out of their school up the park.

It was a great day for us when we learned about it. We laughed and rejoiced. Now the swanks would have to go to St Peter's, where there was no rhododendron garden at the front and no shiny floor in the hall; no hall at all, in fact, just one big room if you pushed the partitions back. And the toilets in the yards, one for the girls, one for the boys, were smelly.

They would go in the afternoon, we in the morning. And we grinned as we left St Peter's and watched them come in disconsolately, afraid, suspicious, dressed in their short blue pants and bicycle stockings and little blue caps that bore the gold school badge on the front just over the peak. They were as afraid of the ragamuffins of St Peter's as we had once been – but no longer now because the attention of the little batesemas was drawn from us to the newcomers.

'Eh, look at the bloody little swanks,' they jeered as the fearsome little fellows came towards us with their books under their arms, neatly dressed, faces well washed and scrubbed, young bodies well filled with food. 'That one there looks just like Lord Muck 'isself.'

'That one', a little fellow who might have been my own age, shrank back and we all laughed. I laughed too, loudly, enjoying the torment and fear that had been transferred from us to them.

Then my attention was drawn to the short, pot-bellied man wearing a raincoat and carrying an umbrella, who was striding with quick, short steps behind them. It was the headmaster of the Hollywood Park School, the one who

had thrust my mother and myself out of his school in such
a humiliating fashion on what was supposed to have been
my first day at school, about three years since.

I don't know if he recognised me. He seemed to glare at
me as he went by and I couldn't help feeling a moment's
fear. But then he glared at all the others too, hating them
instantly for being poor, for wearing ragged clothes and for
being dirty and starved-looking. And for tormenting his
pupils, and for occasionally tearing the blue caps off their
heads and kicking them about like footballs.

He must have complained to our headmaster a lot about
it, because our headmaster several times warned us sternly
against it. But he never caned anybody for it, and there was
obviously no love lost between him and the other headmaster, and there were rumours that they quarrelled
frequently, our headmaster defending us staunchly against
the other's charges

But one other thing that came out of these arrangements
was a new sport – watching the wounded being brought in.
With our afternoons free now we were able to go rushing
up the park brew to the school turned hospital every time
word came that a new load of wounded was arriving. It was
exciting to see them. We crowded as close to the gate as we
could, where the ambulances with the big red crosses
painted on their sides backed in. They did not go beyond
the gate. The wounded were lifted off on to stretchers and
carried in by nurses.

As each one was lifted out, the crowd yelled, 'Hi,
Tommy.'

They were all Tommy. They all waved to us if they could
and smiled weakly. Most of them had come right from the
front. I waved to them too. I waved to one man who was
being lifted out, his entire body covered with blankets and

only his face showing. I shouted, 'Hi, Tommy,' as did all the others.

But it was at me he looked and smiled. And quite distinctly he said, 'Hi, 'arry.'

I stared at him, astonished that he should know my name. And then I gave a little gasp and others around me who had recognised him at the same time began shouting, 'It's Freddy Gordon!'

It was Freddy all right. We were not able to say any more to him. They were carrying him into the hospital. We didn't know it then, but they were only carrying half of him. The other half, both legs, had been left behind at the Somme.

It was all over the street in no time. For once a casualty had preceded Emily's telegram. There had not been time for the War Office to issue the usual message of condolence. The battle wounded had been rushed to England, to the various towns where there was space in the hospitals, and it was by sheer chance that Freddy had been shipped to his own town.

By the time we got back to the street yelling out the news to our parents, shrieking at the top of our voices, 'Freddy Gordon's been wounded – 'e's in th' 'ospital!', both Florrie and Annie were flinging on shawls and rushing up the street. They did not speak to one another, though Annie would have if Florrie had spoken to her. But Florrie would have nothing to do with her or her mother.

Mrs Green watched them both go flying up the street from her doorstep, grinning and showing her toothless mouth and cackling to herself gleefully. She was rubbing her hands together, a sure sign that something pleased her. Had her hopes risen again?

Other women came out on to the street to discuss the matter. Mrs Humberstone lumbered across with her rolling, sailor-like gait and thick arms folded across her ample bosom, to talk to the Jewish women. But some of the latter had crossed over to the opposite pavement and others met in the middle of the street. I have told you how this had happened before. Well, it had happened several times since then, whenever little Emily came riding on to the street. The war, it seemed, had almost completely destroyed that invisible wall, bringing the two sides together.

The women cried with one another, put arms round one another, and it didn't seem to matter whether you were Jewish or Christian, you just wailed and moaned.

As yet, when the news came that Freddy was in the hospital there was only excitement. Nobody knew of anything to mourn then. And even when Florrie and Annie came back they knew nothing at first, although they were struck by the fact that the two women were walking together and talking earnestly, and Florrie seemed suddenly to have developed a great affection for Annie, because she had an arm round her shoulders, and when they got to the Greens' house, Florrie invited Mrs Green, who was standing outside on her doorstep, to come over and have a glass with her.

It was all somewhat mysterious. Mrs Green herself was puzzled – and suspicious. She went with Florrie to have a glass. Why not? Annie was probably relieved not to have to tell her mother – Florrie would do that for her.

Bit by bit the whole street learned. There was shock, disbelief, whispered conversations held on doorsteps, in the middle of the street.

'The poor man . . .'

'He'd be better off if 'e 'adn't come home 'tall.'

'And 'e was such a good soccer player, 'e was.'

'Yis. I saw 'im kick th' winning goal against Cheadle Heath, th' year before he left.'

'Yis, I saw that too. Well, 'e won't be kicking any more balls, the poor man.'

'Not the way 'e is. I wonder what they did with th' legs.'

'Left 'em there, I suppose. Not much good to 'im any more.'

The conversations went on. In my mother's shop they talked of nothing else, and Mrs Jacobs took advantage of the situation to tell once again, as she had done so often in the past, how she had suffered her injury and how her eye had been knocked out, supposedly by a jealous suitor at a dance who, seeing her dance with another man, had jabbed her in the eye with his elbow, knocking it out.

'He claimed it was an accident,' Mrs Jacobs said bitterly. 'The bastard. And he was supposed to be a gentleman.'

The women were irritated and annoyed. They'd heard the same story so often and they didn't believe it anyway. It was Freddy they wanted to talk about and Mrs Mittleman broke in roughly, saying, 'So your eye was knocked out. You compare that to two legs?'

'A leg is worse than an eye?' said Mrs Jacobs angrily. 'Since when?'

And then, seeing that they weren't interested in her or her story, she stalked out in a huff. The other women hardly noticed. They went on talking, Mrs Mittleman saying, 'So what is the shaigets going to do now? What is to become of him?'

'A terrible thing,' murmured Fanny Cohen. She was without a baby for once, but as bedraggled as ever, dangling limply over the upturned orange box she was sitting on. 'What can a man without legs do?'

'Florrie will have to take care of him,' said my mother. 'He'll not go hungry.'

'Poor Florrie,' said Mrs Berger, a short, fat woman who lived right opposite the Gordon shop. 'She was only waiting for the war to be over and for Freddy to come back so that he could take over and let her get married.'

'She'll have to wait,' said Mrs Mittleman grimly.

'Yes,' said Mrs Berger. 'I feel sorry for her. First, it was the mother and now it's Freddy.'

'And what's Mrs Green saying?' asked Fanny Cohen.

They all looked to my mother for this information, because Mrs Green was our fire goyah. But my mother shrugged. It had only happened this Monday, too early yet for Friday and Mrs Green's visit. 'She'll have plenty to say,' my mother said.

'And Annie?' someone else asked.

They all conjectured over that for some moments longer before the group broke up. Perhaps both sides of the street were wondering about it. Perhaps they'd all been curious about the strange friendship that had seemed to develop between Florrie and Annie when they came home from the hospital that day.

We soon found out how Mrs Green felt about the matter. She came scurrying over to our house in response to my call on Friday night and as soon as she started prodding our fire with quick, short stabs of the poker her toothless mouth was chattering. She cackled as she talked. There was a triumphant glint in her eyes.

'Oh, you'd think butter would melt in her mouth, the way she talks now. "And how are ye today, Mrs Green? And 'ow's Annie? And 'ow's little Peter? Come on and 'ave a glass on me. And what'll it be? 'ow's about some Guinness?" Mind you, every time I come in to th' taproom afore this she wouldn't even look at me. Now, seems she can't get enough of me company And Annie's become her best friend all of a sudden. And little Peter warn't nothing but a little bastard and not fit to be looked at. Oh, it's all different now. There was a whole man afore this. Now there's only half a man and a man somebody's got to be taking care of once he gets out of 'ospital. Poor man. He gave his legs for king and country, and I got to honour him for that, but it's Florrie's 'ard luck, not mine and not Annie's. Annie's 'ad 'er share of 'ard luck and there was no pity for her then, and I can tell you right now she's not going to be saddled with a man who 'asn't got legs. Nor me. I'll take Florrie's beer, but not her brother, not the 'alf that's left of 'im.'

'And how does Annie feel about it?' my mother asked.

Mrs Green looked up at her and gave a loud cackle. The flames were now shooting up in the fire and their light danced across her face. 'Once a fool always a fool,' she said. 'The girl's daft. She'd take him without legs, it don't matter one bit to her, she's that much gone on him. And with Florrie cozening to her all the time, she'd be willing to pick 'im up, what's left of 'im, and carry 'im off to the preacher. But I'm not going to let 'er. Not on your bloody life. It's Florrie's trouble, not ours. She'll just have to put off her own wedding to that man in Birmingham a bit longer, but she'll not pile her trouble on my 'ead. Not if I can bloody well 'elp it.'

So that's how the wind was blowing and soon the whole street knew about it and there was much speculation as to what was going to happen when Freddy got out of the hospital. In the meantime the war went on. It was that year the Americans entered the war and new hope rose among everybody. The headmaster's face looked a bit more cheerful, and he even smiled now and then, and came around to the classrooms to ask how many thripenny doughnuts there were in a dozen. At cheder, the rabbi puffed on his long cigarette holder, and paced up and down in front of the fireplace while we recited our Hebrew. His thoughts still seemed far away from us, yet there was less gloom on his bearded face, for the end of the war, which seemed in sight when the Americans came into it, might bring his son home.

Yet the war was not over by any means and little Emily came two or three more times to our street – once to poor Mrs Melrose across from us, bringing news that her husband, that quiet little stocky man whom everyone liked so much, had been killed, and once to the Bergers, their son Benny killed, and another time to some Christian family across the street, just a wound.

There were also letters from the front, with Mrs Finklestein shrieking out stories of new heroism on the part of her husband every time she got one, although she would never let anyone read it. The postman, an elderly man with white wispy hair showing under his peaked cap and with a pronounced limp that came from the Boer War, went from door to door on both sides.

There was one for us on this day and I was with my mother at the door when she took it. There was a foreign stamp on it, and she jumped at once to the conclusion that it was from America and became excited. It was a long time since we had heard from them, the transatlantic mail had come almost to a standstill because of the war.

'Open it, open it,' she said, clasping her two hands together in front of her as she always did when excited. 'Read me what they have to say.'

I did. I tore open the envelope and there were several pages of writing inside. I was sure myself that it was from one of the relatives in America. 'My dear sweet Lily,' I read and stopped, and my mother and I looked at one another, and there was a long silence.

'It must be from him,' she murmured. There was not only disappointment in her face but something else, fear perhaps.

'Do you want me to read it?' I asked.

We looked across the street. The postman was over there now and he was delivering a letter to the Forshaws' house. We watched in silence for a moment.

'No,' my mother said finally. 'It's for Lily. Put it back in the envelope and we'll give it to her when she comes home from work. I'll have to tell her we opened it by accident.'

I did what she asked, though I was curious and wished I could have read it. Lily had never told us what was in Arthur's letters, though she always seemed happy after receiving one. And lately, too, she and Mrs Forshaw had been comparing letters with one another, both usually coming at the same time. My mother had never asked Lily about them.

She was silent now as we went back into the house. I put the opened letter on the mantelpiece to await Lily's arrival and went out to play, and forgot about it. Lily came home, late as usual, looking tired, trailing after my father, and as soon as I saw her I shouted, 'There's a letter from Arthur.'

'Where is it?' She gave a violent start, coming to life immediately.

'Here.' I snatched it off the mantelpiece and handed it to her.

But as soon as she took it from me and saw that it had been opened her eyes went accusingly to my mother. She didn't say anything, though; nor did my mother. My father was in our midst and we did not talk when he was there. Whether he had heard me mention the letter and who it was from, and whether he cared in the least, was hard to say. He was already seated at the table with his head bent low over his plate, wolfing down his food, and it did not take him long to be done and to be scraping his chair back as he rose and went for his coat.

The war had not changed his habits. He grabbed his coat off the hook behind the scullery door and strode out with one sleeve on and the other dangling behind him as he groped for it. He clumped through the lobby and we heard the front door bang after him.

Only then did Lily speak and she said bitterly, 'Did you have to open my letter?'

'I'm sorry,' my mother said. 'I didn't mean to. But I thought it was from America. You can ask 'arry. Isn't that true, 'arry?'

'Yis,' I said and, to make matters still easier for my mother, added, 'It looked like an American stamp.'

She seemed satisfied with the explanation and started to go upstairs with the letter in her hand.

'Where are you going?' my mother protested. 'You haven't eaten supper yet.'

'I don't feel hungry,' Lily said. 'I'll eat later. I want to lie down a bit first.'

But it was clear that all she wanted really was to get away from us for a while to read her letter. She was upstairs for about an hour and then came clattering down the stairs. We had all finished our supper by now and were sitting around the fire, reading. We looked at her curiously as she came into the room. The letter was still in her hand, and her eyes seemed to be sparkling and her whole being was alive. She was in extraordinarily good spirits and, sitting down at the table, said, 'I'm hungry now.'

'Thank God for that,' my mother said, starting to bustle around her with the food. 'Did you get some good news?'

'Yes. They all expect the war to be over soon. They're all talking of coming home.'

'I hope so,' my mother said, and the conversation and the sudden change in Lily's mood gave her courage to ask the question that had been preying on her mind all day. 'When Arthur writes to you does he always call you "my dear sweet Lily"?'

She was probably sorry she had said that when Rose, without looking up from her book, gave a scornful laugh. Lily flashed an angry look at her, then one at my mother. 'You did read my letter.'

'No, just the beginning. That's how we knew it was for you. Then we stopped.' As Rose continued to laugh, she shouted at her, 'You be still.'

'I wouldn't like anybody to read my love letters,' Rose said.

'It wasn't a love letter,' Lily cried. 'It's just the way he talks to me. I'm much younger than he is and he thinks of me as a little girl. That's all it means.'

'What does he say in his letters?' my mother asked, relieved perhaps, but not altogether convinced, and furious again when Rose gave another one of her little meaningful laughs.

'Do you want to hear what he writes?' Lily asked.

It came unexpectedly and surprised us all. Thus far she had guarded her letters from Arthur with the utmost secrecy, snatching them out of the hands of whoever had answered the postman's knock and keeping them hidden somewhere in her room. The offer now actually to read one to us made us look up from our books abruptly and stare at her.

Perhaps my mother was more surprised than any of us. 'Yes, I'd like to hear it,' she said.

'Well, not all of it,' Lily said. 'It's too long. I'll just read you a part that might interest you.'

She had barely eaten any of the food that my mother had put in front of her. She pushed the plate aside, took the letter out of the envelope and unfolded the pages. After some searching, she selected one and began to read, her face alight as she did so, her voice very clear. 'There is no heroism,' she read. 'There is only dirt and mud and cold and wet and men crying like babies and dead faces staring up at you and bodies lying huddled and still and the smell of death all around you and the sound of guns and flashes of fire bringing more death. There is no bravery either. Men have to be pushed over the top, prodded with the butts of rifles, threatened with revolvers by their officers, and they are trembling with fear, and sometimes crying with it, and they go blindly like so many terrified sheep being pushed to the slaughter.

'I sometimes wonder how men ever came to write about the glory of war and painted pictures that depicted this glory. The reality is just the opposite. I have learned this much and I do not think I could go on with it if I did not know what we are fighting for, that this might truly be the war to end all wars. That is what keeps me alive and keeps me going, the thought of the new world that this war is going to create. It will put an end to a lot of misery that existed before this, poverty for one thing, I hope, and particularly the differences that have always separated people one from the other . . .'

Lily paused and looked up at us for a moment as if there were some special significance in what she was about to say next. Then she went on in her calm, clear voice, 'Like religions, for one thing. We see it so clearly on our street, don't we, Lily? It's as if each side belonged to another world, and yet we know that isn't true and we are all very much alike and all very much part of the same world. I am hoping that when I come back – if I come back (we all have the superstitious belief that if we express this doubt our chances of survival are better. It's sort of childish, but I say it anyhow) – all this will be done away with and there will no longer be any separation between the two sides of our street. I am using this, of course, as a metaphor. My horizons are much broader than our street. I am thinking of the whole world. The new world that will come out of this slaughter. But I am thinking also of you and me . . .'

Lily broke off abruptly, as if she had gone too far with the letter, as indeed I think she had.

My mother had caught it, though, and she asked, 'What does he say about you and him?'

'Nothing,' said Lily hastily, beginning to fold the letter. 'It's nothing important.' Then she rose.

'Where are you going?' my mother asked in surprise, looking at her still full plate.

'I'm going over to Mrs Forshaw's to tell her I got the letter.'

'But you haven't even touched your supper. Besides, she got one herself. I saw the postman delivering it to her when yours came.'

'Well, she'll want to know about mine anyway and she'll want to tell me about hers. I won't be long. I'll eat when I get back.'

Chapter Eight

We knew that the war was over long before the newsboy came into our street with his stack of papers clutched under an arm bawling, 'Extra, extra, Germany surrenders. The war's over!'

That would have been Jimmy Lee, of course, a little ragged boy from Back Brook Street, as dismal and vile an area as Daw Bank. He was undersized for his age, which was about the same as mine, eight at the time, and he came every evening when the men and women were home from the mills.

But we knew already, before he came on that chill November day, what had happened, and celebrations had begun on most of the streets, and on ours people had congregated in the middle of the street, with both sides mingling and talking joyously and excitedly.

It was perhaps the last time the two sides would be drawn that close together. After the war was over things went back pretty much to normal, the way they had been before. But in that first flush of victory and happiness and relief, and God knows what other emotions were involved in this great moment, we were all very much one, and we were in a state of euphoria, drunk with our happiness.

Well, there was a lot of real drinking going on. Bottles of stout, jugs of beer appeared on the scene, and they were being passed among the older people. And there were bags of sweets for us and bottles of ginger beer, and much carrying on among us, racing about, chasing one another, shouting, screaming.

It was a regular party and I remember that Mrs Humberstone organised us into a parade – all the kids, the Christian ones and the Jewish ones, all mixed and not in separate groups, marching together round and round the street with flags in our hands, shouting and singing 'God Save the King', and 'Rule Britannia', and 'Pack Up Your Troubles in Your Old Kitbag'.

And there was dancing among the older people. The Forshaws had brought their gramophone right out into the street. They were in especially good spirits, these two. Their son was alive and he would be coming home soon. Mr Forshaw had obviously had too much to drink and it was quite noticeable in the way he teetered a bit as he adjusted the gramophone, and the way Mrs Forshaw, smiling, put her hand on his back to steady him.

I saw Lily in the crowd. She was just as elated as Mrs Forshaw, just as happy as everyone else, her eyes shining, a little flush on her ordinarily pale cheeks. She and Mrs Forshaw talked a great deal. They liked each other. That had been obvious for some time and I saw the troubled look on my mother's face as she glanced at them from time to time.

But this was no time to be worried about anything. I think my mother was just as happy as everyone else. People began to dance in the street to the music the gramophone was squawking out through the big green horn. It had been set up on an empty orange box supplied by my mother right in the centre of the street between our house and the Forshaws', and the disc twirled round and round madly. Now it was giving out an Irish jig, and Mrs Turnbull and Mrs Humberstone went to it. Two heavies hoisting skirts daintily above ankles, feet stepping nimbly, while the crowd clapped in rhythm and laughed and cheered, and there were cries of 'Aaah', and 'Eeeh', as the skirts rose still higher. And then the laughter grew to a roar as suddenly none other than Mrs Zarembar, the chicken woman, joined in, and hoisted her skirts too, exposing her thick, piano-leg-like ankles. A Jewish woman doing an Irish jig. Nobody had ever seen this before and the clapping grew louder, and there were more cries of 'Eeeh', and 'Aaah'.

Nobody was angry with anybody else that day. There were no enmities, no bitterness, and as I said, it was as if the two sides of our street had been welded into one.

Soon, too, the men began to come back, and when Cocky returned at St Peter's we all lined up in the schoolyard and gave three cheers. He stood before us, still in his uniform, the rimless glasses shining just like in the old days. But he was not the same as before. He couldn't seem to speak. He chewed his lower lip, and we noticed that his hands kept clenching and unclenching. The headmaster stood beside him, smiling. Well, he had done nothing but smile ever since news came that we had won the war. Nobody had been caned no matter what he did. And he had gone from class to class wiggling his ears and asking how many thripenny doughnuts there were in a dozen. Now, with Cocky back, his cup was full.

But as for Cocky, whether he shared that happiness or not it was hard to say. For he said little in that moment, except an abrupt, 'Glad to be back' and then his eyes seemed to fill and, looking almost as if he were going to cry, he turned on his heel and walked rapidly into the school.

We all stood silent and uncertain. The headmaster himself seemed uncertain for a moment, then took command of the situation. 'All right, everybody, quick march to your classes,' he shouted. He seemed a little upset.

Another one who came back very soon after the armistice was signed was Mr Finklestein. I saw him striding along Brook Street. He was in uniform and had his kitbag slung over one shoulder, and a rifle over the other. How he had managed to bring his rifle home was a matter of much speculation among us. But he had managed it somehow, and as I watched him he seemed to be marching in a military parade, body erect, shoulders squared, feet going left right, left right. When he came to the corner of our street he halted, saluted, and made a left turn and went right into our house.

I followed him quickly. My mother was standing in the lobby staring at him, thoroughly startled. But she recovered in a moment to welcome him back, though I've no doubt she was wondering, as I was, why he had not gone into his own house first.

He seemed to have loosened up considerably. His body had slackened, and he had lifted his kitbag from his shoulder and placed it on the floor, and he said cheerfully, 'I couldn't wait to get here. I've come for my favourite dish – you know what.'

Yes, my mother knew what – his sponge cake and herring sandwich – and she was able to make one for him, and just like old times he sat in the shop on an upturned orange crate and ate his sandwich, the juice dripping down into his sleeve, licking it off the back of his hand, munching and sighing and saying, 'Ah, this is the life! I thought of this all through the war. It was a dream I always had. I'd be sitting here just like this in your shop eating me sponge cake and 'erring sandwich, and licking the juice off me 'and, and saying what I'm saying now, "Ah, this is the life!" '

But in the midst of his joy his wife came running into the shop. She halted a short distance away from him and stood staring at him as if she could not believe her eyes.

And then, without a word of welcome, there came pouring out of her in her high, shrill voice a stream of complaint and bitterness about her troubles. 'Lily spat at me. Yes, she did. And Doris threw a cup of hot tea in my face. And Louis stole a penny from my purse. And Becky is turning into a thief too, and she threatened me with a knife the other day. There hasn't been a minute's peace in my life. I have no pleasure in my children and it all comes from your family, not mine. And you have no idea what the butcher charges for meat these days. We haven't had a decent meal for years and we've been without shoes, and the sink in the scullery keeps getting stopped up . . .'

On and on she went in the same thin, high, screaming voice that came through the wall. Only this time I could see her face, all tight with passion and her eyes staring wildly, and her little body crouched forward a little, as if she were going to spring at the poor man she was addressing.

A look of pain had come on to his face and he seemed to have lost his appetite. He put down the remainder of his half-eaten sandwich on the counter, passed a hand across his face and groaned.

'My God,' he said, 'I've just come home from the war, I haven't seen you in four years, four years of hell for me, and this is all you can say to me? Couldn't you wait at least until I'd finished my sandwich, and washed up a bit and gone to the water closet and moved my bowels on a real closet for the first time in four years?'

'You've gone through hell?' she shrieked back at him. 'What about me? I've gone through worse hell with those mad children of yours. Yes, yours. They all take after your side. There isn't one in your family wasn't put in a madhouse, and that's what'll happen to your children. But all you can think of is to sit in this dirty little shop and eat herring sandwiches just like all the other dirty Russian Jews. I'm English born and don't you ever forget that.'

He got up, put his kitbag back on his shoulder and adjusted the rifle on the other shoulder and left the shop, and she followed still shrieking at him. A crowd had gathered outside, and they all watched as the Finklesteins went into their own house and the noise of their fighting went on for some time afterwards, the sounds drifting out into the street.

The library was on St Petersgate, a white marble building that always looked so clean among all the other blackened, soot-stained buildings. It was only a short distance from the school and the public baths where we all used to go once a year on the day before Passover. It had a flight of marble steps leading up to the entrance and when Lily first took me there I used to hold her hand going up them, because they seemed so steep

I didn't hold her hand any more. I was eight when the war ended and pretty big for my age. But I still went to the library with her every Saturday afternoon. My two brothers and Rose went to the picture show on Saturday afternoons, but Lily and I preferred the library. We both read a lot and our arms were full as we came out of the library that Saturday afternoon. It was a raw day in early March, with grey clouds scudding across the sky and a wind blowing. It was cold, but we scarcely noticed it in our excitement over the new books we were bringing back home and the anticipation of reading them. We walked down those steps, hugging our books tightly for fear of dropping them.

The library was on the opposite side of the square from the school and we walked along that side. We went past the blackened statue of St Peter and the ancient, turreted building of the public baths, designed almost like a castle, and then down the brew to Mersey Square. Traffic was heavy with horses and carts and lorries and trams, more motor lorries than horses and carts now, and even a few motor cars.

A tram drew up just ahead of us and several soldiers got off, carrying kitbags over their shoulders. It was not an unusual sight these days to see them coming in from Manchester where they had been discharged. Every day brought a new flock. Suddenly, Lily gave a little gasp and stood stock still, staring.

I followed the direction of her eyes, puzzled. She was looking at the last soldier who had got off the tram and at first I didn't recognise him. Then Lily said, almost in a whisper, 'It's Arthur.'

Perhaps he had grown taller, certainly older. I still hardly recognised him. At that same moment he saw us a short distance away and stared too, and then I heard him shout, 'Lily!'

Lily dropped her books and ran towards him, and he ran towards her, and when they both came together he put his arms round her and kissed her, and drew her to him so tightly that her feet came off the ground.

I stood there watching them, not knowing whether to pick up Lily's books or to take in the scene. It was all very strange. Then Arthur released her and waved to me, and ran up to where I was standing and gave me a hug and said, 'You've grown, 'arry. My God, you're a regular big lad.'

He helped me pick up Lily's books and insisted on carrying them for her as we walked along, the two of them in front of me chatting away, and I behind, just like . . . Well, Arthur thought of that too, because once Arthur threw some words at me over his shoulder, laughing: 'Just like old times, eh, 'arry?'

Yes, it was very much like those times when we all walked home from school, when Lily was preparing for her scholarship exam and Arthur was tutoring her. He was intensely happy. That much was clear to me, and so was Lily. They both laughed a great deal, and talked and talked, and seemed excited.

'It's just incredible, you know,' I heard Arthur say once, 'my meeting you like this, you being the first one. Dammit, I don't know if I'm dreaming or not. Here you are, walking beside me, and there's 'arry behind us, and this is Daw Bank, and look, by God, here are the Devil's Steps . . .'

We had just come to them, as dark and odorous as ever, still frightening to me, although I'd gone up them several times when wandering about with my friends and had walked on Wellington Road above. The sight of them made Arthur pause a little and laugh almost with affection in his tone. 'Our old trysting spot,' he said. 'Here's where I'd wait for you to come along. I wish it could have been a bit more picturesque so that I could write a poem about it. Did I tell you that I have begun to write poetry? Well, I have, and some day I'll write one about you and, yes, maybe about this ugly, smelly town. It looks beautiful to me today, though, and you – well, you always were beautiful but you look even more beautiful than ever. God, but I'm so glad to have met you first off. I still can't believe it . . .'

He rattled on, drunk with joy, and Lily looked up at him, smiling, her eyes adoring. She had grown a little since leaving school, but she was still much shorter than him and had to look up to see his face, and watching them from behind I knew the secret that Lily had been trying to keep from us. She was in love with him and he was in love with her. If they had managed to hide it before, they couldn't now and it was just a lucky thing that I was the only one there with them.

For the entire walk they were so wrapped up in each other that I doubt if they were even conscious of my presence, but as soon as our street came into sight Lily halted abruptly, coming out of her dream swiftly, and stood hesitating.

Arthur looked at her enquiringly. 'What's the matter?' he asked.

'Arthur, would you mind if 'arry and I walked on and you followed a bit later? Or, better still, since you must be anxious to see your parents, you go first and we'll follow.'

He reacted angrily. 'Yes, I do mind. I thought we were all done with that sort of bosh. I fought in a bloody war to get rid of it and I'll not go back to it. No, we're going together, all three of us. Come on, now.'

He had taken command of the situation a bit roughly and forcefully, and perhaps it was a good thing he did, otherwise I doubt if Lily would have had the courage to go along with him. She was doubtless thinking of our mother. Fortunately, she was not outside when we arrived at the corner, but others were and all they could think of at that moment was that another of the boys had come home from the war. A flurry of excitement passed through the street, and voices shouted out to Arthur and people came running up to him.

The Forshaws came out of their house to see what all the noise was about, Mr Forshaw holding a jug of beer in his hand. They stared, then saw Arthur, and Mrs Forshaw, usually so calm and undemonstrative, gave a loud cry and ran up to him, pushed other people away, and flung arms about his neck and kissed him and wept, while Mr Forshaw stood by grinning awkwardly, stroking his moustache with one hand, holding the jug of beer in the other.

My mother had come out of the house by now and all she saw was this scene, and she herself went up to welcome Arthur back and shake his hand, as everybody was doing. It never occurred to her that we had been walking home with him, I suppose, but Lily wanted to be sure that she did not find out. About that and something else.

Just before we entered the house she whispered to me, ''arry, don't tell Mam that we met Arthur in the Square and' – her voice growing almost fierce – 'don't tell her that he kissed me. Do you promise?'

I nodded.

She thrust a penny into my hand, not much less than what she got from her week's pay. 'You can buy yourself some sweets,' she said

She didn't have to do that. I wouldn't have told. I had not forgotten that other thing. It was still deeply implanted in my mind – Sarah and Freddy, the ginger beer and the notes inside the bottles, and the terrible discovery in my mother's shop that cloudy day, and Mrs Harris's anguished

cry, and Sarah's screams as she was being beaten, and then
her being shipped off to Australia.

It was still there, along with the frightening conse-
quences that my mother had warned about, the awful thing
that could have happened to Sarah if the discovery had not
been made in time. Or to any Jewish girl or boy.

I had forgotten nothing and yet a penny was a penny, and
history may have been repeating itself as I dashed off
immediately to Mrs Turnbull's sweet shop. How little
things had changed. Poor Mr Turnbull still sat in his chair
outside, shivering in the cold on this day, giving me a
silent, imploring look as I went past him into the shop.

Nothing was different. The shop was empty and from the
back room came the sounds of Mrs Turnbull's voice and
the voices of her boarders, and raucous laughter and the
clink of glasses. Those of her boarders who had survived
the war were back, and those who had not survived had
been replaced by others, rough, coarse, loud-talking men
who wore gaiters and who cleaned out middens and
chimneys.

I rapped on the glass top of the counter long enough to
draw her attention and she came lumbering out,
grumbling, 'Always bothering me. Never give me a
minute's peace, the bloody little buggers.' And seeing me,
said, 'If it isn't little Lord Muck 'isself. Don't tell me you
went and inherited another fortune . . . Well . . . what'll it
be? Don't you keep me waiting all day long. I got other
things to do besides wait on you.'

I made my choice quickly. A pennyworth of clear mixed
gums, and as I went out with my bag of sweets clutched in
my hand, I heard one of the boarders mutter, craning his
neck round the doorway to see me, 'Those bloody Jews,
they got all the money. They were making it by the

bucketful while we was out there in the trenches giving our bloody lives for them.'

It didn't strike me as being any different from all the other things I had heard them say all my life, and I wasn't the least bit disturbed by it. I went home, with my bag of sweets, and this time I shared it with my brothers, though without explaining how I had got my penny. Lily's secret was locked deep inside me.

There was just one moment when it very nearly came out that same day. Perhaps Arthur should have waited a bit. A day or two more wouldn't have hurt. And if only he had waited until after dark when fewer people could see him. But he couldn't wait and he was in a buoyant mood at being home, and so confident of this new world of his that he went striding across the street with a small package in his hand and knocked on our door.

It was teatime. We were all sitting at the table when we heard it, and my mother thought perhaps it was a customer for the shop and hurried to answer it. I think it was Lily who recognised Arthur's voice first. She got up in such a hurry that her cup of tea spilled over. But she paid no attention to it and ran out, and we followed her out of curiosity. We stopped in the lobby behind her. There was Arthur all right, smiling and saying, 'I just brought this for Lily . . . it's a book, something I bought in London and I thought Lily would like it. Would you mind if I gave it to her . . .' It was a book of poetry, a collection of Browning's, as we discovered later.

To my mother, it wouldn't have made any difference what it was. 'She's having her tea right now,' she said. 'I'll give it to her.'

Arthur was looking over her shoulder. He could see Lily standing there. She was staring at him, not daring to speak. He understood, though he must have been terribly disappointed and perhaps a bit disillusioned right from the start of his homecoming. But he didn't press the matter. 'Oh, all right,' he said. 'Just give it to her. And thank you. I'm sorry for interrupting your tea.'

My mother took the package from him, and after the door had closed she walked back through the lobby and handed the package to Lily.

'Why didn't you let him give it to me?' Lily said. 'He saw me standing here.'

'I didn't know you were there,' my mother said and it was the first time I had ever known her to lie, because I'm sure she had known we were all there.

Lily must have felt sure of that too and said bitterly, 'Even if you didn't, you could have called me and I'd have come to the door. He's just come home from the war. I don't know how you can be that way.'

She burst into tears, then, and ran upstairs with her book, and my mother stood looking after her for a moment with that familiar troubled expression on her face, and we all finally went back to our tea without Lily, who remained up in her room for the rest of the evening, probably reading the Browning poems, the love poems written to Elizabeth Barrett.

People had seen Arthur come to our door with the package in his hand and my mother had a lot of explaining to do when her friends gathered in the shop. She passed it off lightly as nothing at all, just a little friendly neighbourly gesture, and whether they believed her or not is hard to say. But soon there were other events of importance taking place on our street that took their minds off this matter completely for a while.

*

The Russian revolution had been over for more than a year now and there was less talk of it than there had been, and not so much mention of it in the newspapers, but it was far from forgotten by our rabbi and in cheder at night he smoked cigarette after cigarette. The long holder itself had become yellow and showed a faint crack at the end from too many cigarettes being slipped in and out, and his hand trembled as he lifted it to his mouth.

He went among us, smoking, more distracted than ever, pointing out a mistake now and then with a yellow finger, but hardly bothering with us, ignoring the giggles and the mischief that went on behind his back. He had to keep moving, it seemed. He could not stand in one place for very long. And so he paced about in front of the fire, sometimes with one hand behind his back, while the other held the long cigarette holder with the burning cigarette in it.

There had been no word from his son in all these years and there were rumours that the rabbi had once contemplated going to Russia to search for him, but had been dissuaded by his wife.

Meanwhile, he was going out of his mind worrying about the boy. He could not rest, at home, in the house up the park where he lived with his wife and daughter, pacing about there too, at his various duties in the synagogue or the cheder or when he performed a wedding or a circumcision, or when he slaughtered the chickens for us on Friday afternoons in the little concrete yard behind the cheder.

He strode through the streets en route to his various duties, sometimes to visit a sick person, or to officiate at a barmitzvah, wearing his long black coat, carrying an umbrella in one hand, and the little ragged batesemas tagged after him chanting, 'The rabbi, the rabbi, the king of the Jews, he bought his wife a pair of shoes . . .'

This time he paid no attention to them. His head was bent and he was far away in his thoughts. The little cobbled streets with their sad rows of houses slipped past him, and he was oblivious to everything. The days, the weeks went by, and finally the letter came. Who sent it nobody knew. It was not signed with a name and it was a hastily scribbled piece of writing in Russian that the rabbi was able to read, since he had come from Russia.

We only heard about this later. It spread quickly among us, how the letter had been delivered by the postman, how the rabbi had stared at it first, the address badly written, many different postmarks stamped on it, and then the realisation that it was from Russia, and tearing it open with trembling yellowed fingers, and his wife clasping her hands together and tense with fear at what the letter might contain.

He read it slowly, for it was badly written inside too, and hard to read. But he read it and to himself at first, with the cigarette holder in one hand, and the wife's eyes glued on his face saw the expression change, then saw the jaw sag and the cigarette holder fall from his hand. She hastily picked it up before the carpet could burn, put it back in his hand and said, 'What is it? What is it? Tell me?'

'It's all over,' he whispered.

He could hardly talk. His eyes began to fill with tears – this is how the wife related it afterwards to others – his eyes filled with tears and his lips trembled and he said again, 'It's all over, God has spoken at last.'

And then he gave her the letter to read, because he could not read it himself. The badly scrawled letter simply said, 'Max asked me to write this to you if anything happened to him and I am sorry to say that it has happened. Max died a hero, fighting for the revolution.'

That was about all it said, but it was enough. There was a funeral ceremony. The letter had failed to say if there had been one in Russia, or if he had even been buried. The rabbi held a funeral. My mother attended and came back dabbing her eyes. It had been sad, too sad for words. The expression on the rabbi's face as he performed the service for his dead son, the trembling of his voice, and the weeping of his wife and the little girl . . .

It was in the autumn of 1919 that this happened. It had taken two years for the letter to arrive from Russia. We were preparing for the Rosh Hashonah holiday. The garden at the back of the synagogue and cheder was filled with crisp red and yellow and brown leaves that had fallen from the trees surrounding the garden. We had leaf fights, dashing handfuls at one another, shouting and yelling. The old-time residents of the once fashionable houses glared at us over the garden walls. The rabbi said nothing. He stood at the bay window of the cheder looking out at us, saying nothing.

The synagogue was packed that first evening of the holiday. Even my father attended on this day. He sat a short distance away from us with a siddur in his hands and his head bent sullenly over it. The siddur was upside down, but he did not know it. Our mother and sisters were upstairs in the gallery. There was hardly enough seating space for all of them, so many of the girls had to stand, and several of them came to the rail and leaned over and giggled and called to men downstairs, and had to be reprimanded and sent to the back of the balcony.

The place buzzed with talk until everyone was settled, then it grew still as the rabbi entered, swathed in his long tallith that covered him from head to toe. All eyes were on him, more so this year than any other, because of the tragedy that had taken place and because of what we had heard was happening to him, and there was a lot of wonder as to how he was going to bear up throughout the longer than usual service.

It was clear from the start that he was not himself any longer. The deep, resonant voice had weakened, and at times was barely audible, and he missed his place several times and had to be helped by other members of the congregation.

No, he was not the same any more and heads were being shaken throughout the service, and eyes met one another, and there was one point, I remember, when my father gave a savage little laugh and muttered, 'I could do better myself.'

People glanced at him sideways, but said nothing. We were careful to keep our heads down over the one siddur we shared. The service dragged on. It seemed longer and more tedious than ever. We were hungry and annoyed with the rabbi's slowness. At last it came to the end, to the final part where he was to blow the shofar that ushered in the New Year.

The rabbi took the ram's horn in his hands and raised it to his lips. It was a yellowish colour, almost like the tobacco stain on his fingers. His hands trembled slightly as he lifted it and there was a deep silence as everyone waited for the wailing sound to come out – a sound that said 'kee – yoah – kee – yoah –'

But there was nothing. His cheeks were puffed out, his eyes strained and all we heard was the labouring breath. It took strength to blow the horn, and he did not have that strength any longer. His cheeks ballooned out desperately and his eyes started out of his head, and a disturbed murmur went through the synagogue. Something was wrong, very wrong, then suddenly the horn fell from his hands and a loud cry went up as he collapsed.

And there was that other thing that came to occupy everyone's mind on the street. This was the return of Freddy Gordon to his home, or what was left of him. They were clearing out the hospital anyway and it was becoming a school again. The soldiers who were better walked out and went home; those who were not and who still could not walk were carried off to other hospitals that were less packed now than before; or else, if nothing further could be done for them they were shipped home, and Freddy was one of those.

They brought him home in an ambulance. We watched as it came and we rushed down to the Gordons' shop to see Freddy being carried out. One of the attendants did it all by himself, lifting the half-body up in his two arms and carrying him as if he were a baby being taken out of a pram, and Freddy smiled at us and waved a hand. Inside the shop old Mr Gordon had risen from his chair and was standing staring, his thick, fleshy cheeks ashen and deathlike in colour. Florrie had come out of the taproom and was standing staring too.

His homecoming had been a bit of a surprise to them. We got this from Mrs Green later. Florrie had been trying to delay it as long as possible. 'She warn't too anxious t'ave him,' the toothless old woman cackled, the Friday after Freddy's return. She spoke to the fire as she prodded with the poker and brought the flames leaping up. 'After all, what's she going to do with 'im? Pickle 'im? He wouldn't be any good to her in th' shop. The old man's just a step away from death's door, and that'd set her free, and that's all she wanted, to get away and marry that man in

Birmingham. He's still waiting for 'er. But now Freddy's in the way. She's been trying to get the hospital to ship him out to one of those soldier homes where they've got a lot of other fellows without legs or arms and things like that. And they were going to do it too, except that Freddy didn't want it and got 'em to send him 'ome, and 'ere 'e is, and I know what Florrie's going to try next. She's working on me Annie to take Freddy off 'er 'ands, but I'll see to it that doesn't 'appen. Not as long as I live.'

She poked furiously and sparks shot up in the fireplace, and all of us listening said nothing. We felt sorry for Freddy. How could you not help it? Especially when Florrie began putting him outside in the wheelchair that the government had given them. There he sat, huddled in blankets, the lower part of his body, the missing legs, well covered. It made people think of Mr Turnbull up at the other end of the street. There he sat too, all day long, looking miserable.

We now had one at the top and one at the bottom of the street. 'Just like two ornaments on a dresser,' said Mrs Humberstone sadly, coming over one day to chat with the Jewish women, about the only one again who did that since the war was over. 'The poor lad. He just sits there.'

She went over to talk to him too and a lot of other people on the street did the same thing. He wasn't yet strong enough to wheel himself about, and he was always glad to have people come over or to stop and chat when they were on their way into the shop.

I went to the shop one day to get a cob of white bread for my mother and his face lit up at the sight of me. 'Ar, lad,' he said, 'You're still growing, aren't you? Bigger than me already, though that wouldn't take much doing, would it?'

He chuckled and looked up at me with something glinting in his eyes that looked suspiciously like tears. But it didn't last long. He kept right on chuckling. 'Remember the old days? When you used to come in for ginger beer for Sarah? Eh? And how is Sarah? You ever hear from her?'

I told him what I knew, what her mother had told my mother, and he nodded, stared straight ahead of him up the street and said, 'Well, that's good. I'm glad to hear it. She deserves her luck. She was a nice girl, Sarah. A good girl. We had some fine times together. When you write to her give her my best. Tell her I still think of her.'

I didn't say anything. I felt awkward, remembering the talk in my mother's shop and the things they'd said about Freddy, and thinking how unlikely it would be for my mother to let me write what he asked to Sarah, if ever we should write to her.

I went in and bought my bread, Florrie waiting on me. When I came out, Freddy reached up for the bag and said, 'Look here, lad, you do me a little favour, will you? Give me a push up the street and I'll hold the bread for you.'

I gave the bag to him and grasped the handles at the back of the chair, and just as we were about to start off Florrie came to the door. 'Where d'you think you're going?' she asked.

'We're taking a little ride,' Freddy said. 'Just up th' street a bit. Maybe I'll stop off and see Annie.'

'That's not such a bad idea,' Florrie said. 'Maybe she'd like to come on back with you and have a glass.'

'Maybe,' said Freddy, 'I'll ask her.' He chuckled, 'I'll ask the whole family, her mother too.'

'That old hag?' Florrie snapped. 'You don't have to bother with her. I can do without her.'

'I know that.' Freddy chuckled again and we set off.

It was easy pushing the chair and I rather enjoyed doing it, and I think some of the other lads on the street, watching, envied me. And I suppose our journey up the street, the first time Freddy had ever done it, attracted a lot of attention. People came to their doors and stared.

And when we got to the Greens', Annie was already out there, looking flustered and glad. 'Oh, hello, Freddy,' she said.

'Hello, Annie. How you be?'

'I'm fine,' she said. 'And how you be?'

'I'm fine. How's little Peter?'

'He's just champion. You want to see him?'

'That'd be nice.'

But before Annie could turn to go in, her mother was there at her back, her eyes murderous and glaring, 'Now, what's this?' she said. 'What's going on 'ere?'

'I'm just visiting,' Freddy said.

'Well, you go and visit somewheres else,' she snapped.

'I don't see what you got against me,' Freddy said, and he was calm enough and even smiling a bit, as if he found the old woman amusing. 'I'm not going t'arm Annie or little Peter.'

'That's right, Mam,' murmured Annie, but her voice was shaky and she was clearly terribly afraid of her mother.

Mrs Green simply ignored her. She spoke directly to Freddy. 'Nobody said you was going t'arm anybody. You just go and visit somewheres else. I know what you did for king and country and I got respect for you, but I got me troubles too and Annie's got 'ers and you got yours, so let's just everybody take care of 'is own troubles and everything'll be all right. I'll 'elp you go back where you come from.'

She thrust her way forward suddenly and snatched the
handles away from me. Freddy handed the bag back to me
in time before Mrs Green started pushing him forward
vigorously back down the street. I ran across to give the
bread to my mother, who had been standing in the doorway
with all the rest taking in the scene, then I ran back down
the street, joining the other boys, who sensed a row about
to start and were excited at the prospect. There was
nothing like a good row between two women to liven
things up for us and there was quite a crowd that gathered
around the Gordons' shop as Mrs Green arrived there with
Freddy.

Florrie had come out with fire in her eyes and hands on
her hips, the typical stance of a Lancashire woman about to
have a fight with another woman. We had seen them
standing like that facing one another when they came out
of the pubs on Saturday night, their faces flushed, their
bosoms heaving, their legs planted firmly on the ground,
their eyes fixed on one another

It was like that when Florrie came out of the shop to face
Mrs Green. The two stood just a few feet apart, both with
hands on hips, Freddy, sitting in the wheelchair in front of
the shop where Mrs Green had deposited him, had a good
view of them. The crowd, ringing them partially on the
pavement and spilling out on to the cobblestones, was
silent.

Florrie spoke first. 'Now what's this all about?' she asked.

'It's all about your brother and you and your little game
won't work, that's what it's all about,' retorted Mrs Green.
Her hair was dangling over her face and her shawl had
slipped down to her shoulders. 'I brought 'im back to you,'
she said, 'where 'e belongs. You're not going to shove 'im
on to me and me Annie.'

'Oh, is that it?' said Florrie and in contrast to Mrs Green she looked almost attractive and bosomy, with her rosy cheeks, the colour deepened now by her anger, the rich golden hair plaited and hanging behind her. 'Seems to me it wasn't so long ago when you'd have kissed me arse just to be allowed to look at me brother and 'ave him call on your daughter.'

Mrs Green gave a cackle. 'And now,' she said, 'looks like you'd kiss me arse just to let your brother talk to me daughter. It's only a pity you couldn't 'ave 'im do that when me Annie needed him for the child 'e gave her and which you said 'e never did but which everybody knows 'e did. It's too late now. Y'aven't got a brother, only 'alf a brother, an' alf-brother.' She cackled again, showing her toothless gums. 'And an 'alf's not enough.'

'First place,' said Florrie, inching forward a foot or so, 'Me brother had nothing to do with that child and you know it. Considering as 'ow your Annie was rolling about in th' park with one after another you'd never know whose child it was. Second place, if it was his, as you say, then a father's got a right to be with his child. So you're stuck either way. And third place, as far as kissing your arse is concerned, I wouldn't touch your arse with a ten-foot pole that's been used for scraping out a midden.'

'First place for you,' replied Mrs Green, 'me Annie never rolled about in th' park with any man. She was just misled, that's all, and by your brother, who's your misfortune now, and yours to keep. And second and third place . . .' She too moved forward slightly, so that the two women were very close to one another. 'When it comes to rolling about in th' park, a whore like you shouldn't be casting reflection on other women's character.'

'Who you calling a whore?' said Florrie, advancing still another inch, her eyes beginning to flash dangerously.

'Who do you think?' said Mrs Green. 'Me shadow? Don't tell me in all those years you spent behind that bar y'aven't found yourself a little sideline?'

It was Florrie who struck first. With the back of her hand and with the crack of a whip, catching Mrs Green on the side of the face and causing her to stagger backwards a little. She quickly regained her balance and struck herself, with the back of her hand and with a similar crack, making the flush on Florrie's cheek an even deeper red.

The two then began to circle each other warily, hands raised in fighting position, and an excited stir went through the crowd, and then a little almost joyous cry went up as the two women lunged at one another in full battle, hands, claws, reaching for hair. At first they were like two horned animals, with horns locked, backing this way and that, head to head, fingers buried in one another's hair; then they began to thrust and jab and scratch and tear – and bite – and they both fell, clutching one another, and rolled on the ground, and bit savagely, screaming with pain, blood covering their faces.

The crowd swelled as more and more people rushed from other streets to witness the fight, and there were roars of excitement and they edged closer and people shoved and pushed and elbowed to see better, while the women fought on the ground, their skirts flying up, showing long drawers and petticoats and flashes of bare flesh, and blood began to stain the rough cobblestones

I do not know how it ended. I was frightened by what I was seeing and I let myself be pushed on to the outskirts of the circle by the wild mob of spectators. I was shivering and sick; then I glanced towards Freddy. He was sitting there, unnoticed by the people. He looked as sick as I felt. He was huddled in that wheelchair, just his head and neck showing above the blankets. Then our eyes met and he motioned to me.

I went over to him and he said in a low voice, "'arry, take me away from here. For God's sake wheel me away somewhere.'

I was perhaps only too glad to get away from the scene. I wheeled him around the corner on to Wood Street. We went past the taproom entrance and to the end of the street to where the steep brew that ran up to where the park began.

When we came to it Freddy said, 'Do you think you could push me up th' brew, 'arry? I'd like to go to the park. It'd be nice in there.'

I said I could do it and we began the climb. We ran alongside the rec at first. It was a large playground at the foot of the park, covered with layers of crushed cinders that sometimes cut badly when you fell. It was here that I had often watched Freddy play soccer for the county team and where crowds used to cheer him. An iron rail separated it from the road that went up the hill, and Freddy smiled a little as he glanced through the rails, doubtless remembering his days there.

'We had some games out there, eh, lad?' he said. 'Oh, I liked me game of soccer. There was nothing like it. And I could play, too. I'm not bragging, but I was a good soccer man. I could kick and head and dribble as good as the best of 'em. And there was nothing like it when your foot caught that ball, and you heard that thud and saw the ball sail right through those goalposts, and everybody shouting and cheering and jumping up and down. But I had legs then, didn't I?'

He was speaking more to himself than me and I didn't say anything. I was having a bit of trouble pushing him anyway as the incline grew steeper, and I was slowing down and gasping a little for breath.

He became anxious and said, 'You're going to make it, aren't you, 'arry lad? You're not going to fail me now. I want to get to see that park.'

He was trying to help me by pushing on the wheels, but his hands were not strong enough to be a lot of help for going up. I kept at it and fortunately his weight was not much of a handicap. I puffed and pushed and sweated, and I got to the top at last and halted, breathing hard. We were at the spot where I had once stopped with my mother on my way to the fancy school, and just as I had done then I turned to look down at the view that lay below us. There it was, the same as before, the same as always, a clutter of streets and endless slate roofs and chimneys, and the taller chimneys of the mills thrusting into the clouds, and all of it seen through a film of the yellowish smoke that hung constantly over the town, its acrid smell drifting up to us.

Freddy looked with me and said, 'That's where we live, down there in that smoke. It's been there all me life. It'll always be there, I suppose. I went to war to save it. Only I couldn't save meself.'

We turned and I wheeled him into the park. It was early spring, a bit chilly and cloudy, but the buds were beginning to show on the trees and bushes. The grass was very green, and it had recently been cut and there was a sweet smell in the air. Freddy drank it in and sighed a bit. Birds were chattering about us.

'Ah, but it smells good,' he said. 'That's what I came for, to smell the grass right after it had been cut and hear the birds singing. It's all so clean, isn't it? There aren't many clean places left in this dirty world of ours. And I tell you something else, 'arry. It makes me think of all the girls I've loved here. So many of them, I can't count 'em. I remember this same sweet smell that used to come up from the grass when I lay with them in the soft darkness, and the stars shining overhead.'

Again, it was as if he were talking more to himself than to me and I said nothing as I pushed him along the path. The park was almost deserted. We went past a thick grove of trees and I noticed one big golden tree that stood out among the others.

He noticed it too and he gave a little chuckle. 'That was my favourite spot, that big golden willow. Its branches spread out like a lady's ballroom costume. It's the most beautiful thing you ever saw and when you get inside that tree it's almost like being in a cathedral. There's something holy about it, I swear. It's big and tall inside, and you feel like you're a million miles away from everything. Trouble is, you can't use it when summer's over. It sheds branches as well as leaves and it's like somebody dying, and there's nothing left but a thin skeleton. But I suppose everything's got to end, eh, 'arry?' Then he added, 'Take me back, will you, lad, I'm getting tired.'

He sounded tired, too, and he started to help me again by pushing on the wheels, this time doing so much better than before, so that we rolled quickly, and soon reached the entrance again and went outside to the top of the hill.

There he made me stop and he looked down the hill for quite some time. He seemed to be brooding over something and I waited until he was ready to go down. But finally, when he did speak, he said rather quietly, ''arry, I want you to do something for me now. Will you?'

'Yis,' I said.

'Go back there into the park. I think I lost my handkerchief. Go back there and look for it, will you?'

'Yis,' I said.

I thought somehow it was a bit strange. I had not seen
him use a handkerchief all the time I had been with him,
and if he had dropped it I would have seen it. But I did what
he asked just the same. At least, I got as far as a few yards
beyond the entrance, then something – I don't know what
it was, but something – made me stop and turn around. My
heart almost jumped into my throat. I couldn't believe
what I was seeing at first. Freddy was starting to
manoeuvre his chair down the hill, pushing hard with his
hands on the wheels.

I rushed back, yelling, 'Freddy, wait for me!'

He must have heard me, but he paid no attention and
went on rolling down the hill. I ran after him, frantic, but
I was too late. Once the wheelchair had gathered
momentum it went faster than I could go and I stopped in
horror, watching it. Freddy had no need now to use his
hands. The chair raced down the steep incline and just as it
got to the bottom I saw the rear end tilt upwards, as if one
of the wheels might have struck some obstacle, then
Freddy's half-body flew out and quite distinctly I heard the
sickening thump as his head struck the ground. The chair
rolled over him and he lay there still, and I remember
hearing my own screams as I rushed down towards him.

Chapter Nine

The hard times began after the war, I remember. The clattering of clogs down the street in the early morning was no longer as loud or as brisk as before. Sometimes there was none at all. The military was no longer ordering uniforms, so trade had slowed down. The tailoring shops were idle, just as the mills were, and the men and the boys and girls who worked there stayed home, and the men sat outside their houses and smoked.

With my father there was little change. He came and went as he always had, sitting at the table alone for his dinner, head bent low, shovelling food into himself then abruptly pushing his chair back with a scraping sound and rising to get his coat hanging on the back of the scullery door, and charging out with one sleeve dangling behind him, off to the pub. Where he got his money was his business.

He gave none to my mother on Saturday afternoons. There was none, he said, so my mother had to struggle as best she could. Her little shop had dwindled to almost nothing. The shelves and bins were practically empty. Not having any money, she could not buy any fresh produce and even if she did, people on the street did not have money to buy. She resorted to her old method of getting new stock, crawling under Pollit's fruit stall and foraging for half-rotted fruit and vegetables.

I went with her often on these missions and even crawled underneath with her several times now that I was a big lad, ten years old, almost eleven, and I remember the smell of the half-fermented apples and oranges and the other things, and the mush that got onto my hands and face, and I remember too the flushed look of triumph on my mother's face when we were able to fill our two straw bags. 'Oh, aren't we lucky?' she'd say.

Pollit took very little from her. He'd have given her the stuff for nothing if she'd let him, but she still wouldn't, still too proud, and he shrugged and pretended to haggle with her for the best possible price. Then off we'd go, and this time I'd be lugging the two bags for her and saying, when she wanted to help me, 'No, I can do it, Mam, I can do it by meself.'

She was not as strong as before. She seemed to have grown heavy round the middle and walked more slowly. In the house she did not rush to answer a knock at the door, even when it was the postman with a letter perhaps from America, and you did not hear the rustle of her skirt as she whirled round to go to the door. I sensed something different about her and the way sometimes people spoke to her, dropping their voices to a whisper if I was around, something that I did not understand.

It would take a little longer before I did, a year or so more before Zalmon would take me and several other boys round the corner and into a dark entry to explain the mystery of life.

But one night I woke up to hear a baby crying. I listened, startled, thinking I was dreaming. But no, it was real and it came from the room next to us, the one where my mother and father slept. Joe and Saul were awake too, listening. They slept at the other end of the bed, and their feet protruded on to my end and sometimes into my face. They were whispering to one another.

I said, 'There's a baby in Mam's room.'

Saul said scornfully, 'Don't you think we know it?'

'Mam just had it,' Joe informed me.

I was a bit taken aback. Then I asked, 'How?'

Saul screamed with laughter. Joe chuckled. He was a little more restrained and more tolerant towards me. 'How d'you think?' he said.

'He doesn't know,' Saul said with the same contempt.

I didn't then, but I didn't ask any more questions. I simply accepted the wonder and excitement of it all. I stared at it with wide eyes the next day in my mother's room. She was lying in bed, looking wan, suckling the baby at her breast. I had seen other women doing this before when they came into the shop. Fanny Cohen had had a new one not many weeks before. But this was the first time I had seen my mother suckling the baby, and I felt strangely awkward and embarrassed, and turned my head away.

My mother's tired face took on an amused expression. 'Don't you like the baby?' she asked.

'Yis.'

'Then why don't you look at it?'

I turned my head slowly and my mother, who may have guessed the cause of my embarrassment, put her breast away inside her nightgown. I could see the baby's face more clearly now. It was red and wrinkled, and looked as if it might be going to cry. It was making faint sounds like a clucking chicken.

'He looks like you,' my mother said.

'Is it a boy?' I asked.

'Yes,' she said.

'What's its name?'

'We're calling him Sidney.'

'Why?'

'That was the name of my uncle who died a long time ago. You always call a baby after someone who died.'

'Why?'

'Because you do. It's the custom.'

'Aren't we going to America?' I asked suddenly.

She seemed puzzled, 'Yes, of course we are,' she said. 'Why not? What's the baby got to do with it?'

'How can you go to America with a baby?'

'Oh, it's easy. A baby can go just like anybody else. When he's a bit older, of course. You'll have to write another letter for me to America. They'll want to know about the baby and who knows, maybe that'll help hurry them up a bit sending for us.'

I believe she really thought that. She was always seeing people through her own eyes and seeing herself mostly, and attributing to them her own gentleness and unselfishness. She was certain they would share her joy in the new baby, and feel all the more need to help her.

I know I certainly believed it myself and was only too anxious to start writing the letter, and perhaps would have done so then, except that suddenly we were both aware of someone coming into the room. We both turned our heads and looked towards the door, and were startled to see my father standing there.

His usually heavy footsteps had been quiet for once, and we had not heard him come up the stairs. He stood there looking down at the floor, his face sullen and scowling as always, not saying anything for a moment, then muttering, always, not saying anything for a moment, then muttering, 'How are you feeling?'

I saw the surprise come over my mother's face and I felt the same thing. I had never before heard him ask this of her. Nor had she, probably. She did not answer his questions but spoke to me quietly, saying, ''arry, go downstairs and play.'

I went, somehow feeling extraordinarily happy. There was peace in our house for once, something I had never known before.

A week later we had the bris. The guests filled our kitchen, and since there were few chairs most of them had to stand. My father had put a bottle of whisky on the table, and he poured a few small glasses, then put the cork on tightly and guarded it for the rest of the time with glaring eyes. There was also sponge cake that my mother had managed to bake for the occasion in spite of her confinement.

Lily was in charge. She bustled about serving refreshments. She had been in charge of the house, as she always had been when my mother gave birth to one of us, from the time when Lily was a child herself. I don't think she minded too much this time. It got her away from the drudgery of the tailoring shop. She rushed about in the kitchen with her cheeks flushed. She still wore her hair long, as she had done when she was going to school, and it swished behind her as she swung from place to place among the people.

The rabbi came at last to perform the circumcision. It was the new young rabbi who had taken the place of our old one. There had been a great deal of consternation among some of the members of the congregation when he first came. He was not only very young, but clean-shaven, and that was what had disturbed many people, especially the old women. They had whispered about it in my mother's shop and I had heard them ask what sort of rabbi could he be without a beard? Wasn't shaving with a razor sinful?

There had been arguments, some defending him. Mrs Zarembar was one of these, but since he had come to live with her as a boarder she had assumed an almost maternal attitude towards him. What was wrong with not having a beard? she wanted to know. What was right with it? Mrs Mittleman flung back at her. But then, oddly enough, Mrs Harris had taken Mrs Zarembar's side, defending the young rabbi's right to be clean-shaven and, since she was an authority on such matters, the decision was in the young man's favour. Nothing more was said about his lack of a beard.

Besides, he had come to be well liked, especially by those with unmarried daughters. It was perhaps one reason why Mrs Harris had defended him. She still had three daughters waiting for husbands to come along and she had already had the young rabbi to dinner in her house. Well, so had other families, except ours, and I think this was the first time that he had come.

Not the first time, though, that he had seen Lily. He had asked me about her in cheder. How old was she? Was she engaged to anyone or anything like that? He had smiled a bit awkwardly when he had asked that and I saw a little colour come into his pale face. It was a rather long, ascetic face and he wore metal-rimmed spectacles. He spoke with a pronounced Russian accent. He had fled from Russia and the Bolsheviks not too long ago, barely escaping with his life, it was believed.

The congregation had decided that the former rabbi's house up the park was much too big and extravagant for a young, unmarried rabbi and had arranged to board him at Mrs Zarembar's house. One of the reasons for selecting her was that the Friday chickens would be close at hand and could be slaughtered by him in her backyard. The arrangement had worked out well so far. The chickens were slaughtered immediately, thus saving us a trip to the synagogue.

Mrs Zarembar was well pleased with her new boarder. And proud. There was no mistaking that as she arrived with him at our house that day. She came waddling in beside him, her rosy cheeks flushed a still deeper hue, the proud smirk on her face. 'Here he is,' she announced, as if she were presenting a new flock of chickens to the company.

They had all been waiting for him and a respectful silence fell over the gathering. They were wearing their best clothes for the occasion, and Fanny Cohen had brought her newest baby along and was holding it in her arms and bouncing it up and down a bit to keep it from crying. The rabbi nodded and bowed slightly to each one, murmuring a greeting, then his eyes came to rest on Lily, who was flitting about in the background and had not paid much attention to his entrance.

He stood there, his eyes following her as she moved about with a tray in her hands, and seemed oblivious for a moment of the rest of them.

My mother had come downstairs with the baby a short time before and was holding him in her arms, and I saw her eyes go from the rabbi to Lily. 'Lily,' she called out, 'please bring the rabbi some refreshment.'

Lily went over to him with the tray, and he took a small piece of sponge cake and smiled at her. 'I don't think we've met before,' he said.

'No, we haven't,' said Lily.

'I'm Rabbi Oslov,' he said. 'My first name is Abraham. And yours?'

'Lily,' she said.

They were all looking, watching, listening. The room was very quiet. My mother's eyes were shining. The rabbi was smiling and did not seem to know what more to say, but his eyes were fixed on Lily. She herself stood there calmly, not saying anything, not having anything to say to him. He had looked at her before this, I know. I had seen him once standing in the doorway of Mrs Zarembar's house as he was about to go in. Lily had just come out of our house and he was watching her as she walked down the street; then he had come into our shop several times to buy fruit and while conversing pleasantly with my mother had kept glancing around as if in search of something. It had not escaped my mother's attention, but she had said nothing. She said nothing now.

The silence in the room was broken by my father's voice, rough and savage. He had settled himself in a corner of the room, away from people, and had been drinking his whisky. 'What the bloody 'ell are we all waiting for?' he shouted.

The room stirred, and the rabbi roused himself, laughed and said, 'Ah, yes. We have a circumcision to perform. Where is the young victim?'

So now my mother brought the baby forward and everyone gathered round, and the rabbi began the prayers and everyone joined in. Then he produced a small case from his pocket and opened it. The knife lay inside, very shiny. The baby in my mother's arms began to cry immediately and Fanny Cohen's baby in the background took up the refrain, so there was a howling from two babies while the rabbi expertly snipped off the foreskin.

I watched, fascinated, and saw the blood come out of the tiny penis, which the rabbi staunched quickly with a towel, but not before a stream of urine shot up into his face. He gasped and laughed and looked about for another towel, and it was Lily who handed it to him quickly and he wiped himself.

He was still laughing as he handed it back to her, saying, 'God has strange ways of speaking to us. It could have been His reprimand for my delaying the ritual.'

'Perhaps it was the baby's reprimand,' she said. 'He may not have liked what you did to him.'

'That', said the rabbi gently, 'he should not have objected to. It has made him a Jew, something that he will be proud of some day, don't you think?'

Lily gave no answer and I think this must have troubled the rabbi a bit. But then there were other things about her that troubled him, the most important being that she did not attend the synagogue.

He used to ask my mother about it when he came into the shop on the pretext of wanting to buy some of her faded fruit and the question always embarrassed her. She had no answer to give; she didn't know why and she was worried over it. Lily had not been going for a long time and there were other things that bothered my mother, like reading strange books that she would not let any of us see, and going to lectures and meetings of various sorts and refusing to explain what they were about.

She may have suspected that it had something to do with Arthur and sometimes, when Lily left the house to go to one of her meetings, she would peer through the window to see if Arthur was leaving too. As if he would be so foolish as to depart at the same time, knowing that not only she but the whole street would be watching.

Besides, Arthur was very busy these days. He had started going to the University of Manchester to study law, and we caught glimpses of him mornings hurrying to catch the tram and coming home in the evening with his big books tucked under an arm.

So my mother's fears must have been allayed a lot as far as this business was concerned and with the young rabbi showing an interest in Lily a new hope, another dream, must have taken possession of her. Other mothers may have had the same hope for their daughters – the competition was keen, not only on our street but up the park where the rabbi could have been certain of a rich dowry. But it was Lily he wanted and he seemed to be making no bones about that, despite the family he could see with his own eyes and must have heard talked about by many people – a father who drank and cursed and abused his wife unlike any other Jewish father, a mother struggling to make ends meet with a little bit of a shop that sold faded fruits and vegetables, five growing children and now still another to increase the mother's burden, a late-born coming ten years after the last one, to add to the din, the quarrels, the poverty.

Who would want to get mixed up with a family like that?

It must have been whispered in his ear more than once. And yet, with all the rewards being dangled before him, he couldn't seem to look at any girl except the one in this family. True, the other girls being offered him were no great beauties and some of them were a good deal older than he was. But he himself was no bargain when it came to looks – frail and thin and wispy, looking as if a strong wind could blow him over – so the joke went in the tailoring shops. And that walk of his! He had a mincing gait that gave him a slightly effeminate air. And he had a big nose, and thick-lensed glasses through which he peered at you myopically, making you feel that he was not quite seeing you. And worst of all, he had a sight lisp.

But he was a rabbi, a man of God, and he pleased everyone with his performance. He did everything that the other rabbi had done (and for less money since he was young and unmarried and did not require a big house or have to support a family), and he was brisk and efficient at his duties; and in addition he delivered a sermon every Saturday.

As a rule, we used to leave promptly when the service was over. But now we remained seated while the rabbi spoke to us. It was mostly about Zionism, and Chaim Weizmann and the great pioneering work that man was doing to bring about the Jewish homeland in Palestine, and he spoke of the need for all Jewish people to make that their goal and to help the cause. He spoke passionately and with fiery eloquence, and when he did, all the frailty, the mincing gait, even the lisp seemed to vanish and he became a giant standing before us, with his eyes flashing, and we all listened spellbound; and before he was done the old women were weeping in the gallery and the men were gripping their hands.

He was obsessed with this topic. When he was with people he could speak of nothing else. In cheder, too, he spoke of it to us, and he organised us into groups of Maccabees and sent us out to collect money for the cause from Jewish homes. He was altogether different from our other rabbi. Well, he was young to begin with – perhaps not more than twenty-two or so, perhaps old to us but young enough – and there were times indeed when he actually became one of us and laughed and joked; and once, catching Zalmon bouncing a ball in the back row, instead of boxing his ears as the other rabbi would have done, he invited Zalmon to throw the ball to him and suddenly we were all having a wild game of catch right there in the cheder, with much hilarious shouting and shrieking.

In the midst of it all the tall, gaunt figure of Max Korer, the treasurer, appeared in the doorway. He was standing there taking in the scene with a grim, disapproving look on his thin, gloomy face. A hush fell over us, and the ball rolled over towards his feet and we all watched it.

If the young rabbi felt embarrassed, he did not show it. He ran to pick up the ball, a smile on his face, and said cheerfully, 'Come in, Mr Korer, come in.'

'Is this how you conduct a Hebrew lesson?' Mr Korer asked.

'Not always,' the rabbi joked. 'Most of the time we are busy with our books, but for once I thought I would give their minds a rest and exercise their muscles. They will be still better Jews if they can gain some physical strength.'

The treasurer was not amused. In fact, he was furious. He turned on his heel and stamped out. Later, there was a great to-do over the matter. There was talk of sacking the young rabbi.

But he had his champions and my mother was one of them. In her shop, where the argument raged pro and con one day, she defended him loudly, her cheeks flushed. 'What do they want from him?' she demanded. 'He works hard all the time and for the little money he gets for it he is doing plenty. What if he plays ball now and then with the boys? Better than he should be shouting at them all the time.'

Old Mrs Harris was inclined to agree with her. Huddled in her shawl, she adjusted the wig under it slightly and nodded her head in agreement, muttering something

indistinct. But Mrs Jacobs threw her hands and one eye up
to heaven and cried out, 'God in heaven, what is happening
to us? What is the world coming to? What kind of rabbis is
God giving us?' She had been fiercely opposed to the rabbi
from the start because of his lack of a beard. No rabbi could
be worthy of his calling if he did not have a beard, she had
maintained. Now she was more sure of it than ever. 'This
is a rabbi?' she said. 'What sort of a rabbi is it that does not
have a beard, first of all, and second of all, spends his time
playing ball in cheder with the children?'

Mrs Mittleman had not been sure about the matter until
now but, disliking Mrs Jacobs as she did, she swung over
immediately to the defenders. 'So what of it?' she said,
'What's wrong if he plays ball a little with the children? I
have no objection, I can understand, though,' she added a
bit slyly, 'why some might object, especially those who
have a son who would like to be married.'

'What's that?' Mrs Jacobs bridled and turned to face her,
the one good eye flashing fire. 'Are you perhaps talking
about my son?'

'Your son?' said Mrs Mittleman innocently, shrugging
her shoulders. 'I wasn't even thinking about your son. I was
just saying, there are a lot of mothers who might be jealous
of the rabbi because he is young and so eligible and is
getting so many offers.'

'Well, I'm not one of them,' snapped Mrs Jacobs. 'And I'll
have you know my Rafael has plenty offers.' The others
avoided looking at one another, but they all wanted to
laugh, knowing that the one-eyed woman was indulging in
dreams. Mrs Harris especially kept her eyes down.
Desperate though she was to find a match for her
remaining unmarried daughters, the gawky idiot son of her
neighbour was the last one she'd ever consider. But Mrs

Jacobs continued defiantly, 'My Rafael doesn't have to worry. All he has to do is snap a finger and the girls would come running. He is now head presser at the shop. True, the shop has been idle for a few weeks and he is not making so much as he used to. But when things get better he will be making plenty.'

No one said anything further. As far as they were concerned the discussion was over, and they began to drift out one by one. My mother was left thinking. A week later she invited the rabbi to Friday night dinner. It was a further attempt to show her support for him. But it was time. Others had invited him to Friday night dinner. My mother had hesitated only because she was afraid, first of my father, who would have to be there, and second of Lily herself and whether she would want it.

But she decided to take the chance without consulting either of them first and the rabbi accepted her invitation with alacrity.

Friday night dinners were always the best of the week. They were like holiday feasts and the whole atmosphere was festive. We came home from the synagogue into a house that smelled of chicken soup and freshly baked cakes. The table was decked out with a crisp, snow-white cloth, and set with the best dishes and cutlery. In the centre the candles burned in the shiny brass candlesticks that my mother had smuggled out of Poland. The fire glowed in the grate, with pots simmering over it.

The rabbi came home with us that Friday night, chatting cheerfully all along the way, with everyone envying us. He sniffed and sighed as we came in and, rubbing his hands together briskly, said, 'Ah, what lovely smells.' Then he called out, 'Good Shabbes, good Shabbes!'

My father was there, a surprise to my two brothers and myself who were unprepared for his presence. He was already seated at the table, with his head turned to one side, and if he answered the rabbi's greeting it was barely audible and just a mutter of something. Rose and Lily did a little better, although Lily was noticeably cold, and her eyes looked red and swollen, as if she had been crying.

Well, she had. My mother had had enough trouble getting my father to be there for dinner and if it hadn't been for the new baby she might never have got him to do it. But since the baby's arrival he had been a little easier for her to handle. As for Lily, however, she had run into a storm of protest. Lily, outraged when she heard at the last moment that the rabbi was to be a guest for dinner, had wanted to leave, had bitterly accused my mother of trying to make a match for her, had burst into a torrent of tears, had carried on like that, to my mother's despair, until my father intervened, roaring that if she didn't shut her bloody mouth he'd shut it with his fist.

All that took place only moments before our arrival and if the rabbi sensed anything in the rather tense atmosphere he gave no indication of it. He said a blessing first before the dinner began, then chatted cheerfully about various things, the weather, nothing of importance, but just something to make us feel at ease with him. He was never without words. He was really a personable fellow and it was no wonder most people liked him. He directed his attention to Rose. 'I hear you are to become a dressmaker,' he said to her.

'I am a dressmaker,' said Rose stiffly.

'Ah, I beg your pardon,' he apologised. 'I thought you were still learning. What kind of shop do you work in? Is it a big one?'

'It's not a shop,' Rose said in the same stiff tone. She had difficulty speaking to people and never looked at them when she did. She was much like my father in many respects. She had problems getting on with others and was a loner on our street, without friends, aloof and superior in her manner. Since working in the dress shop she had also affected a haughty, artificial way of speaking that was supposed to be upper class, She still, I am sure, lived in her dream world, fantasising less about dukes and duchesses and lords and ladies, and more about the rich women of the world who were patrons of the dress shop where she worked. Someone had once told us that they had seen her wandering about the streets up the park, pausing every now and then to look at one of the fancy houses there, and I have no doubt that in her mind she was living in one of them, dreaming as she walked along by herself.

It was in her fancy upper-class British tone that she answered the rabbi now. 'It is an establishment, not a shop,' she said. 'I work for Madame La Cossita and we are very exclusive. Madame La Cossita accepts just a select few as her clients. Lady Bramhall is one of them.'

The rabbi tried to look properly impressed. I am sure he was not deceived but he was polite, nodding and saying, 'Ah, yes. It must be very interesting to work for a place like that.'

But then the whole effect for Rose was spoiled when my father gave a sudden ugly little laugh and said, 'It's just a bloody shop like any other shop, except they charge ten times more and give their workers ten times less than any other shop. They're a bloody bunch of cut-throats and for the few farthings a week she gets from them she'd be better off staying at home.'

Rose's face froze. She sat there for a moment saying nothing, then suddenly, abruptly pushing her chair back with a familiar scraping sound that was like his, she left the table. A few moments later we heard the door bang as she went out of the house. It was not the first time she had departed like this after a quarrel. She would wander about a bit in the dark by herself, perhaps up the park, among the houses that were lit now, many of them, with the new electric lights, then she would return and go silently upstairs to bed.

There was a brief, awkward silence after her departure, before my mother started to apologise. The rabbi dismissed it with a wave of a hand and said gently, 'She is very young. And she has a lot of pride and there is nothing wrong with that. We are a proud people. Pride has always been a characteristic of the Jews. Some day we will really have something to be proud of, a nation of our own. What do you think?'

He addressed this last question to Lily, who had been helping my mother serve and had just placed another dish in front of the rabbi. He had turned his head and spoken to her over his shoulder. It was the first time, too, that he had spoken to her since the greeting, though I know his eyes had been following her as she moved about the kitchen, bringing the food to the table and taking dishes back into the scullery.

Lily, silent all this time and evidently still hostile to the visitor, answered him rather loudly, and with an abruptness and vindictiveness that startled us and brought a worried frown to my mother's forehead. 'I'd rather not think of it, if you don't mind,' she said.

'Why?' The rabbi looked a bit astonished. 'Don't you want a homeland for the Jews?'

'There are too many nations already,' Lily retorted. 'What do we need another one for – to divide the working class still more? The enemy of the Jews is not the Christians, it's the bosses. Instead of running away, they should stay here and fight with their fellow workers for the freedom they want. Anti-Semitism comes out of the system, like all the other evils, poverty and hunger and war and disease. If you destroy the system you destroy all those things.'

We looked at her in amazement. Where had all this come from? We had never heard her say anything like this before. I myself didn't understand half of what she was saying with such passion, with eyes flashing, but I could see the horror on my mother's face and I noticed that even my father was staring at Lily with something like incredulity in his eyes, and I knew that Lily had said something awful.

But the rabbi himself was nodding and smiling a little, almost as if in agreement, 'Ah,' he murmured, 'then you are a Socialist, But so was I. I was even a member of the Bolsheviks. I thought as you did that if you got to the root of the evil – capitalism, the Czar – and the workers took control, everything would be all right, for the Jews especially. But I found out differently. When the revolution was over, when the fighting had stopped and the workers were in control – Lenin, Trotsky, Kerensky first, of course – things would be fine for the Jews. I was soon disillusioned. The Jews, I discovered, were still regarded as Jews. Not wanted, not welcome any more than they were under the Czar. Perhaps persecuted even more, because the lust for blood had been sharpened by the revolution and, with the whole country still in turmoil, new scapegoats were needed and there we were, the scapegoat always ready at hand. If I had not run away I would have been killed.

Many of my friends were and, mind you, this was after the revolution was over. Now tell me, Lily, what do you have to say about that?'

'I say you are a liar!' Lily flashed back at him.

I heard my mother gasp. I heard her say 'Lily!' and even make a move as if to strike her.

But the rabbi intervened, holding up a hand. 'No, no, no,' he said. 'Let her speak. It is good for her and for all of us. I am not a liar, Lily. I have no reason to lie. Believe me, I have no reason to feel any love or loyalty to the Czar and everything that he represented. No one could have been more overjoyed than I was when he was overthrown. I could never forget how we suffered under his rule, the persecution, the pogroms. My father was killed in one of them. I saw him killed, Lily, with my own eyes when I was a little boy. They came in the middle of the night, the Czar's Cossacks, and they burned our houses and the synagogue, and they took out the men and shot them, and the women, the young girls, they raped. I went through all this, so why shouldn't I want to see a revolution come about and the workers in control? But I swear it did not change things for me and for my fellow Jews. That I swear to.'

'They turned on you', said Lily, 'not because you were a Jew, but because you were a rabbi, just as they turned on priests and ministers. You represented an institution that has always supported the capitalist powers and is used by them to keep the workers subdued. You were one of the evils that they had to get rid of.'

The rabbi shook his head sadly. 'Religion is the opium of the people,' he quoted. 'You see, I have read my Marx too. But do you know, Marx himself was an anti-Semite. If you read him as closely as I have you will find it in his own writings . . .'

'Oh, what bosh!' cried Lily. 'What a lie! If anyone can say a thing like that, then he is truly a liar.'

'I will find the passages for you,' the rabbi said, smiling. 'I will be glad to point them out to you, but not tonight. I think I have spoiled the Shabbes enough for you already.' He spoke this last to my mother and had begun rising. 'I apologise.'

'It's not your fault,' my mother cried. 'It was Lily's. She had no right to talk to you like that. She should be the one to apologise.'

'No, no. Lily was just speaking her mind. She is a thinker and I admire her all the more for it.'

He left and we were silent for a moment after he had gone. My father broke the silence by rising abruptly, going to the scullery door and getting his coat, and by putting it half on, then striding out with the sleeve dangling behind him and his right arm groping for it. The front door slammed shut after him.

His abrupt departure only added to my mother's distress. His presence tonight had given her so much to hope for. But all that had been crushed in this moment. Things were just the same as before. Except with Lily. There was something new in what Lily had revealed tonight that frightened her.

When he had gone and the house was silent again, she turned on Lily and said in a low voice, 'Are you really a Socialist?'

'Yes, I am,' said Lily.

A little groan escaped my mother and she put her hands to her face. What could be more horrible? Was there anything worse than being a Socialist? And was this the meaning of all those strange books she had been reading, and those strange meetings and lectures? But I know what other thoughts were in my mother's mind that night and probably keeping her awake. What other secrets was Lily hiding?

Chapter Ten

We were all growing up. Fast, very fast. There were now only two of us going to school, Saul and myself. We went separately, by ourselves or with our friends. There was no need any longer for my mother to fear we would be attacked by the ragamuffins. We were big and able to take care of ourselves.

I was ten and in Cocky Rawlings's standard five class, and the tallest boy in the class. Saul was a bit taller than me, and Joe an inch or so taller than Saul, so that we made steps and stairs when we stood alongside or when we walked off to the synagogue together. There was even less room in the bed now for all three of us, but we had to manage, with a great deal of kicking and shoving during the night.

Joe had left school and had been barmitzvahed already. He went into the tailoring shop, to work next to Lily and my father, but he had his heart set on becoming a journalist and my mother encouraged him. He had such beautiful handwriting, she boasted to all the women in her shop. For this reason alone he should be working for a newspaper, instead of learning the tailoring trade, and she kept urging him to write to newspapers for a job.

At last, unbelievably, one answer came out of all the letters he'd written. It was from a big newspaper in Manchester, asking him to appear for an interview. There was so much joy among us. It was almost as if he had the job already.

The day he went for his interview was an exciting one. He put on his best suit, a blue serge with the first pair of long trousers he'd ever worn, bought for his barmitzvah. He had a waistcoat with it too, and he wore one of my father's stiff collars and a tie. He came downstairs to show us and my mother's face glowed with pride. 'Oh, you look so beautiful,' she said. 'How can they help but give you the job?'

He was a handsome boy, there had never been any question about that, and it had been growing more and more noticeable as he got older. Girls had already begun pestering him with invitations and he had gone to party after party. That morning he looked at his very best and much older than his years. Lately, since working in the shop, he had begun to sport a cane and wear a monocle. He wanted to take these with him to the interview, and there was some arguing between him and my mother before she got him to give up the idea.

Then off he went, strutting confidently down Brook Street, on his way to Mersey Square and the tram that would take him to Manchester. He looked almost as if he might be carrying the cane, swinging it about, with the monocle screwed in his eye, as I had seen him do when I had once come upon him and a friend of his in the park, saying, 'By jove, by jove!'

We waited. My mother was holding her breath. Was this to be the first lucky step towards good fortune? Every time there was a sound at the front she jumped up. The hours passed. It was evening and still he had not come home.

'He must be working,' she said. 'They must have given him the job. He's a journalist.'

It was right after tea that he came home. We saw him walking along Brook Street and even from a distance it was clear to us that he was moving very slowly and that there was something wrong. We all stood outside watching him, clustered together anxiously, the concern growing as he came closer.

Now it was obvious that there was something very, very wrong. His clothes seemed to be torn. His stiff collar was hanging off his neck and the tie was dangling down all askew. And one sleeve on his fine blue serge suit seemed to be ripped. And his face . . .

His face was battered and he was crying. The sick feeling must have settled deep inside my mother and in all of us. I heard her whisper, 'Oh, my God,' and she put an arm round him and led him inside. We followed and there he broke down completely, sank into a chair and burst into bitter sobs. His story came out gradually, bit by bit, with intermittent sobbing between the words.

He had gone to Manchester and he had come to this newspaper office, a big place with a lot of roaring machinery somewhere in the building. The girl at the reception desk had taken his name, and that of the man he wanted to see, and told him to wait. So he sat down on a bench and waited. And waited and waited and waited. Other people came and went, but he seemed to have been totally forgotten. Employees went out to lunch, but he remained sitting there. He was hungry, and the stiff collar dug into his neck and hurt, but he was afraid to loosen it for fear he might be called in any minute. He had to wait still longer, much longer, though, and it was not until mid-afternoon, when he had begun to feel that he could not take any more of it, that the girl finally told him to go in.

He went into an office where a heavy-set, white-haired man with a bulbous nose sat at a large desk and the first thing the man said to him as he sat down was, 'You're a Jew, aren't you?'

'Yes,' Joe said.

'Well, I can tell you right now you aren't going to get a job on a newspaper. No newspaper will hire a Jew.' The man's voice was slightly hoarse and he looked across the desk at Joe with bloodshot eyes. He wore no jacket and no collar, and his shirt was open at the neck. The desk was cluttered with papers and Joe kept hearing the rumbling of machinery. 'I'm doing you a favour telling you this,' the man said, 'I'm going to save you a lot of time and trouble writing letters. We're a humanitarian country. We gave you people refuge when no other country would have you. But don't take advantage of it and start pushing yourselves into places where you aren't wanted. Stick to where you belong, in the tailoring shops and pawn-shops and the markets. Remember that and you'll be all right . . .'

'And is that what he sent for you for?' my mother asked in a whisper. 'Just to say that?'

'Yes.'

I saw my mother clench her hands and compress her lips. She couldn't speak for a long time.

But that wasn't all of Joe's misfortune that day. Coming off the tram at Mersey Square, sick with despair and disappointment and hunger – he hadn't eaten all day – he made his way slowly across the square and crossed on to Daw Bank and then under the viaduct, and just as he was passing the Devil's Steps it began – the jeering, laughing voices, familiar sounds and words: Jew, kike, van-squashers, who killed Christ?

Joe had always been more afraid than any of us and not much of a fighter, but he had never been caught like this alone and in his best clothes. He was terrified. Then he made the mistake that we had always been warned against – he started to run – and it acted upon them as it would on a pack of wild dogs. The next moment they were on him. There were about six of them and he went down under all of them, screaming. They pummelled him mercilessly, ripped his clothes, until finally a man coming out of the pub under the viaduct came to his rescue and chased them off.

Joe stumbled away, crying, his face bloodied, his fine blue serge suit in rags.

Yes, we were growing up, and when school broke up for the summer holiday that year I was all done with Cocky Rawlings's class and ready for Miss Penn's standard six, and the headmaster had talked to me about becoming ink monitor and studying for the scholarship exam. 'You're not as bright as your sister was,' he said, looking down at me from the tall desk where he sat. 'But you're about the best of the lot here, which isn't saying much, because most of 'em have the brains of donkeys. But at least you know how many thripenny doughnuts there are in a dozen . . .' He winked, but kept his face looking severe and the red ears stuck out. He gave them a little wiggle and went on without changing expression, 'You might talk to your mother about it and see whether she'd want it or not. I wouldn't care to have the same thing happen as did with Lily. You talk to her and let me know.'

There was no hesitation on her part when I told her. Her eyes lit up. A new hope, a new dream came into her mind.

This would make up for the last disappointment with Joe, for all her disappointments. 'Oh, yes,' she said. 'Tell him yes. And he mustn't worry. What happened to Lily won't happen to you. They're all working now and we'll be able to manage.' But then a slight hesitation came over her, and she lowered her voice and said, 'But don't tell your father. We won't say anything to him about it yet.'

There was hardly any need for her to say that. I never talked to him, nor he to me. I recall one time coming home from the library with a stack of books under my arm. I almost ran into him as he was coming out of a pub called the Red Lion on King Street. We both started and stopped short. We looked at each other for a moment, then dropped our heads. Not a word was spoken. He seemed to be fumbling in his pocket for something and I thought perhaps he was going to give me a penny. But no, if he was he changed his mind abruptly and with a little muttered sound charged past me, almost shouldering me aside.

I didn't care. I was used to him by now. He had seemed to change a little after the baby was born, and had spent a bit more time at home, and had even shown some interest in the baby, peering down at it in the crib with a cigarette smoking in his mouth. But now he was the same as before, coming and going, ignoring us all, except for a look at the baby now and then.

I went on my way that afternoon not thinking of him. The summer weather had begun. The skies were clear and the sun shone, baking warmth into the cobblestones and narrow pavements that ran along both sides of our street. We felt the warmth in the evening as we raced up and down the street, often barefooted at this time of the year.

I was not like Lily. When I was told about the scholarship exam that I would be taking I did not start burying myself in books. I rushed outside as soon as tea was over to play. I was no longer one of the smaller boys hanging on the fringe of the group. I was one of the big boys. Zalmon, my brothers Joe and Saul and a few others had left the group, too old to be playing in the street. They were workers now in the tailoring shops, bent over their machines all day, coming home to eat their dinner and then going out to a picture show or to walk through the park with a girl.

I was one of the older boys now, one of the leaders of the pack, along with Philly Cohen and Benny Mittleman, and on a summer night we led a group of smaller boys down to the rec to play a game of piggy stick. It was the one game you couldn't play on the street; we'd tried it and smashed too many windows, and it had been forbidden.

But on the rec there was plenty of room and we headed for it that night in a noisy, chattering bunch, carrying our sticks and piggies. I had made my own, spending hours whittling the little piece of wood into the shape of a pig's snout on each end. It was one of my most treasured possessions and I clutched it tightly as we went down to Wood Street, then turned left on to Wood Street and past the Gordons' taproom. The door was opened by a customer just then and I caught a glimpse of Florrie inside, standing behind the bar, with her face flushed and her hair all stringy and hanging loose down over it. She was not half as attractive as she used to be, and she had grown heavy and careless with her appearance ever since Freddy had died that day when he went careering down the hill in his wheelchair.

I thought of that first night when I had gone in there to buy a bottle of ginger beer for Sarah, and how pretty she was then when she stood in the doorway and stared at Freddy writing his note. That night came back very clearly to me at that moment, and chiefly I suppose because this night was very much like that one, soft and balmy, with the flush of sunset in the sky, and people sitting outside their doors smoking their pipes and cigarettes, and the edges of buildings beginning to turn dark against the sky. It all flitted through my mind very quickly and was gone by the time we reached the rec.

The place swarmed with shrieking children. There were all sorts of games going on, balls, shuttlecocks flying into the air, and the thud of boots against soccer balls mingling with the shouts and cries. Over at the iron fence some of the mill lads were playing pitch and toss, kneeling down on the crushed cinder ground, eyes intent on the coins that were being thrown, some of the losers glaring up at us as we went by and muttering, 'Garn, you bloody Jews.'

We hurried past them, seeking out a place for our game. There was an empty spot close to the edge of the grassy slope that ran down from the park. It was not exactly ideal for our purpose, because the piggy could easily fly over into the park and get lost among the bushes and trees, but it was the only one left for us and we began playing with warnings to watch out for the park.

For an hour we played without any mishap, then I made the mistake of letting Shloime Roseman use my piggy. Shloime was only about eight or nine, but he already showed promise of becoming another Zalmon. He was thin and short and wiry and mischievous, and constantly in trouble at school and at cheder. And he loved to fight and wrestle. He'd already had several fights with batesemas and had come out the victor in all of them. He was a good batter at cricket and especially at piggy. He didn't have a piggy of his own, so I had lent him mine, although with some qualms. As soon as he came up to bat, I moved far back to catch the piggy, knowing the distance he could hit.

He placed the piggy on a little stone, with the snouts raised. He spat on his hand – always a warning sign – then gripped the stick tightly, bent down and tapped one of the ends causing the piggy to fly upward, and when it was in mid-air he swung and struck. There was a crack like the sound of a whip and the piggy went soaring. But right where it was not supposed to go, into the park among the trees and bushes.

I gave a loud yell of despair and raced after it. The others went on with the game while I crashed through the overgrown bushes and grass. I had a fair idea of where the piggy had gone and made my way straight up the incline, searching the ground as I went along. It was like a jungle. I don't think the gardeners ever touched this section of the park. Vines grew everywhere, wrapping themselves round the trunks of trees and overgrown bushes and crawling along the ground. My feet got tangled in them, and there were thorny bushes that scratched my hands and face as I beat my way upwards, looking here and there for the piggy.

Suddenly I was facing an enormous tree. It was a mass of gold and I realised this was the golden willow Freddy had spoken of. I remembered he had said it looked like a beautiful big ballroom gown, and that's exactly how it was, its branches drooping gracefully down as if from a hoop and trailing along the ground. A sweet aroma came from its yellow leaves.

I stared up at it, fascinated, then heard the murmur of voices. They came from within those branches and I crept slowly forward to look. I parted several of them with my hand and peered in. It was like a cathedral inside, Freddy had said, and that's how it struck me, although I had never been inside a cathedral. But I knew it had to be something big and awesome, and that's how this was, and dim. It took me some time to make out the two figures lying close to one another, a man and a woman, and then I knew as I listened that they were Arthur and Lily.

I could make out what they were saying now, too.

'Oh, I'm sick of it. I'm real good and sick of it.' This was Arthur's voice. 'I hate this secret business, arranging meetings where nobody can see us, hiding under this tree, like a pair of thieves.'

'I know, darling.' It was Lily speaking now, quite clearly Lily, and she had called him 'darling'. 'I hate it just as much as you do. But what can we do?' She sounded quite hopeless.

'What can we do? I'll tell you what we can do.' Arthur's voice was angry. 'Instead of skulking about like this we can just simply come out in the open and tell 'em how things are between us and that we want to get married. That's what we can do.'

'No, no, we can't do that. Not yet.' Lily seemed frightened.

'Why not?'

'I think it would kill my mother.'

'It won't kill her. She'll get over it in time. Oh, this is such a lot of damned foolishness, this Jew-Christian business. I thought we'd be all done with it when the war was over. I was so sure of it! But it's as bad as ever.'

'I know,' said Lily, with the same hopelessness as before. 'We'll have to wait, that's all.'

'Wait for what?'

'There'll be a better world You'll see. It's got to come,' said Lily.

'My God, Lily, you don't want to wait for the revolution, do you? It's got to come, that's for sure. I'm as much a believer in it as you are, and I know once we get rid of capitalism we'll have a damned better world and all these things that separate us will be gone. But it's going to take some time yet, Lily, and I don't think we should wait. Not for the revolution, dear girl.'

'Just a little longer then, Arthur, please, darling,' she begged.

'Look,' said Arthur, sitting up suddenly, 'I know you're putting it off mostly on account of your mother . . .'

'What about your mother?' Lily interrupted.

'Oh, she doesn't feel as strongly about it as yours,' Arthur said.

'But she does feel something,' Lily said.

'Yes, there is something My father too. I've spoken to both of them about you. I've told them pretty much how I feel.'

'And they weren't too keen on the idea, were they?'

'No,' Arthur admitted reluctantly. 'I suppose there's a touch of bigotry in them too. They advised me to think about it carefully,' he added bitterly. 'I haven't talked with them about it since. I don't intend to. I was going to say just before that I'll be graduating in another year, then I'll be getting a job in some law office and that's as long as we're going to wait. We're going to get married then, no matter who says what. How about that?'

'All right,' said Lily slowly, still thinking.

'You promise now?'

'Yes, I promise . . .'

'Well, then, let's seal that with a kiss.'

He took her in his arms, and there was a considerable silence while they clung to one another in a long, passionate kiss. I could have stolen away, and I think I was about to, but just then I caught sight of the piggy. It was lying only a foot or two away from me, off to the side. I crept towards it, but unavoidably stepped on a twig. There was a crack and they separated quickly.

'There's somebody here,' Lily whispered.

They saw me and I tried to run. But Arthur, springing up, had caught me by the arm and swung me round so that he could see my face. 'It's 'arry,' he shouted.

Lily's face must have turned white. She got to her feet, straightening out her dress, and came over to us. ''arry,' she said in a whisper, 'what are you doing here?'

'I was looking for my piggy. We were playing on the rec and it got hit up here and I went looking for it, and it was right in here.' I was as scared as they were.

They didn't seem to know what to do for a moment. Nor did I. Arthur had released my arm and we all stood looking at one another. Then Arthur said, 'Well, I suppose the fat's in the fire now.'

'No, it isn't,' said Lily. 'You aren't going to tell, are you, 'arry?'

I could very easily have asked 'Tell what?' but there was no use pretending. They knew I'd heard. I hung my head and muttered, 'No.'

'That's a good lad,' Arthur said.

As we walked away together, Lily spoke earnestly to me. 'Arthur and I love each other,' she said, 'and we're going to get married some day, but I don't want Mam to know about it yet. You know how she feels about marrying a Christian. You remember Sarah, don't you, and how terrible that was to her?'

I nodded. How could I have forgotten it?

'It's not really terrible,' Lily continued. 'Not if you're in love, and Arthur and I have been in love for a long time.

It doesn't matter really what you are if you're in love. I'm telling you this, 'arry, because you're a big boy now, and you're my brother and I know you understand, don't you?'

'Yis.'

She put an arm round my shoulders and gave them a squeeze. 'Thank you, 'arry,' she said.

'And thank you from me, too,' Arthur said. 'I'm sorry it has to be this way. I wish I could be your brother too.'

I didn't say anything to this. The light was fading. The jungle of trees and bushes was a mass of shadow. The sky above it seemed very white in contrast. From the distance below there came faintly the echoing sounds of children playing. They were still at it and would be as long as there was a little light left in the sky.

'You can go and join your friends now,' Lily said. 'And remember what I said about not telling anybody.'

I left them there. I don't think they were going back to the tree. They would have stayed much longer, probably, if I had not come along. But I had spoiled their tryst and they would go home, each taking a different route when they came to the top of the hill, making sure they did not arrive in our street at the same time.

I went back down the slope with my piggy in my hand, but by the time I got to the rec my friends were gone. I drifted about for a while, looking at the various games going on, then went home.

They did not go back to the park after that night. They were afraid of discovery. At least Lily was. Arthur himself might have welcomed it. But Lily, however independent she might have sounded at times with her new Socialist philosophy, was in deadly fear of being caught and despite her promise to Arthur I think the problem was far from resolved in her mind.

A year must have seemed a long way off to her, a good, comfortable distance away, during which time any sort of miracle could happen. Who knows what wild thoughts may have been going through her troubled mind – even that she could talk my mother into altering a belief that was thousands of years old.

In the meantime she was taking no chances. It was fortunate that I had been the one who stumbled on them in the park that night. The next time they might not be so lucky. Yet they had to see each other, be with each other. They were terribly in love. So it was decided to meet somewhere out in the country – much as Freddy and Sarah had done, and probably for the same reason.

The place they chose most often for their trysts was the Seventeen Windows, a quaint old inn out in the Derbyshire Hills, given that name because it had exactly that many windows, seventeen of them. I know, because I counted them every time I went there.

Lily had taken me, whenever she went there, to lull any suspicion my mother might have about her spending a day in the country by herself. Nor was it strange that she should have chosen me to go with her. We had more in common, with our liking for books and music and things like that, than any other two in the family and we went often together to the library, and once she had taken me to the theatre to see a performance of *A Christmas Carol*.

It was quite natural that she should have taken me out to the country on a Sunday afternoon and I think on the whole my mother was rather pleased with the idea. The one thing she would have liked, though, in addition was for

Lily to have asked the young rabbi to go along with us. He would have liked it too.

He was in the shop one Sunday afternoon when Lily and I were on the point of leaving and, seeing us about to set off and learning where we were going, he said wistfully, 'Ah, but it must be very beautiful out there. I have never seen the Derbyshire Hills.'

My mother took Lily aside and whispered, 'Why don't you ask him to go with you?'

'No,' Lily whispered back fiercely.

The rabbi had engaged me in conversation, but we could both hear what was going on. The rabbi, however, smiled and pretended not to hear.

Lily was silent and furious for a while as we left. But she soon got over it, and laughed and chatted as we went along. Her spirits were always high on these trips filled, I have no doubt, with anticipation and eagerness to see Arthur, though she might have spotted him a dozen times that day already peeping surreptitiously through the window.

We took the tram at Mersey Square. I loved this part of the trip especially, sitting on the top deck with the sun shining on my head, feeling the rumble of wheels beneath me, seeing the town slip by and the countryside beginning.

I was eleven years old and I had never been far beyond the town, and just riding on a tram gave me a sense of adventure and being far away. We got off at a little holiday town called Marple, which was as far as the tram went, and began walking. I loved this part too. The Derbyshire Hills rose all around us, undulating against the sky. We crossed through fields and woods, and alongside little brooks that trickled quietly and glittered in the sun. Flowers grew in abundance everywhere. Fields were filled with shining

buttercups and daisies, and there were thick beds of
bluebells. A rich scent rose from it all, and we both sniffed
it eagerly and smiled at one another as we walked.

We came at last to the crest of a grassy hill, and there
below was a little valley with the Seventeen Windows
nestled cosily in among the green landscape, surrounded by
hills. It was a gabled structure, perhaps two hundred years
old, but still sturdy, its brick tawny with age, its seventeen
windows glittering in the sun. There were flowers all
around it and tables were set up outdoors at the front, and
as we approached, within minutes after coming down from
the crest of the hill, the proprietress, Mrs Fogg, came out to
greet us.

She seemed as old and quaint to me as the inn itself, a
tall, thin, gaunt woman wearing a sun bonnet and a white
apron over her dress, always with a pleasant smile of
greeting that showed large buck teeth, and hands stretched
out to receive us. 'Ah, and how be ye?'

Her accent was not Lancashire as ours was. I believe it was
Welsh and it is very difficult to try to reproduce here. I know
that her husband had been a Welsh coal miner and had been
killed in a mine explosion. That had been many years before
all this and before she came to own the Seventeen Windows.
She had, however, acquired quite a following, and her tables
and the little bar inside the inn were well filled on a Sunday
afternoon. I had been surprised when I first came here to see
how many people Lily knew. I learned later that it was a
Sunday gathering place for Socialists and Labourites, and
Mrs Fogg herself was a Socialist.

As she greeted us with the warmth with which she
greeted all her guests, smiling and showing her large
prominent teeth, she said, 'Your friend's here already.'

'Oh, is he?' said Lily.

She spoke casually, as if it were of no great interest to her. But I could almost hear her heart pounding, and when Arthur appeared just then coming out of the inn, her heartbeat must have quickened still more. But both she and Arthur restrained themselves as they met, making it seem as if they were mere friends, smiling and just shaking hands, although Arthur did not let go of the hand that he shook and they remained like that for a few moments longer, chatting about the weather, smiling at one another, while Mrs Fogg bustled off elsewhere.

Arthur held on to the hand as they sauntered to a table. I followed behind them. They were as oblivious of me as they were of all the other people around them. For a while, that is, because it wasn't long after we had seated ourselves and had begun to eat the cucumber sandwiches on thin white bread that Mrs Fogg's girl served us, along with a pot of tea in a cosy and the plate of scones, that people began to come over from the other tables and there was a big noisy circle around us.

There were discussions and arguments, about Socialism and anarchism and the Labour Party and the man they all referred to as 'Jimmy', but who was Ramsay MacDonald, the young leader of the Labour Party that so many of them belonged to. It was all over my head. I listened, but scarcely understood what they were arguing about, why the Socialists didn't like the Anarchists and why the Labourites didn't like either of them, and why, even though they seemed to disapprove of one another, they all congregated together. And then there were the supporters of the Communists in Russia, and this seemed to confuse matters even more for me.

Perhaps all I cared about really were my cucumber sandwich and tea and scones. I was ravenous by the time I got there and I devoured most of what was put on the table, Lily and Arthur eating very little. They broke away from their friends after a while and went off by themselves, and it was always understood that I was to take care of myself during that time. I did that by wandering about the grounds and looking at the big vegetable patch that Mrs Fogg had at the back of the inn, and the chicken coop that was usually filled with clucking hens and one big strutting, fierce-looking rooster. She also had several plump white rabbits that were fun to watch.

After about an hour Lily and Arthur came back from wherever they had been, Lily always looking a bit dreamy and leaning her head against Arthur's shoulder, and their two hands clasped together, and sometimes Arthur's other hand round her waist. We began the walk back home, with the two of them in much the same position and I behind them. I could see how Lily kept her head on his shoulder for a while, and how his hand tightened round her waist, and I am sure if it had not been for me they would have stopped and kissed.

I heard Arthur murmur, 'I don't know if I can wait a whole year. It seems like a terrible long time.'

'Yes, I know,' Lily sighed.

'Then why must we?' he asked.

Lily hesitated, then said, 'Arthur, how would we live? And where?'

I couldn't see Arthur's face, but I am sure it must have had a perplexed frown. These were questions, perhaps, that he had never given much thought to. But he did try to answer them. 'I could get digs in Manchester,' he said. 'I should be doing that anyway, because the last year is going to be a hard one, and I shouldn't be wasting time travelling back and forth every day. I need all the time there is for study.'

'Could you afford it?' Lily asked gently.

It was a question more difficult to answer and Arthur hesitated. 'I know Mam and Dad's been finding it hard enough as it is,' he admitted. 'And they wouldn't be able to help me out any more than they are doing right now, especially with the mill being slow. I'm not on full scholarship, you know, like I was at the Grammar School. It's only part scholarship and I've got to pay the rest. Well, Mam and Dad have been doing that so far and it hasn't been easy for them. I wouldn't ever ask them for any more – they wouldn't have it anyway. But I'm thinking, if we got married and lived in Manchester I could take on some tutoring work. I've thought of doing that before now, but it would have meant staying in the city until very late and the trams don't run at night. But I could do it if we lived there.'

'And I could work too,' Lily said thoughtfully. 'There's lots of tailoring shops in Manchester, and I know the trade well enough to work anywhere.'

'That would do it then, wouldn't it,' Arthur began eagerly, but Lily stopped him with a finger to her lips and turned her head to look at me. He looked too.

But I was pretending not to have been listening and had bent down to pick some flowers in the field we were crossing. They went on and I did not get the rest of their conversation for a little while because I had really become occupied picking flowers. The two of them went on ahead, and after I had gathered an armful of buttercups and daisies that I would give to my mother, I ran after them and was able to listen again.

They were walking very slowly and talking earnestly. Arthur was saying, 'Oh, I'm sure of it, I'm absolutely sure, and as far as it's interfering with my studies – well, there's nothing could interfere more than the way I feel now, wanting you, knowing you're right across the street from me and I can't even talk to you, thinking of you all the time, daytime, night-time. It's been driving me mad, Lily. Yes, I'm sure this is what I want. The only question is, do you want it?'

'Yes I do,' Lily said, and her voice trembled a little. 'I think about you all the time the same way you do of me and it's torture for me too. I want to marry you and be with you all the time. The only thing is, I don't want to hurt my mother. I don't care about my father. He doesn't matter. But I do care about my mother.'

'Yes, I know,' Arthur said, 'I know all about your father. But I wouldn't worry. I told you before, your mother would get over it in time.'

Lily shook her head. 'I don't think so. I don't think she could ever get over it. It just wouldn't be possible for her to get over it.'

'Why d'you say that?' asked Arthur.

'Because of what she believes and what all Jewish people believe.'

'And what's that?'

'If a Jew marries a Christian he or she is considered dead.'

'What!' Arthur was incredulous.

Lily nodded her head slowly. 'She told us that a long time ago. I remember it so clearly. It was during the time they found out about Sarah and Freddy. You remember that, don't you?'

'Yes.' It was not something that Arthur would have wanted to remember. He spoke rather shortly. Clearly, he didn't regard it as a parallel and would just as soon she had not mentioned it. 'That was just a bloody bit of foolishness. Freddy was always after some girl.'

'Yes, I know. But my mother was terribly frightened over it. She was suspicious of you and me even then, even though I wasn't much more than twelve and you fifteen. I think she wanted to impress it on me especially. I'm sure she was looking at me when she told us of the terrible thing that could happen to a person who strayed from the fold. And I really got an eerie feeling when she said it. I think we all did, because she made it sound so real. Dead. That was the word she used. You became dead if you married a Christian. I was angry with her too, and I remember I said it was a lot of bosh and stamped out. But it really made an impression on my mind and I've never forgotten it.' She shivered a little and drew closer to Arthur, and he put an arm round her waist.

'You wouldn't forget it,' he said. 'They put a lot of superstitions in our minds when we're kids and it's just the right time for them to stick. But you're not going to let that make any difference, are you?'

'Oh, no. I'm not a bit superstitious. I'm really not. I'm just thinking of what's in my mother's mind. She believes it. I'm sure she does.'

'I'm sure she does too. But I promise you she'll forget all about it once she sees how really alive you are.' Then, anxiously, he asked, 'What's the matter, Lily?'

They had suddenly come to a halt and I halted with them. Lily had put a hand to her heart, as I had seen her do several times before. 'It's nothing, really,' she said. 'Just a little pain. I think it must be too many of Mrs Fogg's scones.'

'Shall we sit down and rest a while?' Arthur said. 'You seem to be short of breath too.'

'No, I'm all right. I'll soon catch my breath. I was a little frightened, I suppose, talking of that old business.'

'Well, we won't talk about it anymore,' Arthur said. 'It's all nonsense, you know. But are you sure you're all right?'

'Yes, I'm quite all right.'

After a little while we walked on. Lily didn't say any more about the pain she had felt, but I noticed she walked much more slowly than before, and I think the cheerfulness she put into her tone as they continued talking – about other matters this time – was forced.

Again we separated just before we reached our street, Lily and I going ahead. Lily seemed very tired and still walked rather slowly, and as we came near our street she said, 'Don't tell Mam I got that pain.'

'I won't,' I promised, knowing that I was not to tell anything, not just this incident.

My mother's eyes brightened when she saw the flowers I had brought her, but then they became concerned as she looked at Lily's face. 'Don't you feel well?' she asked.

'I'm all right. Just a bit tired.'

'You're so pale.'

'That's because I'm tired. I'll go upstairs and lie down for a little while.'

As soon as she had gone my mother turned to me and asked, 'Did anything happen?'

'No,' I said.

Then she began asking the usual questions: how was the trip? Whom did I see? Were there a lot of people there? She was prying, unmistakably, and I always made sure I did not mention Arthur's name. Nor, for that matter, did she. Perhaps she was afraid that if she asked if Arthur had been there I would say yes. Maybe I was too. I could not have lied to her so directly as that. So we fenced a little, until she allowed her suspicions to be lulled, and then her attention was drawn to the flowers I had brought her.

She had arranged them in a glass jar that had once been used for pickles but now served as a vase. She had placed them in the centre of the table and they spread out in a huge bouquet, exuding a fragrant smell that was like perfume.

She looked at them with delight on her face and said, 'Aren't they beautiful?'

I was pleased and said, 'Yis.' Then I asked, 'Can I go out now and play?'

'Yes,' she said. 'Go out and play, but come back soon because I want you to write a letter to America.'

As I ran out, she was still standing there looking at the flowers.

There was so little beauty in her life, and so little hope, that even the slightest thing like a bouquet of buttercups and daisies could give her enormous pleasure and put her in a gay mood. She was in that sort of mood when I sat down at the table with her later and she began to dictate to me. But there were other things that contributed to it, I soon found out, all the little fragments of hope that had been accumulating over the past few months and that were trembling inside her.

'My dear mother-in-law, father-in-law, brothers and sisters-in-law, and all the dear little children, just a few lines to let you know that we are well and hoping to hear the same from you . . .'

Her letters began in the usual way and my pen scratched industriously on the ruled notepaper for a while until she paused to gather her thoughts for what she was going to say next and I had an opportunity to dip the pen in the ink bottle once more.

Now, continuing and unable to wait for all the pre-liminaries about news of the street she usually gave, she plunged right into the good news that was bursting inside her. It must have surprised the relatives in Chicago, accustomed as they were to our tales of woe, our misfortunes and pleas for steamship tickets – although you can be sure my mother did not forget this last towards the end of her letter. But for the greater part it was an outpouring of the joy she felt . . . 'For once God has smiled down at me,' she dictated. 'I know what it is to be happy. Do you remember in my last letter I wrote and told you of the new rabbi, a young man who did not have a beard? How we were all so suspicious of him, because he shaved his face every day, which Mrs Harris claimed was against the Jewish law. Well, all that was cleared up. The rabbi explained at a meeting of the synagogue committee that he did not use a razor, but a powder that he rubbed on his face in the morning and that took off the hair. Well, even then not everybody was certain about it, so a letter was written to the chief rabbi in London, and the reply came stating that only the use of the razor was forbidden and the use of a powder to remove the hair was well within the law.

'So this matter was settled to everybody's satisfaction and we soon found out what a good rabbi he was, how well he led the services in the synagogue and how well he taught the boys in the cheder, and how well he did everything, even the slaughtering of the chickens and the animals for the kosher butcher, who says that he has never seen a rabbi before cut the throat of a cow so quickly and cleanly, with just one swift movement. He does so well at circumcisions too . . .'

Now, at this juncture a sputter of laughter came from my mother's mouth and she had to stop her dictation. I have told you before how my mother always enjoyed a good laugh and how sometimes when she and Fanny Cohen were together they would go into fits of laughter, bent over with their heads close together, their bodies shaking all over. Well, this grew into one like that, and although I didn't quite understand what it was that had set her off, I couldn't help joining in.

So then we both laughed for a while, and finally my mother wiped her eyes, sobered and said, 'Let's go on. Never mind that part about the circumcision. Cross it out.'

I did so and she resumed her dictation, 'I like the young rabbi very much. He is nice and pleasant, and you can talk to him without feeling uncomfortable. Since he's unmarried he has been invited wherever there are daughters. I have had him to dinner once, and I am sorry to say things did not go so well because he and Lily got into an argument about politics. But that hasn't stopped him from coming again. Actually, it is the shop he comes into to buy fruit, but that is only a pretence. He comes really hoping to see Lily. If she is not there he always asks about her. It's quite clear that he prefers her to all the other girls he has met – and aren't they and their mothers jealous! But who cares. I am very excited about it myself.

'I keep thnking what a wonderful thing it would be for her. After all, what has she got to look forward to? She works in the tailoring shop all day and hates it, and she comes home at night and goes right to bed. Once in a while, on a Sunday, she goes into the country with 'arry. That is all the pleasure she gets. What sort of life is that for a young girl, to see no young men, to go out with no one but her eleven-year-old brother? And now there is this chance for her. Oh, what a match that could be. A rabbi! . . .'

I stopped writing. Her words had trailed off and she was staring over my shoulder. I turned my head to see what she was looking at. Lily was standing in the doorway. She was in a dressing gown and slippers, and her face seemed very white. Her eyes were fixed on us with burning intensity. 'It's no use,' she said in a low voice.

'What's no use?' my mother asked and her voice trembled a little, showing she was frightened.

'I heard everything.'

My mother took in a deep breath. 'All right, so you heard,' she said. 'What of it? What's wrong with what I said? I'm writing to them in America. I want them all to know. I'm full of joy that this is how the rabbi feels about you.'

'Well, that isn't the way I feel about him. And I'm not going to marry him. There's not going to be any match. You can tell them that.'

'Oh, Lily, Lily . . .' My mother looked at her appealingly. 'Don't be foolish. This is such a wonderful chance for you. He's such a nice young man. You could be so happy with him, so much happier than I ever was.'

'It's no use,' Lily said. 'You've got to stop thinking of it.'

'Don't you want to get married?' my mother asked.

'I'm going to get married,' Lily said, but I think her courage failed her then, because she added quickly, 'some day.'

'Some day?' my mother murmured unhappily. 'And have you picked out the man yet?'

There was a pause, and I held my breath and looked at Lily, and thought she was going to say it. Now. She looked at me and knew what I was thinking, and there must have been a moment of desperate uncertainty for her, aware that this was her opportunity, but still afraid.

Then it was settled for her. A voice spoke. 'Yes, she has him picked out all right.' And it was followed by a cynical little laugh.

We all turned. Rose had come into the room. She did not look at any of us; nor were her words addressed to anyone in particular. She went about preparing herself some food. She did this often, as if she were a boarder in the house, much like my father, eating alone, ignoring us. When she spoke to anyone it was to a wall, as she was doing now.

'Oh yes,' she was saying with that peculiar little laugh, 'she's picked him out all right and she'll marry him, too.'

'Who?' asked my mother.

'Who d'you think? Who d'you think she's been going with all this time? I saw her today coming back from the country with him, where she's supposed to have been with just her little brother.'

'Who? Who?' demanded my mother in a loud voice.

'Ask her. Why don't you ask her?' And again that laugh.

My mother turned towards Lily. There was terror on her face. And Lily's was whiter even than it had been before.

'Don't pay any attention to her,' she muttered and flashed a look of hatred at Rose, who had seated herself at the table now. and was beginning to eat the little food she had put together, while staring at the wall opposite her and saying amusedly, 'She's supposed to be the bright one of the family. The brilliant one. And the beautiful one. The winner of scholarships. Look at her. She slaves away in a dirty little tailoring shop for a few pennies a week and she's going to marry a bates, and she'll spend the rest of her life on this street, and before you know it she'll be running to Gordon's Saturday nights to fetch a pint of beer for her husband.'

'Who is it?' shouted my mother, interrupting her. I had never heard her shout like that before. Joe and Saul had just come in and they were both staring at her. 'Who is it she went to the country with? Who did you see?'

I think Rose was a little frightened, but she held her ground and repeated stubbornly, 'Ask her. Let her tell you.'

'Tell me!' Once more my mother swung on Lily, her eyes flaming.

Lily broke down. She put her hands to her face and sobbed. Then, in a choking voice, she said, 'Tell her, 'arry,' and ran out and up the stairs.

My mother turned towards me now. They were all looking at me, waiting. Even Rose had turned her head and was watching.

'Who was it?' my mother demanded.

I was no longer bound by any promise. Lily herself had told me to tell. 'Arthur,' I said.

A groan escaped my mother. She began to wring her hands distractedly. After a moment she asked, 'Has she seen him there before?'

'Yis,' I said.

'He was there every Sunday?'

'Yis.'

'And she's going to marry him?'

'Yis.'

'She told you that?'

'Yis.'

'Oh, my God, my God.' She began to pace up and down, still wringing her hands. Then suddenly she stopped pacing and said almost harshly, 'Sit down at the table. I want you to write a letrter.'

She had forgotten completely about the other letter we had been writing. It was never finished and never sent. I tore it up afterwards. It was this new one that we sent: 'My dear mother-in-law, father-in-law, brothers- and sisters-in-law, and all the children, just a few lines to let you know that we are well and hoping to hear the same from you . . .'

In spite of her agony and her rush to say what she had to say, she did not forget the preliminaries, but as soon as they were done she raced on to say, 'And now I must tell you of the terrible thing that has happened to us, a calamity worse than anything yet and one that you must share with us, because the disgrace must fall on you too should Lily carry out her plan.' She spoke fiercely, trying to stem the tears that were coming to her eyes, her voice choking a little, while the other three round the table sat and listened, and my pen scratched quickly to keep up with the flow of her words. 'I must tell you right now that Lily is planning to marry a Christian boy. He is the one who lives across the street, Arthur Forshaw. This all began when they were still children, and I did not pay too much attention to it then and let it go on. I even let her write letters to him when he was in the war. God has punished me for that. I found out today that she has been meeting him secretly in the country and they are planning to get married. Perhaps I deserve this. I don't know. I should have been more strict with her and not let her write to him when he was in France during the war, I think that really got things going for them. Well, now the awful truth has come out, and I am sure you will feel the way I do, that this shame must not fall on our family . . .'

Yes, she was crying now, and I had to pause while she pressed a handkerchief to her eyes and finally got sufficient control of herself to be able to go on, though in a broken voice interrupted now and then by further outbursts of tears . . . 'All these years I have begged you to send for us, but I no longer do that. I ask that you should send for Lily. Let her go alone and I promise I will never ask for anything else after this. Please, dear relatives, save her from this terrible calamity. I do not want to sit shiveh for my daughter. I do not want her to die . . .'

And now she could not say another word. She was utterly bereft of speech and gave way completely to her tears, while the rest of us looked on helplessly, not knowing what to say or do.

Chapter Eleven

Well, now, there is just this one more summer to talk about, because it was to be the last I was to spend in England and at the start it did not seem very different from all the other summers before it, warm and sunny at times, rainy at other times and all of us growing up.

One thing I do recall in particular – the Forshaws stopped playing their gramophone for us. On those lovely evenings when everybody sat outdoors watching the sun set behind the square brick tower of the India Mill, they no longer left their door open so that we could all hear the music. They kept their door closed and they themselves never sat outside.

Everybody knew, of course. There were no secrets on our street. The women who came into my mother's shop waited for her to talk to them about the thing they all knew, about my sister and Arthur Forshaw. But she never did, and there was such misery on her face they all felt sorry for her and there were often long, uncomfortable silences in the gatherings.

I think there was a watchful air throughout the whole street. They knew on the other side, of course. The distance between us may have widened considerably then.

Suspicious eyes were cast from one side to the other, without much being said. There were other girls like my sister who had now reached marriageable age, and boys too, and parents were worried. The Harrises still had three girls not married, all of them languishing during evenings in the parlour, waiting for a suitor to knock on the door.

And Mrs Jacobs sniffed and said, 'They'll wait. My son is not good enough for them. So they'll wait.'

Across the streets the noises from Mrs Turnbull's back room grew louder. The new crop of boarders she had taken in after the war ended was not much of an improvement on the previous bunch. One of them was a little chimney sweep named Willie Cheevers, his thin, pointed rabbit's face and hands perpetually blackened from his work. He came out of the sweet shop one Saturday night seeking trouble, a mug of beer in his hands, his teeth showing in a malicious grin, his feet unsteady. He tottered over to the kerb and fixed his attention on Mr Harris, who sat beside his wife wearing a bowler hat, reading a Jewish newspaper in the fading twilight, and began the mocking litany with which we were all so familiar. 'Eh, Ikey Moses, you vant to buy a vatch? If you vant to buy mine vatch, then buy it, and if you don't then take your snotty nose avay from mine vindow.'

The boys in the back room, hearing him, roared with laughter. Mr Turnbull, sitting behind him on the stiff-backed chair placed up against the wall, gaped blankly at his back, with a thin thread of saliva hanging from the lower lip. The two Harrises pretended not to hear, and Mr Harris kept his bearded face buried in the newspaper. The rest of us on our side also pretended not to hear.

But Willie was bent on mischief that night and he kept up his jeering, taunting jibes, going so far as to approach the

Harrises still closer and into what might have been considered border territory. Then suddenly I saw someone leap out of one of our houses. It was Zalmon, but a grown-up Zalmon, bigger than ever and burly, now a presser in one of the tailoring shops. I don't think anyone was more startled than Willie himself. Zalmon seized him with both hands and lifted him off the ground as if he were a rag doll, shook him violently, then hurled him to the ground.

It was the first time anything like this had happened on our street. Everybody watched with bated breath. Not a word was spoken by anyone. People simply watched and all you heard while it happened were the faint cries of some children playing at the lower end of the street.

Willie himself said nothing. His eyes were fixed fearfully on Zalmon as he picked himself up and slunk back into the shop, and Zalmon waited until he had gone inside, then with a shrug of his broad shoulders went back to his own house.

It came at last. I mean, the letter from America in answer to my mother's. Perhaps it came sooner than we had expected, sooner at any rate than most of the answers to her letters. I was home when the postman knocked on the door and ran to answer the knock. As soon as I saw the letter I knew where it was from and dashed into the house shouting, 'It's from America.'

I saw my mother draw in a deep breath and her voice shook a little as she said, 'Open it and read it.' But then she snatched it from me and opened it herself, took out the letter and looked inside the envelope, and the disappointment that came into her face was deep and bitter. 'There is no ticket,' she muttered.

But I read it for her anyway.

'My dear daughter-in-law,' I read, 'just a few lines to let you know that we are all well and hoping to hear the same from you . . .'

It was the usual polite, conventional opening, what we ourselves had written, but suddenly the tone changed, startling me as I read. 'Now, what the hell is this you write to me about your daughter wanting to marry a shaigets from across the street? Don't you have a broom in the house? Couldn't you take it and beat her until every bone in her body is broken? And where is the father while all this has been going on? But I shouldn't ask. I know where the father is. Never mind him. You say you want to send her off to America and get her away from the shaigets, and you want me to send you a ticket for her to come here . . .'

There was a new paragraph This was a well-written letter in fine handwriting. She herself could not have written it, but had doubtless dictated it to Uncle Sol, the youngest of the family and the one they always referred to proudly as 'the high school graduate'.

'In case you don't know it,' I went on, 'I am not the Bank of America, nor did I bring the crown jewels with me when I left England. I don't have a mansion and a staff of servants or a limousine to go to the grocery in. When we ride anywhere it's on a trolley car, and we have to take our own garbage out like everybody else. You might also want to know that you are not the only one who comes to me for money. When Abe needed a new set of false teeth, guess who he came to for the money? When Morris couldn't meet the payments on his furniture, guess again who he came to for the money? When Barney got a rupture, I'll give you another guess who he asked for the money for the operation. On top of all that Dora has just got herself engaged to some schlemiel who hasn't got an extra pair of socks to his name and still she wants a big wedding in a hotel. And now you want money to send your daughter to America.'

I paused and looked at my mother, and wished I didn't have to read further. Her face had taken on that sad, hopeless look that I had seen so often before. However, I had to continue until it was all over.

'I should say to you what I have decided to say to all the others who come to me for money from now on. Go to blazes. I have myself to look out for. But I've got to admit your situation is serious and something has to be done. I know I would not like the disgrace of having a Christian in the family. So for this reason I have decided to do something for you. I am going to arrange to have a steamship ticket sent to you. I will not give you the money to buy one in England because your husband would only drink it up. I will have an agent here make arrangements with an agent in Manchester, and you will receive the ticket from him. But when Lily comes here she will get a job and pay me back each week until the ticket is fully paid for. And you are not to bother me again with your troubles. As I said before, I do not own the Bank of America . . .'

But by then a cry of joy had escaped my mother and she had thrown her hands heavenwards to give thanks to God, much as Mrs Jacobs had once done in her shop. I remember also how she rushed to tell everybody in her shop that afternoon and the clamour of joy that broke out among the women. How flushed and excited and almost delirious with happiness my mother was all afternoon, and how her voice shook when Lily came home and she told her the news, news she was certain would make anyone share her joy. 'You're going to America,' she said. 'Just think, to America.' It would make up for everything, she thought.

But Lily said nothing. She listened in silence and said absolutely nothing, and went upstairs, and I heard the slow tread of her footsteps.

Later on my mother called up to her to come down for dinner. Lily called back, saying she wasn't hungry. I suppose my mother was disappointed. Perhaps she'd half hoped that Lily would forget everything in the excitement of going to America. But evidently she had not. And her worry increased as Lily remained silent in the days that followed. She said not a word about going to America, and when the topic came up she would leave the room and go upstairs.

Then the ticket finally arrived and this was an occasion for another outburst of joy on my mother's part. Here it was, actually, the thing she had been waiting for all her life, a large pink-coloured slip of paper that would give Lily passage on a steamship to Quebec, thence to Chicago by rail, together with a letter and instructions from the agent in Manchester. She showed it to Lily as soon as she came home from work that night. Her own face shining, she thrust it into Lily's hands, made her take hold of it and look at it, feel it, stroke it, as she had done. 'Now you're practically on your way to America,' she exulted.

But it was the same as before. Silence. Lily obediently took hold of the ticket and looked at it, but said nothing. Her face was stony.

My mother grew a little angry and impatient. 'Aren't you glad that you're going to America?' she said. 'My God, any other girl would give her right arm to be going. And you – you don't seem to care at all.'

Then suddenly tears came to Lily's eyes and she burst out, 'I don't want to go to America.'

My mother looked at her aghast. Perhaps this was what she had feared all along, but she refused to believe it. 'What are you saying?' she cried. 'You don't know what you're talking about. You don't want to go! Why?'

'I don't want to go. I want to stay here.'

'Why?' She knew, but she was asking the question just the same. 'Why don't you want to go?' And then she said angrily, 'Is it because of him?'

'Yes.' Well, she had asked and she had got her answer. It was out now, the thing they had both been trying to avoid all these weeks. It was quite fully out in the open and Lily made no attempt to hide it any longer. 'It is because of him. I love Arthur. I want to be with him.'

It shocked my mother, even though she had known all along. 'You're mad,' she said. 'You can't marry a goy, you know that. You're going to America, that's what you're going to do.'

'No, I'm not,' Lily cried, 'I'm not going.'

She turned and ran out of the room towards the stairs, and in doing so she almost bumped into my father, who had come in unnoticed by all of us. He turned to watch Lily run out, then turned back to my mother and muttered, 'What the bloody hell's going on here?'

He may have heard part of the argument as he was coming in through the lobby. He already knew that Lily was going to America, thanks to his mother's assistance, and he had said very little about that. But he did not know anything about the real reason for her going. My mother had never discussed it with him; nor had anyone else. But now, in her agony, she was ready to turn to anyone for help, so she told him the story and as he listened we saw his face darken. With anything else, with any other problem my mother might have had, talking with him would have been utterly useless. He would have been completely indifferent, perhaps he would have sneered contempt. But with this it was different. I watched – we all watched – as the rage took possession of him, the colour in his face darkening even more. Then suddenly, before she was hardly done with her story, he whirled and started for the door.

My mother seized hold of him, alarmed. 'Where are you going?' she asked.

'I'm going to talk to the goy across the street,' he hissed. 'I'm going to ask him where the bloody 'ell does he come off going with my daughter – with any Jewish girl.'

'No,' my mother cried. 'No, you mustn't. There'll be a fight and that'll make it still worse.'

'Get the bloody 'ell out of my way.'

'No, no!'

For once, for once in her life, she fought him, wrestled with him, and for once he gave in to her. But he was not done with it. If he could not talk to the goy, then he could talk to his daughter. He went to the foot of the stairs and called up. 'You,' he shouted. He never called any of us by name, only in this fashion 'You, come down here.'

Lily must have been afraid. Who wouldn't, summoned by that hoarse, enraged voice? She came slowly down the stairs. As soon as she reached the bottom stair his hand lashed out and he struck her across the face. It was like the sound of a whip. Lily staggered back and put a hand to her face. But she still had not uttered a sound. She stood there facing him and his hand lashed out again and again. In all these years, despite his violent temper and rages, he had never struck one of us before. We watched petrified, my mother wringing her hands and letting out cries as if she were the one being struck.

All through the entire thing Lily remained silent, and when at last it was over she turned and ran up the stairs, and the rest of us went back into the kitchen, and my father ate his dinner not saying another word himself, and when he had done he rushed for his coat hanging behind the scullery door and strode out still putting it on, the door banging shut after him.

Now the days that followed were strange, for Lily remained silent through all of them while she seemed to submit to the things that had to be done, to getting her photograph taken for the passport, to filling out various forms, to having clothes made for her and standing still while my mother fitted them on her. She hardly said a word to any of us, to anybody at all. She went to work in the morning and came home at night looking as tired as usual. She hardly ate anything during this time and indeed she looked ill, and my mother worried sometimes about it and talked about it with the women in the shop, and they all reassured her. Jeumy would be all right once she got to America.

That was the answer, of course, and my mother tried not to worry. Once, when Lily came home and said she could not eat, but just went upstairs to lie down, my mother sent me up after her with a tray of food, some hot soup and a plate of meat and potatoes that I carried carefully up the stairs.

I knocked on the door, and when Lily saw the tray she frowned and said, 'Put it on the dresser. I'll eat later.' She was not lying down. She was sitting on the edge of the bed and was sorting through some books that she kept in a cardboard box, her bookcase. ''arry,' she said, 'I'm going to give these books to you when I leave.'

I was delighted, of course. I'd never had any books of my own other than those I got out of the library. There was one with gold leaf on the edges. 'Can I have that one too?' I asked.

She shook her head, smiling. 'No, not that one,' she said. 'I'm taking that with me.' It was the book of poems that Arthur had brought her when he came back from the war. She picked it up and fingered it a little, then started to cry.

I stood there awkwardly, not knowing what to say or do. Then I heard a knocking at the front door below. There was the sound of footsteps in the lobby going to answer the knock and a few moments later my mother called up, a little excited, 'Lily, you have a visitor. It's the rabbi. He wants to see you.'

I think it was just about a week before Lily was to leave. All sorts of people, even some from up the park, had been coming to say goodbye to her. Lily frowned at my mother's message and immediately called back, 'I can't see him now.'

'Please, Lily,' my mother begged, and we heard the rabbi's voice saying apologetically he'd come another time, and my mother saying, 'No, no . . .', then begging Lily once more and adding, 'He's brought you something. He can go upstairs and give it to you. You don't have to come down.'

'All right,' Lily said, finally, reluctantly. 'Let him come up then.'

He came very quickly with light footsteps. I wanted to go, but Lily grasped my wrist and said fiercely, 'No, stay here, 'arry.'

The rabbi entered the room awkwardly, then saw me and looked as if he wished I was not there. But he smiled and said hello to me too, and to Lily he said, 'I'm sorry you're not well.'

'It's nothing much,' Lily said, 'I'll be all right.'

'I hope so,' he said. 'You don't want anything to interfere with your journey and you have a long one ahead of you.' She had not asked him to sit down, though there was not even a chair in the tiny room and the only place he could have sat was on the edge of the bed next to her. I myself had been standing all this time. The rabbi too stood, holding a small wrapped package in his hand. 'I was sorry when I heard you were leaving us for America,' he continued. 'America is a wonderful country, but for selfish reasons I wished you could stay here.'

Lily said nothing. He knew, of course, why she was being sent to America. That information would have been given him by his landlady and perhaps a great many other people. But I doubt if Lily felt any embarrassment over it.

'Yes, I'm very sorry,' the rabbi went on. 'You and I don't agree on a great many things, and yet we have one thing in common that would eventually have overcome all our differences. We are both Jews.' He smiled.

Lily still didn't say anything. She was sitting with her head bent slightly towards the floor, wishing, I suppose, that he would soon leave.

The rabbi continued, smiling a little, 'Although I must admit I enjoyed our little arguments. There's something very refreshing about a good argument over a vital issue. I sometimes get very tired of people agreeing with me all the time, and the trivial things that occupy their minds. It's just a pity that you and I couldn't have got to know each other a little more. There were so many things we could have talked about.'

Lily spoke at last in a very low voice. 'I don't think we could ever have found anything to agree on.'

'Except the one thing I reminded you of before,' the rabbi said. 'And that is the most important of all things.'

'Not to me,' muttered Lily, still not looking at him.

'Ah, but it will be,' the rabbi assured her. 'Some day you will find that out. There is nothing more important for any of us.'

Lily refused to talk further and the rabbi handed her his package. 'I brought this for you to read on your journey. It is a book. I know you like books. This one is a very famous book. I hope you will read it.' Then he held out a hand. 'And I will say goodbye to you now, and wish you a safe journey and a good, happy life in America.'

Lily took his hand and he held it for a moment, then turned and walked out of the room, and both Lily and I were silent as we listened to his footsteps going down the stairs, and waited a bit longer while we heard our mother escort him to the door, then close it after him.

Lily unwrapped her package. Inside was the book. It had a black leather cover and on it in gold lettering were inscribed the words 'Old Testament'.

Well, now, there was that Sunday when Lily put on her white dress.

It was just two days before she was to leave for America. My father would take her to Liverpool. After all, this was a man's job, a father's job, and he was taking his responsibilities seriously for once. My mother could have had no quarrel with that, though she would have liked to go to Liverpool herself to see Lily get on the boat and sail off to America. What a thrill that would have given her! But there was not enough money to take her to Liverpool too.

But she was busy packing for Lily and that in itself gave her vicarious pleasure. She loved every moment of it. Somehow, she had managed to get hold of an old metal trunk and was putting Lily's things into it, all her clothes, all her belongings, including her books, except the ones she was leaving for me. She would have left the rabbi's book behind if she'd had her way, but my mother insisted on putting that in too. She was proud of the gift the rabbi had given her daughter; she had spoken of it to everyone.

And then they came to the white dress, the one my mother had made for her when she had won her scholarship and was to have gone to the Grammar School. She had never worn it, but it was still in good condition, and my mother saw no reason why it should not go in with the other clothes. 'Who knows,' she said a bit sadly, 'you might still wear it for some special occasion.'

Lily was staring at the dress. Suddenly she said, 'Don't pack it now. I want to wear it today.'

'Today?' my mother said, amazed. 'But what for? You're not going anywhere special.'

'I want to wear it,' Lily said stubbornly.

'If it still fits you,' my mother said, giving in.

'It will fit,' Lily said.

Yes, it did, and it looked as beautiful on her as it did that memorable day when she first put it on, when my father had dragged her by the hair to the workshop. All of us, except Rose, who turned away contemptuously, admired her in it when she came downstairs in the white dress, her long dark hair hanging down to her waist, much the same as that day years before.

'Take good care of it,' my mother said. 'They'll want to see you in it when you get to America. You must put it on for them as soon as you get there.' Then she asked, 'Where are you going?'

'Just for a walk,' Lily said. 'Would you like to come with me, 'arry?'

'Yis,' I said promptly.

I remember as we were leaving, my mother called out to us, 'Don't be long, Lily. You've still got a lot of packing to do.' Then, just as we reached the door, she added, 'Better take an umbrella along. It might rain and you don't want to spoil your dress.'

Lily pretended not to have heard this last. So did I. We both hated to carry umbrellas. Besides, Lily seemed in a hurry.

It was not the most perfect of days. Warm enough, yes, but with clouds in the sky, and the sun peeking in and out of them. Yet we enjoyed walking, and people all along the street standing in their doorways called out their admiration for Lily's white dress and how lovely she looked in it.

We had soon left the street behind and I saw we were heading for Mersey Square. 'Where are we going?' I asked.

'You'll soon find out,' Lily said, a bit mysteriously.

It was not until we boarded a tram that I discovered we were heading for the country and the Seventeen Windows. I was a bit startled. I hadn't forgotten our last trip there, and my mother's discovery and the row that followed. Lily had not been there since.

Nor did I think she'd ever go again, nor see Arthur again, and so far as I knew she had not seen him since that day.

'Won't Mam be angry?' I said.

Lily was silent for a bit, as if mulling over my question. I waited a moment before asking her again, 'You won't want me to tell her, will you?'

For a little while longer she still seemed to be thinking. Then she said, 'Yes, you'll tell her, if you want.'

Her answer struck me as strange and I puzzled over it for some time before saying, 'Will Arthur be there?'

'Yes.'

'I can't tell Mam about him,' I said.

'Perhaps you will.'

This too was strange and left me more puzzled than ever. But I didn't say anything further. Lily's whole manner seemed strange, for that matter. She did not chatter, as she usually did when we were on these outings, and laugh with excitement over the anticipation of meeting Arthur. She was silent and lost in her thoughts all the way, and when we got off the tram and started walking through the countryside she seemed nervous and kept glancing back, as if afraid someone was following us.

The sun kept up its game of hide and seek through the clouds, and once indeed there was a light shower of rain and it pattered softly on the leaves as we hurried through some woods. But it soon stopped and a fresh smell rose up from the earth.

Lily drank it in deeply. 'I love this place,' she said suddenly, breaking the silence between us. 'Do you?'

'Yis,' I said.

'Wouldn't it be nice to live here all the time?' she said. 'To be able to step out of your house and smell all the flowers and trees.'

'Yis,' I said.

'Perhaps some day I will,' she said confidently, 'And you'll come to visit me and stay over, and we'll have long walks through the woods and fields.'

'But you're going to America,' I reminded her.

'Yes,' she said, and that was all, and she became silent again, and remained silent until we had climbed the hill and came to the top where we could see the Seventeen Windows below.

Then Lily stopped and I looked at her, wondering. She had become nervous again and was hesitating, as if she did not want to go further. She put a hand to her heart and I could see an expression of pain on her face.

'What's the matter,' I asked anxiously, 'do you have the pain?'

She'd had it before in the house, and my mother had asked the same question and sometimes made her lie down on the sofa. She dropped her hand and took hold of mine, and clutched it hard and I could feel its coldness. 'It's nothing,' she said. 'I've just got to stop for a while.'

Her face had gone pale too, and we both stood there with her hand holding mine tightly. But after a moment she seemed to recover and we went on.

Just as we neared the bottom of the hill Mrs Fogg came forward to greet us. She was wearing her usual garb, a long, blue-striped dress that was almost like the striped petticoats the women who worked in the mills wore, a white apron over it and a white bonnet that was fastened under her chin. She was smiling and showing her large buck teeth, and as she approached she reached forward with both hands to touch Lily. She held her off a moment and said, 'How beautiful you look. Just the way a . . .'

But Lily stopped her, putting a finger to her lips and looking at me.

'Doesn't he know?' Mrs Fogg whispered.

'Not yet.'

'Perhaps he should.'

'Later.'

This talk went on between them in whispers, but I heard it all right and couldn't help feeling puzzled by it. We went on, Mrs Fogg walking beside us with her long, masculine stride and chatting away in her hoarse voice about the weather, her flowers, various things which I am sure were designed to take my mind off anything I had heard.

When we came to the inn there seemed to be more people about than usual and they all gathered around Lily, embracing her and saying things that I did not quite understand. It seemed to me that something very unusual was about to happen, whether I was supposed to know about it or not. Then Arthur appeared, emerging from the inn, and I thought he was dressed unusually well, wearing white flannel trousers and a dark-blue blazer, a cricket shirt with a school tie, looking very handsome and tall, and smiling.

He went straight towards Lily and the others drew back a little to make way for him. He took Lily in his arms and kissed her. It was a long kiss and everybody watched. I watched too, feeling embarrassed. Arthur had never kissed her like that before in public. But for once neither one of them seemed restrained.

Someone said, 'That'll do for the while, Arthur,' and everybody laughed and the couple broke apart.

Then Arthur came over to me and put his arms round me and said, 'We're going to be brothers, 'arry.'

'He doesn't understand,' Lily said.

'Haven't you told him yet?'

'No, but I'm going to now. 'arry, come with me.' She led me away from the group and over to one of the tables on the lawn, and we sat down opposite one another. She leaned across towards me and spoke earnestly, saying, ''arry, you must try to understand what this is all about. I'm going to marry Arthur this afternoon. I know Mam doesn't want me to marry him because he's a Christian and I know this is going to hurt her very badly. But I can't help it, 'arry. I love Arthur and he loves me, and this is all that matters to us. I brought you here because I wanted one of my family, at least, to be here at my wedding, and when you go home I want you to tell Mam you saw me getting married and how happy I am. You'll be going home alone, because Arthur and I will be staying here tonight. Later on we'll be going to Manchester to live, and I'll be working there and Arthur will be finishing his studies at the university. But we will be coming back to the street tomorrow to get our things and I'll talk to Mam then, and maybe she won't feel so badly about it all. Do you understand me?'

I nodded. But I was a little bewildered by it all and there was something else that hadn't been explained. 'But aren't you going to America?' I asked.

'No.' She shook her head. 'Mam will know that I'm not going.'

Arthur came strolling over to us. 'Everything all right?' he asked.

Lily nodded, ''arry understands. It's a bit of a shock to him, I think, but he'll get used to it and so will they all.'

'I'm sure of that,' said Arthur. 'Can we get married now? They're all waiting for us.'

Lily rose, and I got up with her and followed them. The wedding ceremony took place there on the lawn in front of the Seventeen Windows. There was nothing religious about this ceremony. The man who performed it was an official of the Socialist Party, a short, stocky man with red hair, and the words he spoke had very little resemblance to those of any ordinary marriage ceremony. Arthur and Lily stood in front of him, holding each other's hands, and I must say they made a very lovely couple, Arthur so tall and handsome in his white flannels and Lily beautiful in her white dress and her dark hair flowing behind, and everybody gathered around them silent and still; and in the background, as the red-haired man intoned the words that were to unite the couple, were the sweet, faint sound of birds coming from the trees and there was a rich scent of flowers all around us.

There was something very beautiful in the setting that has always stuck in my mind, and when it was over the silence was suddenly broken as everybody swarmed around the couple to congratulate them, and then they all burst into the 'Internationale', singing it in loud, hearty voices and standing erect, and then there was much laughter and Mrs Fogg's waitresses began bringing out refreshments and drinks, and then it started to rain, and there were little screams and shouts as everybody rushed inside to keep from getting drenched.

It was a heavier rain than before, but it didn't dampen spirits. Inside, everybody crowded around the tables that had been pushed together to make one long one. Lily and Arthur made me sit right near them, and Lily made sure that I had plenty of Mrs Fogg's watercress and cucumber sandwiches that were being served, along with her custard tarts and scones and pots of tea and glasses of champagne and stout and porter. I had never eaten so much in my life, and my face grew red and swollen with contentment, and all around me there was talk and laughter and singing, the singing being mostly revolutionary songs, and one cynical, irreverent piece that I have always remembered:

> Long-haired preachers come out every night,
> Try to tell us what's wrong and what's right.
> When you ask them for something to eat,
> They will answer in voices so sweet,
> You'll get pie in the sky when you die.

I heard that sung by the red-haired man who had married Lily and Arthur, with all the others joining in towards the end, accompanied by much table thumping.

It was over at last, for me, that is. Lily thought I should start back before it got dark. Arthur said he would walk me part of the way to the tram and we set off together, after Lily had kissed me and hugged me and wept a little, and told me again to tell Mam how happy she was, and she would see her tomorrow and talk to her then about everything, and not to feel too badly about her not going to America.

Arthur had to pull me away from her, otherwise she might have held me still longer. I had to trot to keep up with his long stride. He seemed anxious to get away from the inn, but I think it was chiefly because he had something to say to me. The rain had stopped and the sun had come out again, though it was low in the sky. You could hear the dripping of the trees as we climbed up the hill and a fresh, sweet smell rose up from the grass.

Arthur began talking when we were halfway up the hill. ''arry,' he said, 'I can't tell you how happy I feel today, how good everything seems and how right. But I know it must be very puzzling and strange to you. Especially to a lad coming from our street where there's those two sides and each side is supposed to be different from the other. That's how we grew up on that street, isn't it? That's how it used to be with me when I was your age. But it's all wrong. It isn't like that at all. We're not very different from one another, not different at all, in fact. We're all just human beings with the same needs, the same desires, the same feelings as one another. It's all a lie about us being different. It's something they cooked up so we'd be fighting one another instead of them, the ones who keep us down and make their fortunes off our labour, the same ones who send us off to war when they get to fighting among themselves over the spoils. You'll find that out some day, they'll be calling on you to go to war for them, you can be sure of that, because there's going to be lots more wars in the future.

'I got in one myself, and I saw men getting killed and wounded and crippled and all that, and I must have killed a lot myself, and I'm just sick every time I think of it. Because we were fighting one another instead of those who'd sent us out there. Oh, they're clever, those capitalists. It's hard to beat them at their game. They've got us fooled with words like patriotism and duty and honour, and they've got us divided up into classes and religions so that one figures he's better than the other.

'But it'll all change, 'arry. Believe me, it will. People get smarter. The human brain has a potential for development. Some day it will grow big enough so that everybody will see and understand the truth, and then they won't act like a bunch of sheep. Then that wall that separates the two sides of our street will crumble, just like the wall of Jericho. Maybe Lily and I gave it a little push today. But one day you'll hear a trumpet blow and then it will all be gone. Oh yes, 'arry, we're going to have a better world. Things won't always be the way they are now. There'll be good times for all of us, not just a few. Mind what I say now. I promise you there'll be a better world than the one we're living in today . . .'

He was drunk. He had one arm round my shoulders and leaned down to speak to me, and I could smell the champagne on his breath as he spoke. But he was drunk with happiness as well. I had never heard him speak so much and so rapidly without a pause, and I myself never said a word all the time.

Before we knew it we were at the tram stop. Arthur came to with surprise. 'I never intended to go this far,' he said. 'But I did and now I'll say so long and you can get on the tram, and don't you be afeared, 'arry, of what you have to say when you get home. Your mother will listen to you. She's a good woman, your mother. I like her a lot and respect her, and you can tell her that if you want.'

I sat on the top deck of the tram going home. It started to rain again and I was all alone up there, and when the conductor came up to get my penny he grumbled and asked if the bottom deck wasn't good enough for me and muttered something under his breath that I managed to catch. It was, 'You Jews are all alike.'

It was still raining when I got off the tram at Mersey Square and by the time I got home I was soaked. My mother looked at me in consternation and said, 'I told you to take an umbrella, but you didn't listen. Where's Lily?'

Then I told her.

Death was darkness. I had learned that already in the one or two funerals I had attended on our street, one during the war when Sam Harris was killed and the Harrises sat shiveh and my mother took me in there to sit with them. So I already knew. The window shades were all drawn down. The mirrors that might have caught a gleam of light from somewhere were covered over with dark cloth. Everybody sat in the darkness in their stockinged feet.

And now I was sitting in my own house in my stockinged feet in the darkness, with my two brothers sitting beside me, and Rose sitting next to them holding my baby brother, and my mother and father on the other side of her, and other people – neighbours – sitting about the room, some on upturned orange and apple crates, because there were not enough chairs. And everybody was very still, my mother especially. How terribly silent she was, with her head bent towards the floor. I kept looking at her, wishing she would move or say something.

My father, sitting beside her, seemed fidgety and uneasy. He was not accustomed to sitting in a room with his family and with all the other people from our street around us. He had not been allowed to shave, because that was part of the ritual of mourning too, and he kept running a hand over the bristle on his chin and it made a slight grating noise.

The neighbours who came in had all glanced at him first, some seeing him in the house for the first time. All of them were a little afraid of him, only dared glance sideways at him and quickly averted their eyes. Yet he would have been glad if someone had spoken to him; it would have relieved some of his tension and for once he might have been polite.

People kept coming and going softly, and in the darkness you hardly knew who it was. I recognised old Mrs Harris, though, with her wig plastered tightly over her forehead and a shawl over her head. I saw Mrs Mittleman too, and Mrs Jacobs, the latter weeping and rocking to and fro as she sat down, though it was altogether possible her tears were false and inwardly she was exulting, the way she had done when the discovery came about Sarah and Freddy. 'My son is not good enough,' she would be saying to herself. 'A goy they consider better.'

Fanny Cohen sat straight in her chair, her face stolid. She had come alone, without any of her children. She had left her recently born baby in the care of the older ones. She had been sitting here all day, loyal to my mother, refusing to leave her side. She had tried speaking to her, but my mother had not answered her either. She spoke to no one, not even to us, not even to the baby, who tried to climb up on her lap and had cried when she ignored him. Rose had then picked him up in her arms and cradled him in her lap. How strange she too had become in this moment, so suddenly passionately devoted to the child, a mother all at once. She clutched him tightly, rocked him, whispered to him, kissed him. I had never seen any such emotion come from her before. I stared at her.

But mostly my eyes were fixed on my mother with anxiety, and I wished she would say something, do something other than just sit there, like someone who had died herself. Perhaps this fear struck me that she too would die if she continued to sit there like that.

It had begun after her shriek, that fearful, penetrating shriek that she had let out after I had told her yesterday. It struck terror in me, in everybody in the house, even my father who was there at the time, and everybody on the street, for they all heard it. On both sides people came to their doors to see what had happened, heads stuck out of windows, women came rushing to our house, surrounding my mother, who was tearing at herself with her hands. I remembered in my shock seeing Mrs Harris do the same thing out on the street years earlier.

Now it was happening to my mother, always so gentle, so quiet, and transformed suddenly into a madwoman who was trying to destroy herself. They forced her hands behind her back so that she could not harm herself further. Gradually her struggles had ceased and she had lapsed into this deadness.

The day wore on. It was a Monday and I could hear children coming home from school. I heard their shouts and cries and laughter, and I felt envious of them. I wished I could be with them, not sitting here in the darkness mourning for my sister Lily, who was supposed to have died because she had married a Christian.

As soon as they heard the children coming home, many of the mothers who were sitting with us got up and left, and for a while there were very few in the room other than ourselves and it was lonelier than ever. But now some new ones were coming in. The front door had been left open and the newcomers walked directly into the lobby, and we heard their footsteps as they approached, then the two entered the room, and all our eyes went towards them and remained fixed there.

It was Lily and behind her was Arthur. He was hesitating and obviously afraid to come in, so he hung back a little. But Lily herself came straight towards my mother.

She saw the condition my mother was in, with her head sunk on her chest, and became distraught immediately, fell on her knees before her, took both my mother's hands in hers and cried, 'Mama, what's the matter? Are you ill? Look at me, Mama. This is Lily, your daughter. I'm not dead, Mama. I'm not dead. Look at me, Mama. Talk to me. Say something. Oh Mama, Mama.'

She burst into tears. She might just as well have been talking to a wall for all the response she got. There was nothing showing on my mother's face, no sign of recognition, no acknowledgement of the voice, and Lily kept pleading with her, begging her to listen, to say something, and we all sat there numbly, too frightened and too shocked ourselves to be able to do or say anything.

Lily grew still more distraught, and Arthur came up to her and put his hands on her shoulders and tried to get her to leave. 'Your mother's ill, Lily,' he said. 'We'll come another time. Let her alone now.'

But Lily refused. She shook his hands off. Her eyes would

not leave my mother, nor would she give up trying to reach her. 'Mama, Mama, look at me,' she kept repeating. 'I am Lily, your daughter. I'm not dead, Mama. I'm alive. I'm married; Arthur is my husband now. We love each other. We're both very happy. I came here to tell you that. I want you to be happy too. Mama, lift up your head and speak to me. Please, please. Speak to me. I love you too, Mama. I don't want you to be angry with me. Oh, Mama, please, please . . .'

There was no response from my mother. Nothing at all. It was as if she had not heard her. She remained silent, with her head bent. Lily kept on pleading until Arthur finally bent down and lifted her up and led her away, and I could hear Lily still crying as they went out into the street and the door had closed after them.

Chapter Twelve

What followed after that forms a sad chapter in the history of our street. It was very much like the time they had discovered the romance between Sarah Harris and Freddy Gordon, with all the Jewish people fearful that the same thing could happen to their daughters. Only this time it was much worse, because it had happened again and with a marriage – God should only forgive! And this time, too, the Christians may have been just as shocked and as fearful for their own daughters and sons.

A distinct coolness sprang up between the two sides. Not even Mrs Humberstone came to cross over and chat. But the worst part happened on Friday when I was sent out to call Mrs Green to come and stoke our fire and take off a pot. I was innocent enough as I stepped out on to the pavement and called across the street, 'Oh, Mrs Green, will you come and do the fire?'

The door was closed, and I waited for several moments and was about to call again, thinking she had not heard, when it suddenly burst open and she came running out, her hair awry and scattered about her shoulders, her face showing she had been drinking a lot. However, she did not cross. She stopped at the kerb and yelled across at me, 'You can do your own stinking fire. If we're not good enough for you, then you're not good enough for us. Yah, you bloody Jews. Who killed Christ, anyway?'

I ran back into the house to tell my mother and her face whitened with anger. She seemed for a moment as if she might go out and answer Mrs Green, but she halted. This was the Shabbes, no time for a fight. But what to do? We would have to go scouring around among the other fire goys and goyahs and see if one of them would come. But what if they all felt the same way about us?

In the midst of our dilemma there came a knock at the door. I went to answer it. Outside stood Mrs Forshaw, smiling a little. ''arry,' she said softly, 'go and ask your mother if she'd like me to come in and do your fire for you. Tell her I'll be glad to do it.'

I did as she asked. I think my mother was a bit stunned when I told her. My brothers and sister who were in the house at the time looked at me in astonishment too. It was the last thing in the world we could have expected. We had given no thought as to how the Forshaws might have felt about all this, but if it had occurred to us we would have assumed they didn't approve of the marriage any more than my family did.

But here she was as friendly as could be and offering to help us out of our predicament, Accepting her offer, however, would have meant we were returning her friendliness and all that went with it – accepting the marriage too.

But if we didn't at least let her take care of the fire, it could have led to an even worse sin. We would have had to do the fire ourselves. And the pot of chicken was boiling furiously and threatened to spill over unless it was taken off the fire quickly. What to do must have presented an agonising choice to my mother.

At last she decided, 'I have to go out in the yard to hang out some washing,' she said. 'Tell her to come in and take the pot off the fire and let her put some more coal on and stoke it up a bit. And don't forget to give her the penny. Let me know when she's gone.'

She would at least be out of the room while Mrs Forshaw was here and avoid having to talk to her. I went back to the door and let her in. She smiled pleasantly at everyone, and asked about the baby and how he was doing, and said nothing about my mother's absence. She did her work quickly and efficiently, placing the boiling pot of chicken carefully on the hearth, then briskly shovelling coal on to the fire and stirring it up with the poker. As if she had done this many times before.

But when it came time to take the penny, proffered by my sister, she refused, saying, 'Thank you so much, but I'm only too glad to be able to do this for you.'

She made no mention at all of my mother and went out swiftly, and when we called in my mother from the yard and told her and gave her the penny back, she was silent and did not utter a word about it, and I wondered what she was thinking.

I told Lily and Arthur about it when I went to see them in their new home in Marple. They had originally planned to move to Manchester, where Arthur was to have studied law at the university, and Lily would have gone to work in one of the tailoring shops there. But the plan had been altered for a reason I did not know then but would find out soon enough. Arthur instead had become a teacher in the Marple school and they had rented a quaint old cottage with a thatched roof that was not far from the Seventeen Windows. In fact, it was Mrs Fogg who had arranged the whole thing for them, finding both the cottage and the teaching job for Arthur.

Since I had been to the Seventeen Windows several times already, I knew the countryside well and could find my way there easily. I was eleven now going on twelve and could go by myself. My mother always knew where I was going, and did not object. She simply said nothing and, since Lily's name was never to be mentioned in the house, all I said was that I was going to take a walk to Marple, though of course it was understood whom I was going to see there.

I liked the little cottage with its narrow doors and low ceiling and the cosy fire that was always burning with a kettle singing on it, and almost as soon as I got in there would be tea and crumpets with jam for me and for them too, with all three of us sitting at the table in front of the fire with its dancing flames lighting our faces. I sometimes wished I could live there with them. It was so quiet and pleasant and cheerful – although Lily's face was always touched with anxiety as she asked me the same question when I first came in: 'How is Mam?'

What could I say in reply? I knew how Mam was really. I saw her crying sometimes when she thought nobody was watching her. She still grieved over her daughter who was supposed to be dead. But I did not tell that to Lily, because I knew she was heartbroken herself and probably cried too sometimes.

When I came I would rather have avoided talking about the street at all, especially our own family, but this time I found myself telling them of the Friday-night night episode with Mrs Green, and how Arthur's mother had come to our rescue. I had thought perhaps there was a touch of humour in the whole situation and they might get a laugh out of it. But it had just the opposite effect.

They were both silent and glum for a moment, sitting there and staring into the fire, then Arthur suddenly burst out with, 'Damn!'

I saw Lily place a hand over his, as if to restrain him. But he broke away from her, rose abruptly, and began to pace up and down on the wide floorboards. He was furious. 'Damn,' he said again. 'Damn and blast it all. When is this world going to grow up? When are people going to learn that we're all alike and nobody's any better or worse than anybody else? How many wars do we have to fight and how many more millions have to be slaughtered before the world gets some sense in its fat head?'

'I'm afraid we might have to wait a bit longer than we used to think,' Lily said sadly.

'How long is that?' Arthur asked angrily, still pacing. 'For ever, perhaps. That's what it could mean. We've got to stop talking about waiting and do something now. Now, dammit! If we want change and to turn wrong into right we've got to do it now – not wait. And I tell my kids that at school, hoping some of them will remember it when they get out and join the ranks of the wage slaves.'

'Be careful, dear,' Lily said in a low voice, casting a look at me.

'Be careful of what?' Arthur demanded.

'Your headmaster might not like it.'

'Be damned to him,' Arthur said. 'I don't care if he likes it or not.'

'Don't forget, while you're damning him,' Lily said, still keeping her voice lowered, 'that we have certain responsibilities and you've sacrificed enough already.'

'I'm not forgetting anything,' Arthur said, but he too

kept his voice down, though the bitterness was still there.

Lily quickly changed the subject then, asking me if I'd like more tea and crumpets, and I had the impression that there was a lot they'd said already that was not intended for my ears and there was much more behind it that I did not know.

But it was soon out, and it was something that could not have been kept secret for long, and it explained why they had given up Manchester and Arthur his law studies. It had been imperative that he find work of some sort to support Lily and the baby she was going to have.

No, it was not secret for long. I could not help noticing on subsequent visits the change in her figure, the swelling shape that she had developed in front, and at nearly twelve I had already been told how babies were born. Zalmon had taken a group of us around the corner on to the backs where we played our games of soccer and cricket, and explained the mystery that had always baffled us. He gave a graphic demonstration of what had to be done by the male parent, and told us that he had made his discovery in the Bible that we read in cheder. There was a passage that said, 'And he went in unto her . . .' We ourselves had paid no attention to it, but we knew everything now.

I understood what the swelling in Lily's stomach meant, but I said nothing to my mother and I am sure she did not suspect anything until the baby was born. She had her own baby to think about, and even if she had not shut Lily out of her mind she could not possibly have imagined her having a baby too.

It was born just a day before I came for one of my visits, and I was startled when I stepped into the cottage and heard the crying of a baby coming from the room upstairs.

Arthur had let me in and he grinned at my surprise. ''arry,' he said, 'you're an uncle now.'

Then he told me and led me upstairs, and I saw Lily lying in bed with the baby in her arms suckling at her breast. She gave me a warm smile and motioned to me to come closer, putting a finger to her lips.

I was embarrassed at seeing her breast exposed, just as I had been when I saw my mother feeding our baby too, and I tried to avoid looking at the breast and keep my eyes on the baby as I went up to the bed and peered down at it.

'Who does he look like?' Lily whispered.

'I don't know,' I said. It looked just like any baby to me, very red and wrinkled.

I heard Arthur laugh behind me and Lily said in the same whisper, 'Look in the mirror, 'arry, and you'll see it there too. He's the image of you. Isn't he, Arthur?'

'No doubt of it,' Arthur agreed.

I was a bit astonished. I didn't see how it could look like me. They both seemed to enjoy my bewilderment. Lily said, 'You must tell Mam. Tell her I want her to come and see her grandchild, will you?'

I nodded and said, 'Yis,' while still keeping my eyes on the baby that was supposed to look like me. And I kept my word.

As soon as I got home, I said to my mother, 'Lily had a baby. It's a boy and he looks like me.'

There was a long silence. I looked at her. I did not have to look up to see her face any more. I was big for my age and at eleven I was taller than she was. I saw a strange expression on her face. There were things I saw that did not have any meaning for me. But she must have been going through a great emotional upheaval. The daughter who was supposed to be dead had given birth to a child and that meant she had to be alive herself. How could it be denied? And yet her religion told her that she was dead.

I broke the silence, saying, 'Lily told me to tell you that she wants you to come to see her and your grandchild.'

'She said that?' my mother whispered and her throat seemed constricted, as if she were having difficulty talking.

'Yis,' I said.

Then she said something that surprised me. 'You must go across the street and tell the Forshaws that she had the baby.'

I did that promptly and I think I must have been the first one from our side to have crossed over to the other in a long time.

The door was answered by Mr Forshaw. His brows arched in surprise at sight of me. He had a pipe in his mouth, a mug of beer in one hand. A grin of welcome quickly spread over his face. 'Well, if it isn't 'arry,' he said. 'Come on in. Look who we've got, Margie.'

This last to his wife, who was busy at the fire with some cooking. She came over to me immediately and said, 'Well, if this isn't a nice surprise.'

'Me mother sent me over to tell you that Lily had a baby,' I said, a bit embarrassed by all this welcoming and by being in a Christian house.

'Oh, we know all about that,' Mr Forshaw explained. 'We've been over to see our new addition to the family already. Don't make any mistake about that, lad. We've been expecting it for some time now.'

'Yes, we have,' Mrs Forshaw said gently.

I might have known that from the things Arthur and Lily had said. They had been coming regularly to see the couple, just as I had, and perhaps even more often.

'It was very nice of your mother to send you over to tell

us, though,' Mrs Forshaw added, and I've no doubt they were as surprised as I had been at the request. Perhaps, knowing my mother's concern for other people this should not have surprised them. But they seemed glad that she had sent me. It could have meant to them a sign of reconciliation and acceptance, and perhaps that's what it was.

Mrs Forshaw made me sit down and have some tea and biscuits, and it was then that Mr Forshaw, putting down his beer mug in favour of the tea that his wife served, said, 'We're having a little party, aren't we? But maybe we ought do better than this. Have a regular big party. Invite the whole bloody street. What d'you say to that, 'arry?'

My mouth full of biscuit and gulping down the hot tea, I managed to say, 'That would be real champion.'

'Champion, eh?' He turned to his wife. 'What do you say, Margie?'

Her reply was a little more reserved than mine. 'Do you think the people on the street would want to come?'

'You give 'em enough beer and they'll come if it means getting up in the middle of the night. I think we ought to have it. And it'll be for both sides. They don't drink much beer on that side, so we can have pop. And there'll be eats, of course. I won't mind spending a few pennies on this. It could mean a whole lot to Lily and Arthur too, and they'd be able to show off their baby to everyone. It's a fine baby. They say it looks like you, 'arry. I couldn't tell myself.'

'Yes, it does,' Mrs Forshaw put in. 'It's the image of 'arry.'

'Well, I've got nothing against that. But you speak to your mother and father about having a party here on the street. We couldn't have it without them. We wouldn't want to. That right, Margie?'

'Yes,' she said.

I ran back across the street and blurted it out excitedly to my mother. 'The Forshaws want to give a street party to celebrate the baby. But they want you to agree. They won't 'ave it unless you agree.'

There was no answer from my mother. She just looked at me. Then she went into the scullery and busied herself in there. I don't know what was going on in her mind, but she must have been very confused. A tug of war was taking place within her, between her religion and her heart. How could she agree to celebrate the baby with a party when she had not even seen it yet, when she refused even to acknowledge that the mother of the baby, her daughter, was alive?

I know that she talked about it with my father when he came home from his pub that night. I am not sure just what went on down there, but as I lay in bed I could hear the familiar shouting of an argument and I did what I had always done at these times since I was a child: I pulled the covers over my head to blot out the sounds.

I am sure that it was over Lily and the baby, and the party too, that they had been arguing, and my mother may have tried to get him to do what her heart and conscience were telling her to do, but he wanted none of it. If nothing else, drunk or sober, he clung tightly to his religious beliefs, and Lily was to remain dead.

In the morning my mother's face looked drawn. The baby and I were the only ones home now on weekdays, and since there was no school that day for a reason I forget, a holiday of some sort, I was able to dawdle over my breakfast. My brothers and sister, already over twelve and considered grown-up, were at work, the two boys in the tailoring shop, my sister in her fancy dress shop.

My mother seemed absent about everything and did not appear to pay much attention to me or the baby, and I am sure she was still struggling with her conscience as to what she should do.

Then suddenly her mind was made up. 'I'm going to take our baby to Fanny Cohen to look after while I'm gone, and you'll take me to Marple. I want to see Lily and her baby,' she said, speaking abruptly, as if in a hurry to get the words out of her mouth before changing her mind.

I was only too glad to go, even though I'd been there yesterday. My brother was delivered to Fanny Cohen and we set out for Marple. We took the tram. The route that I walked so easily would have been too much for her. As it was, the tramline ended quite a distance from our destination, and there was still a fair bit of walking to do through fields that were filled with flowers, and a brook to cross and a farm to pass with cows grazing in the pasture. It was pleasant scenery – I'd always loved it and found it part of the pleasure of going to see Lily and Arthur – but I doubt if my mother saw much of it.

She was lost in thought all the way, with her head bent a trifle, and somehow it reminded me of other walks we'd taken together, bent on some errand, like the one we once took to the market when the shop was in her thoughts, or the time I had my first pair of clogs and she took me to the school up the park. I was only about four years old then and held her hand as we walked, and sometimes I had to trot to keep up with her if she was in a hurry. It was very different now. I walked briskly at her side, taller than she was, and if any hand was held it was hers in mine when we had to cross over a stile and a row of stones that formed the bridge over a brook, or if she stumbled over some rocks.

We finally arrived at the cottage and I let her look at it from the outside for a moment to see the strange place in which our Lily now lived. How different it was from the row of houses in which we lived, with its quaint old thatched roof and the garden of flowers all round the house giving off a rich scent. It was like something out of a fairy tale.

How it affected my mother is hard to say. She did not speak, but she did look, and then we went inside. Arthur was home because of the school holiday and he looked startled when he saw my mother. But he quickly recovered and cried, 'Well, well, well. What a nice surprise this is.'

'I came to see my daughter,' my mother said, speaking in a flat tone and hardly looking at him.

'Yes, of course,' Arthur said. 'And you will see her, and the baby too. Let me take you upstairs.'

We followed him up the narrow stairway whose treads were bent from centuries of feet. When he came to the door he leaned in and we heard him say, 'Lily, I've got visitors for you and you're going to be pleasantly surprised.'

He straightened up and moved aside to let us in. My mother went first. I was behind her, conscious of the shock Lily must be feeling. She was in bed, with the baby in its cradle at the side of the bed. Her eyes were riveted on my mother, as were my mother's on her. There was a brief and breathless halt when neither seemed to know what to do or say. Then Lily let out a cry: 'Mam!'

I heard my mother begin to sob, then their arms went out to one another and they were both together, both weeping. It took them a long time to get over it and few words were said, though there was much that was unspoken between them, and I stood watching, stirred myself by what I was seeing.

Once it was over Lily said, 'Don't you want to see the baby, Mam?'

'Yes.' She was still wiping her eyes, but recovered from the emotional outburst and now she turned her head towards the cradle and smiled. The baby was awake. It looked back at her.

My mother laughed. 'He knows me already,' she said.

'Yes, he does.' Lily laughed too, happily. 'Would you like to pick him up and hold him, Mam?'

'Would it be all right?'

'Yes, of course.'

She had been wanting to do that all along, you could see. She bent over the cradle and took the baby in her arms and held him up close to her, and there was an expression on her face that I had seen before. It was the one we saw when she looked at her own baby, or any one of us, and it was one of deep love.

I think Lily saw it too and I noticed that her eyes filled with tears. 'Do you like him, Mam?' she asked.

'Who wouldn't?' my mother said. 'He's a lovely baby. Have you picked a name for him yet?'

Lily looked troubled for a moment, then she said, 'We're thinking of calling him James.'

A little darkness crossed my mother's face. James was not a Jewish name. She put the baby back into its cradle carefully and sat down again. 'Why are you calling him James?' she asked.

The troubled look remained on Lily's face. She knew that this was dangerous ground and she did not want to spoil the reconciliation that had taken place. 'Of course,' she said awkwardly, 'everyone will call him Jimmy' – as if that made any difference. 'James,' she said, 'is the first name of our friend Ramsay MacDonald. Not many people know that. They all call him Ramsay, but his friends call him Jimmy. He's the leader of the Labour Party, you know, and some day he's going to be prime minister. We all admire him so much and that's why we want to name the baby after him.'

There was a brief silence after this. I don't think my mother was happy about it. Jewish people named their babies after some deceased relative. We had named ours Sidney, after one of my mother's relatives.

However, perhaps she too felt the same way as Lily about spoiling the occasion. She dropped the subject, but then, unfortunately, went on to something even more controversial. 'Are you going to have a bris?' she asked.

Lily must have been dreading this question. It would be the natural thing for my mother to ask. (A Jewish child, as had happened when my brother was born, was circumcised when he was eight days old and this made him a Jew. The event was generally celebrated with a party.) She looked desperately towards the door where Arthur was lolling up against it.

He had been saying nothing until now, simply watching and taking it all in. But now, seeing the look Lily gave him, he came forward to her rescue, smiling. 'My father asked me a similar question,' he was saying. 'Not quite the same, but very much like it. He wanted to know if we were going to have a christening.' He was speaking gently to my mother, although she was not looking at him. 'I don't suppose you know what a christening is,' he said. 'In a way it's very much like a bris. It admits the child into his religion. There's a baptism and the minister sprinkles what is supposed to be holy water on the child's forehead and by that ritual he becomes a Christian. Then he's given a name, and all this is usually followed by a celebration of some sort, a party.'

'We could have that, at least,' Lily said. 'We could have a party for the families.'

'Mr Forshaw told me he wanted a big party for the whole street,' I blurted out, speaking for the first time.

'Oh, did he now?' Arthur said, turning his attention to me. 'And how did you find that out?'

'I sent him to tell them you had had the baby,' my mother explained.

'Well, they knew all about that,' Arthur said. 'But it's a good thing 'arry went in or we wouldn't have known. A big party for the whole street. It doesn't sound like such a bad idea. What do you think, Lily?'

'I'm not so sure about that,' Lily said, hesitating. 'I was thinking of just a private little party for ourselves. I'm not sure all those people on our street would want to come.'

She was saying pretty much the same thing that Arthur's mother had said and Arthur's answer was similar to his father's, 'Oh, I wouldn't worry about that. They'd come all right. And there couldn't be a better way to bring both sides together for once. The more I think of the idea, the more I like it. What about you, Mam? What do you think?'

My mother spoke slowly and again without looking at him. 'If there can't be a bris then I suppose a party will have to do.'

And I think that settled it.

When the one-armed pedlar came to our street the following Friday, trundling his cart and slow-moving donkey, bawling lustily through the one good hand cupped over his mouth, 'Be–boo–ragbone!' he may have been surprised at the swift response that came from both sides of the street. They had been waiting for him with their bundles of rags and meat bones saved for a week, and now they rushed out and surrounded his cart and began jostling and scrambling with eager hands in the cart for the newest, brightest colours of sandstone.

As soon as he had gone they were on their hands and knees in front of the doorsteps with buckets of water and the rectangular slabs of sandstone decorating the pavement in front of their doorstep until, when they were done, it looked like two rainbows with all the different colours running down on either side from top to bottom.

And with that there ran a current of excitement through every house. It was only the start of how our street was to be decked out for the party that was to be held on Sunday. They were all coming. There had been no question as to that and they all took a hand in the preparations, some with the decoration, some cooking special dishes, some baking cakes, everybody contributing what the family could manage to the party. The Forshaws would supply the beer and my mother would practically empty her shop to bring the fruit, which was all she could afford. As for my father, having been won over finally to the idea, he promised to bring a bottle of whisky, but never kept his promise. His presence alone, he said, was enough, considering, he said, he was doing everyone a favour just by coming.

Somehow, someone got hold of long strips of bunting and several Union Jacks that had been used somewhere in Armistice celebrations, and they were strung across the buildings on both sides, with the flags sticking up on the chimneys. And there were boxes and buckets filled with flowers set out on windowsills. Never had our street looked so bright and beautiful, and we were all ecstatic over the way it looked; and people from other streets, like Back Brook Street and Bann Street and Wood Street, came

to peer round the corners and look in wonder at the
unusual sight.

Old Mr Bebb, our landlord's handyman, who was so good
at climbing up roofs and replacing missing slates despite
his age and trembling hands, had brought out several
sawhorses and placed old doors on them to make one huge
table set up in the middle of the street on the cobblestones.
There was a tablecloth made from leftover rolls of wallpaper with a flower pattern, and on this were piled all the
goodies that people had contributed to the affair. Most
prominent were the two kegs of beer that the Forshaws had
bought – from the Gordon shop, of course – and right next
to them was their gramophone with its big green horn,
something a lot of people had only heard but never seen
until now. The music began playing immediately,
summoning those who had not yet arrived to the party.

The weather was just perfect. Everyone agreed on that.
The sun had begun shining from early morning and the sky
was a deep blue. It was a Sunday sky, of course, the mills
not working and no smoke coming from their tall stacks to
darken it. And since it was early May the air was soft and
balmy.

It couldn't have been a better day and yet I noticed there
were some people who were slow in coming out of their
houses, and when they did come there was a tendency on
the part of either side to stick together, the Jews all
gathering on one side of the improvised table, the
Christians on the other. It was still the same way: old Mr
and Mrs Harris, he with his bowler hat on over his
yarmulke; right opposite them Mrs Turnbull and several of
her boarders, the latter noisy and laughing and half drunk
already with the beer that Mr Forshaw was pouring out
liberally. Mrs Humberstone was on that side too, along

with Mrs Jackson and Mrs Melrose, the two war widows. Mrs Green and Annie were there, and so was Florrie Gordon, and everybody noted how carefully she and Mrs Green kept their distance from each other, the way it had been ever since they'd had the big fight several years earlier.

We clung together also, the Harrises and the Blanks and the Cohens and the Finklesteins and old Mrs Zarembar, all of us pretending to be at ease sitting so close to the Christians from across the street, but still with the invisible wall between us and a certain tenseness yet there.

Then suddenly there was the clop clop of a horse and carriage as it came into the street, and all heads turned towards it and a great shout went up, because this was Lily and Arthur arriving with the baby. Everyone rushed towards it, my mother and Mrs Forshaw foremost in the crowd that gathered around the shiny black cab whose driver sat perched aloft with his silk top hat sticking up and the whip in his hand, gazing down at us aloofly.

There was just this one awkward moment as Arthur and Lily were alighting. She had the baby in her arms, and both my mother and Mrs Forshaw reached up to take it from her. Lily, still standing on the step, hesitated, not knowing which one to give it to. Mrs Forshaw solved her dilemma by taking it from her and giving it to my mother, smiling. But she remained close while my mother proudly showed it to others.

Eventually she came to my father. He had joined the party later than the rest of us and for a while my mother had feared that he would not come at all. But he had come, without the bottle of whisky he had promised, and the moment he emerged from the house his eyes fell on the two kegs of beer and he wasted little more time striding over there.

This had happened just a few moments before the cab arrived. In the commotion that followed, both he and Mr Forshaw remained seated there, ignoring everything that was taking place, getting to know one another over repeated and quickly downed mug after mug of beer, and seeming to enjoy one another's company tremendously to judge from the talk and laughter that went on between them, and the occasional toasts they made to one another. People were too busy then cooing over the baby and shaking Lily's and Arthur's hands to notice the two men at the beer kegs, but I was looking and thinking I had never seen my father laugh before or talk with another man, and wondering if this was the way he was in the pub after he left our house at night – quickly while still putting on his coat and with one sleeve dangling behind him, in a great hurry to get away from us.

I did not have much time to think of all that before my mother reached him and Mr Forshaw with the baby. Mr Forshaw sprang instantly, though a bit unsteadily, to his feet, touched the baby with a hand and said, 'Gaw, he's a nice litle fellow, isn't he?'

'What do you think of your grandson?' my mother said to my father.

He had remained seated, with his head turned away from the baby and the beer mug in his hand. 'My grandson?' he said. 'What d'you want me to say?'

'You can at least say hello.'

'Hello?' He laughed. 'You say it for me. I'm too busy.'

My mother saw that he was drunk already, and did not bother any further with him. Nor did it spoil by much the pleasure she was getting out of this whole thing, the way things were going. For with the arrival of Lily and Arthur and their baby, a lively tone had sprung up in the gathering.

The awkwardness had vanished. There was mixing between the two sides. They were talking and laughing with one another, the Jacksons and the Cohens, the Finklesteins and the Melroses, and certainly Mrs Humberstone back again with everyone, going from one to the other slapping backs and shouting in ears. Even old Mr Harris was joking with Mrs Turnbull, though old Mrs Harris continued to maintain her reserve and kept adjusting her wig more tightly.

The kids were having a great time, running wild on the street around the table, yelling and screaming, wrestling with one another, both Jewish and Christian kids playing together for the first time that I could remember.

The gramophone continued to make itself heard over the din, and then came a lively tune that made one of Mrs Turnbull's boarders get up and do a clog dance. He was a tall, thin fellow wearing gaiters and corduroy britches with a fancy handkerchief wrapped around his neck. His clogs rattled over the cobblestones with his quick, agile movements, throwing off sparks, while everyone roared applause and clapped hands in time with the music.

There was more dancing after that by other people, and lots more drinking. By this time Mr Forshaw was too unsteady on his feet, and too deeply immersed in his own drinking and his new-found companionship with my father to be able to pour beer into mugs, and my father who was in a similar state would never have offered to help anyway, so Florrie took over the bartending.

Florrie had put on a considerable amount of weight in the past few years. She was no longer the attractive, well-shaped blonde girl I could remember, but a heavy, double-chinned woman with large, jouncing breasts under her dress that seemed to be dragging her down. She was still unmarried, the salesman from Birmingham long since forgotten. But despite all her heaviness she handled the serving of the beer well, keeping up with the almost ceaseless mugs being thrust at her for refills.

'And one for me too, lass, if ye don't mind.' This from Mrs Green, who was a scarecrow beside her, thinner than ever and stooped, with grinning, toothless mouth and witchlike hair scattered over her shawl. She was the only woman among them wearing a shawl. The others all wore their Sunday best. It would be talked about later. But what else would be talked about was the way everybody watched, wondering if something was going to happen, and how nervous Annie looked.

Mrs Green's tone couldn't have been more polite, but people could not forget the fight she and Florrie had had several years ago and the hostility that had existed before and afterwards. In fact, until today, until that very moment, not a word had been exchanged between them. So they watched and held their breath a little, because both women were hot-tempered and quick to act on impulse. Florrie could very well have given Mrs Green the beer she asked for – but right in the face. It wouldn't have surprised them if she had done that, and Mrs Green would have gone for her with both claws, and then the party would have turned into a real donnybrook.

But no such thing happened. In fact, Florrie was quite nice about it and even smiled a bit, and made sure her mug was filled right to the brim.

And Mrs Green said, 'Ta, Florrie. But if ye don't mind, I'd like to drink a toast to ye. So 'ave one with me, will ye?'

'Why not?' Florrie said and filled her own mug, and they toasted each other.

Everybody watched in astonishment. Here were two

mortal enemies who'd once fought in a way that would have been to death if others hadn't pulled them apart, now drinking a toast to one another.

'T'yer good 'ealth,' Mrs Green said, raising her mug of beer.

'T'yers,' Florrie said, raising hers.

But that wasn't all. In her beer-sodden state, Mrs Green sought reconciliation elsewhere. She now tottered over to my mother, beer mug in her hand, and said, 'Now, me good lady, if you want me to do yer fire for yer just you send 'arry out to call me, and I'll come quick and on th' double, and if I can't come fer being crippled or some't else, then me Annie would come, and you never got to worry about yer fire, I promise you that. And I tell you something else. You didn't kill Christ. I know who did but I'm not telling. But you didn't and anybody says you did's a liar, and you just send 'im over to me and I'll give 'im what's what.'

Afterwards my mother and her friends would have a good laugh over this in the shop, but at the moment she just smiled and nodded and, seeing the condition Mrs Green was in, agreed with everything she said. And I think, too, it must have added to the satisfaction she felt about the whole day. It was not only that it had brought the two sides of the street together in a bond that would last for quite some time, but it had brought Lily back to her. Lily was a living creature and she had added to her own life with another, and that's what completed the day for her.

I think I must have felt something of that myself. I know I was aware of a strange sense of peacefulness and contentment as I lay in bed that night. The party was not yet finished for just a few of the men who lingered over what was left of the beer. They were laughing and talking, and occasionally broke out into a song. Somehow I did not mind their drunkenness. My father would come stumbling in later, but I would not mind that either and I would not have to pull the sheets over my head to blot out the noise.

Eventually the street grew quiet. The last of them had gone in. The last door had banged shut. The lights in all the houses had gone out and the two rows of houses were in darkness, save for the pale greenish light thrown by the gas lamp on the upper corner.

It was very still in our house and soon I fell asleep.

Epilogue

We left England in the summer of 1922, a year after our big street party. My mother's dream had finally come true. Unbelievably, the tickets had arrived. We lost no time in making our departure one hot July day, all of us trailing down the street carrying our torn luggage that my mother had bought cheaply in a second-hand shop. She carried Sidney in her arms as we left, and people from both sides of the street stood on their doorsteps waving to us and shouting, 'Ta-ta! Good luck in America!'

But I never really left the street. It was always there in my mind through the years that followed, with vivid memories of the people who lived there, and its two sides facing one another, sometimes like two enemy camps and close friends at other times. I longed to go back and see the place again, but I was busy growing up in America, first in Chicago, then New York, going to school and getting a job and getting married and having children, and lots of things.

Forty years had passed by the time it was possible for me to go. Perhaps I might have gone sooner if the ones I was so desperately anxious to see were still there. But the three of them, incredibly, were gone. First it had been Lily, a heart attack only five years after her marriage to Arthur, then

Arthur himself not more than two years later. Jimmy had been brought up by Arthur's parents, with whom we had been in correspondence for a long time, and it was through them we learned that Jimmy had been killed in the war.

All of this did much to destroy my mother, in addition to the fact that the poverty she had fled in England pursued her to America, and her dream never blossomed into its fullness of the wealth and luxury that were supposed to be part of America. Her life ended on a cold winter day in a dark, unheated, small tenement flat in the Bronx. My father was drunk on that day and after the funeral I never saw him again.

With all this unhappiness, together with the death of my older brother Joe of cancer, I had little appetite for pleasure travel anywhere. But all these things passed and the thought of the street persisted constantly, and at last I was ready and able to go, with my wife, of course.

I had told Ruby much about the place already, and in addition had written a series of sketches for a magazine about the street and my life there, so she was familiar with it by now and just as eager to see the place as I was.

We left our two children in competent hands and flew to London. After one night at the Cumberland, recovering from jet lag, we lost no time boarding a train for Manchester. We could have travelled there much faster by plane, but I wanted to see the countryside for the first time in my life. We had never been able to afford trips of any sort during the twelve years that I had lived in England and I had seen very little of the country.

I feasted my eyes on everything I saw through the window of the train and my only regret was that a misty drizzle had begun to fall, obscuring my vision a little. It was still drizzling when we got to Manchester.

Fortunately, I had brought an umbrella along and we got under it as soon as we stepped out into the street. We were able to get a taxi immediately and the trip to my town took less than half an hour.

I had told the driver to let us off at Mersey Square, the centre, so that I could walk the route to the street and see all the familiar places I had passed on my way to and from school. But when we got out of the taxi we had to stand for several moments under the umbrella while I looked around. I was lost. I did not recognise anything.

Gradually, however, it began to come back to me. There had been some changes. The old tram station was still there, but it had been rebuilt and converted into a bus station. There were no more horses and carts, but swiftly moving automobiles and rattling trucks and big lumbering buses all in a ceaseless heavy flow of traffic that swirled about us.

Perhaps the biggest change was the river. It had disappeared, along with the bridge on which we used to pause as we came home from school to peer down and watch the grey water rats climb up the walls of the cotton mills that lined the river banks. Now, all that had been covered over and turned into a wide concrete promenade.

But everything else was becoming recognisable. I had my bearings now, and with Ruby's arm tucked in mine, and the two of us keeping close together under the umbrella, we started out, I excitedly pointing out familiar old landmarks.

There across the street was the jam works. Smell it? Same sweet smell of strawberries that used to torment us when we were coming home from school hungry. And there's the Devil's Steps that we were always warned against. First, there was the smell – the people, both men and women, used it as a toilet when coming out of the pub right next to the Steps – and then you never could tell who might come pouncing out of them at you.

We went past the Devil's Steps and under the old viaduct on to Daw Bank – with its ancient crumbling houses still there, and the middens in front of the houses still overflowing with garbage. Pew! You held your nose as you went by. Old Biddy was no longer there, of course. I had written about her in my sketches, and how she used to glare at us and mutter evil words as we went by. But there was something else missing.

The row of Jewish tailoring shops that had been built on stilts behind those ancient houses was no longer there. I led Ruby over to where they had once been and we both stared aghast. In place of them was a huge hole. A man passing by halted and told us the workshops had been destroyed in an air raid during the war. In that angry moment I wondered, perhaps unreasonably, if the workshops had been singled out by German planes because they were Jewish, and with uncanny precision they had managed to make a direct hit on them. But another thought troubled me even more. What about our street? Had that been hit? The man did not know. A lot of places had been hit, but it was the mills and the engineering works they were after mostly.

We hurried on, faster than before. We turned on to King Street, still a busy little thoroughfare of shops of different kinds. I would have liked to linger, but we were in a hurry. Nevertheless I managed to catch a glimpse of shops that I had known before, which were still there – Kemp's fish and chip shop, Owen's bakery with its delicious assortment of vanilla cuts and custard tarts displayed in the window, and Hamer's shoe shop where my mother had bought my clogs.

I would come back later, I thought, and I would go into Kemp's and buy all the fish and chips I had once dreamed of; then I would go into Owen's and buy the vanilla cuts and custard tarts that I once could only look at through the window with the saliva running from my mouth and the warm smell of the bakery in my nostrils. But there was no time for that now.

We were on Brook Street and the next street we would come to would be ours – if it was still there. My heart pounded as we approached, and my footsteps quickened still more and Ruby barely managed to keep up with me, though she understood how I felt.

We went past the backs, where we had played our games of soccer and cricket, and reached the corner and our house. The street was still there, and I gave a great sigh of relief and joy. It was there intact, with its two rows of houses facing one another across the cobblestones and the roofs shining in the rain. But as we stood there with the rain drumming on the umbrella over our heads, I sensed immediately that there was something wrong.

The street was empty, devoid of any signs of life and there was a deep silence broken only by the sound that the rain made. And as I looked up and down the street I saw that the houses were empty too. There were no curtains at the windows, no blinds of any sort, and there did not seem to be any smoke coming from the chimneys. What about my house in front of which we stood?

I had wanted so desperately to be able to go inside and see the place, but it too obviously was empty. I tried the door. It was locked. I looked through the window where my mother used to display her faded fruits and vegetables, with the bad parts turned away from view. I could see the room that was supposed to have been our parlour and became a shop instead. It was bare and empty, the wallpaper was peeling and the fireplace did not even have ashes.

I was filled with disappointment and totally perplexed. What had happened here to make everyone leave? Then Ruby pointed out something at the top of the street that I had not noticed. In the first few houses there on both sides doors and windows had been pulled out and were leaning up against the walls. Slates that had obviously come from the roofs were stacked against the wall also.

'It looks as if they're starting to tear the place down,' Ruby said.

She was right. I saw it now, and my disappointment was complete. Yet, as she pointed out, it was a good thing we had come before it disappeared altogether. And a good thing too that it was a Sunday when the workmen were not busy with the demolition.

There didn't seem to be any point in lingering further, and we were about to turn away when the door in the house directly opposite us opened and someone came running out calling my name: ''arry!'

I stared at the woman who was running towards us huddled under a black shawl. I had seen her come out of the house that belonged to the Greens and I could have sworn it was Mrs Green. The same thin skeleton frame and the same bent figure that used to come in answer to my call to do the fire on Friday nights and Saturdays. And as she came closer I could see the same toothless mouth.

She finally reached us, breathless. 'Oh, 'arry, I saw you through the window and I knew it was you right away. I'm Annie. Do you remember me?'

So it was not her mother after all. But I didn't tell her of the impression I'd had. 'Of course I remember you, Annie,'

I said, shaking her hand, 'I'm so glad you're still here.'

I introduced her to my wife, and explained to Ruby that Annie and her mother used to be our fire goyahs, a term that Annie understood and which made her laugh, exposing the toothless gums still more. I asked Annie if there were any more houses being lived in.

'No,' she said, 'I'm the only one left. I'm not supposed to be here either, but they gave me a few more days till the wreckers get to this part of the street. They're tearing it down, you know, to make way for a big public housing project.' She added sadly, 'The street'll be gone for ever. Things'll never be the same.'

So that was it! That was what all the emptiness was about. I was shocked at first. And disappointed. But then I wasn't sure. Perhaps, putting sentiment aside, there was something good in all this. Perhaps tearing this place down wasn't such a bad idea.

But before I had time to think about all this, Annie was urging us to come into her place and get out of the rain and have a cup of tea. I looked at Ruby and she gave a quick nod of assent. She was as anxious as I was to get out of the rain, but especially to be able to see what the insides of these houses looked like.

We followed Annie across the street and into her house, and as I entered a wave of nostalgia struck me, for it was identical to the one in which I had once lived, the same square wallpapered room with its shabby furniture and the blackened fireplace occupying most of one wall, and a fire glowing in the grate. The only difference between this and ours was the large crucifix on one wall.

And as I glanced around at all its meanness, I thought that the one thing that had not changed here in all these years was the poverty. My eyes caught sight of the framed photograph of a young soldier on the mantelpiece. I guessed who it was, her son Peter. He had been a child when I left, still her great shame, supposedly fathered by Freddy Gordon. But I wanted to be sure.

'Is that Peter?' I asked.

'Yis.' She was busy bustling around, preparing tea, putting cups and saucers on the table and a plate of biscuits, while Ruby and I sat down.

'How is he doing?' I asked.

'Peter's gone. He was killed in the war . . .'

She had her back to me, putting the kettle on the fire to boil. I couldn't see her face, but I could detect that this was something she didn't want to talk about.

'I'm sorry,' I said and Ruby murmured the same thing.

Annie made no further comment and went right on to talk of other things. There was so much to tell me and she had evidently kept abreast of everyone who had lived on the street, even those who had gone elsewhere to live, to other cities and other countries, and had in some cases kept up a correspondence with them. I imagine it did much to ease the loneliness she had felt after her mother's death, and then her son's, and when people she had lived with all her life were gone – everyone gone, except Annie herself.

She spoke with the broad Lancashire accent that I myself had once possessed and that had become a strange language to me. I had to strain to follow her and I'm sure Ruby was having the same difficulty. We both leaned forward at the table as she spoke with dropped aitches and words slurred together, but we managed to catch most of it. This one I had known had died, that one had died, and this one had moved here, and that one had moved there . . . Obviously, there had been a lot of changes on the street after I left with my family, but it was clear also from what she said that the configuration had remained much the same, with the Jews on one side and the Christians on the other. If one Jewish family moved out, another came to take its place and it was the same on the other side.

And when the war came it was a lot like that other war, only much worse because of the incessant bombing and the constant fear hanging over them that drew the two sides closer together than ever before. The destruction of the Jewish tailoring shops on Daw Bank had a profound effect upon them, with the same thought that I myself had: if the German planes could pick off deliberately a row of Jewish shops they would do the same to the row of Jewish houses.

'Oh, we was that afeared for 'em,' Annie said. 'We didn't want that t'appen t' our Jews. We'd've taken 'em into our houses if they'd come, but none of 'em wanted to do that.'

I smiled. I couldn't picture any of them accepting such an invitation, yet it was such an unprecedented offer I couldn't help feeling a little amazed. I just wished she hadn't spoken of us as 'our Jews'. I didn't think I cared much for that.

But the important thing was that the street had not been hit, despite all the damage done to the mills and to other streets in the surrounding area in the almost constant air raids. Annie told how old Mr Harris refused to go to the shelter when the sirens went off. He was then living alone in the house with its handsomely furnished parlour, his wife having died and the daughters all married off. They tried to get him to go to the shelter, but it was no use. He stayed there alone in the house reading his Jewish newspaper, and some of the more superstitious people on the street believed that it was because of his presence the street had been saved, the Germans having been afraid that he would put a curse on them if they dropped their bombs on him.

I smiled again. I was sure the old man had already heaped many curses on them, and if you wanted to be superstitious about it those curses had their effect on the outcome of the war. But there were other things on my mind. I wanted to know about the Forshaws. They had written to us for a number of years, so I already knew of the tragedies in their life, the death of Lily, then Arthur and finally of Jimmy. But there had to be more to tell of what had happened to them.

Yes, there was. Annie's face took on a sad look. 'Oh, those poor two people,' she said. 'You know, they were always a cut above th' rest of us, they'd been real 'igh class once before the drink got the better of Mr Forshaw, but they never let on as to that and they acted as if they was just one of us. I liked 'em and so did everybody else, and we were all sorry when Mr Forshaw started to go down still more than he already was. I suppose it was Jimmy getting killed that was the final crushing blow. They'd loved the boy so much. He was just like his father, as nice a boy as you could want, and just as clever too, winning the scholarship and everything, and getting ready to go to university when the war came and he joined up. Didn't have to draft him. He joined up right away and he was killed right away, just as soon as he got over there in France.

'After that, Mr Forshaw took to 'is drinking real bad, and I suppose it was the drink killed 'im. And so Mrs Forshaw was all alone, like a lot of the other women on th' street, and you'd think all of this would've done 'er in too. But, no, it was just th' opposite. She seemed to come alive more than she'd ever been. What she did was join the Labour Party, if she 'adn't been in it already – I'm not sure about that because she never spoke much to anybody on th' street – but they gave 'er a job, and afore you know it she was talking at meetings and she was going around knocking on doors and telling 'em to vote Labour. And when the Labour Party got in power back then, around 1946 I think it was, she left th' street and went to live in London and got a real important job with th' party. And they say she had a lot to do with getting that Public 'ousing bill passed, and 'aving our street knocked down and new 'ouses put up with electric lights and water closets inside and bathtubs and everything. I 'ear she died. I'm not sure. But she was a good woman, and she meant well, even if she did take th' street away from us.'

'I'm sure she did,' I said and looked at my watch. It was getting late. We must have been sitting there for at least two hours talking and we had consumed I don't know how many cups of tea and the time had passed so quickly I had not noticed it. In the meanwhile it had grown dark outside with overhanging clouds and the room had darkened with it, and the fire glowed, reminding me of my mother's shop on a rainy day when the women would come in to sit and talk.

But it was time for us to go and it was difficult parting with Annie. She was so much alone, living there all by herself in that empty street, and I could feel her sadness and loneliness as I embraced her and kissed her and assured her that we'd try to come back to visit her in her new surroundings with electric lights and a bathtub and water closet and everything that only the rich once had. She laughed even though there were tears in her eyes and said, 'Yis, I'll be living like th' Queen of England, won't I?'

We laughed too. We thanked her for her hospitality and her fine tea and biscuits, and we stepped out under the umbrella. It was coming down hard now, and drumming heavily on the umbrella over our heads. I took one last look at my old house as we crossed, then we struck out along Brook Street.

It was late when we got back to London and our hotel. We were both very tired and went straight to bed. Ruby fell asleep almost immediately, but I could not sleep. I tossed and turned all night, thinking of our visit to the street, the things that Annie had told us, my recollections of the past, the images that brought people back to life, my head fairly bursting with all of that.

I knew that I would never see the street again with all its bleak houses facing one another. The wreckers would soon take care of that and perhaps, too, they would dismantle the invisible wall along with it. But maybe that had been done already. When Ruby and I entered Annie's house, I think that must have been one of the few times in the history of the street that anybody from our side had gone into a house on the other.

I thought a great deal about that and finally the night was over and it was dawn, with thin grey light creeping into the room. But even then the street was still there and I heard the sounds I used to hear when I was a child lying in bed in the upstairs room of the house on our street. It was the sound of wooden clogs marching. It began very quietly as the first pair of feet stepped out on to the hard cobbled ground. Then it grew louder gradually as more clogs joined in the march, and louder still like the movement of a symphony rising to a climax, and a violent crescendo as they reached the mills with a simultaneous blast of whistles from all of them. Then there was silence and my eyes would close and I was asleep.